KENYA COWBOY

With very few exceptions, the characters in this book are real persons; likewise the events, incidents and situations are factual. Accordingly it has been the author's zealous endeavour to ensure absolute fairness, good faith and integrity. Where prudence and discretion have persuaded the author otherwise, certain characters have had a mantle of anonymity thrown over them. True identities have been disguised and rendered fictional. In these few instances any resemblances with real persons is to be regarded as coincidental.

Published in 2008 by 30° South Publishers (Pty) Ltd.
28 Ninth Street, Newlands, 2092
Johannesburg, South Africa
www.30degreessouth.co.za
info@30degreessouth.co.za

First edition published in 1999 by Avon Books
Second edition published in 2001 by Covos Day Books

Cover photograph © Corbis (Mau Mau suspects interned after Lari massacre)
Design and origination by 30° South Publishers (Pty) Ltd.

Printed and bound by Pinetown Printers, Durban

ISBN 978-1-920143-23-7

KENYA COWBOY

A police officer's account of the Mau Mau Emergency

Peter Hewitt

About the author

Born in Windsor with the Great Depression looming, his adolescent years were passed in Reading, also on the Thames. Aged eighteen, following an MoD engineering apprenticeship, he was conscripted and served for eight years in the Fleet Air Arm. Upon release he entered the Colonial Police Service, a career change that took him first to Kenya, followed by tours in Cyprus and Nyasaland. His police career concluded with a nine-year spell in the Royal Papua New Guinea Constabulary. Retuning to England in 1972 he took up an appointment with the Foreign and Commonwealth Office, where a succession of postings took him to diplomatic missions in Sierra Leone, East Berlin (GDR), Guyana and Lisbon—until a surfeit of 'foreign parts' prompted him and his wife to settle in the north London suburb of Cockfosters. The next five years or so saw him employed in the relatively tranquil environs of Barnet as one of the borough's school officers. There was to be, however, one final call of the wild that he felt unable to resist and so took off again for Sierra Leone where he was engaged by a large diamond-mining company in a senior security role. This post-colonial swansong persuaded him that retirement might be the preferred option. Since then he has alternated between Cockfosters and a 'bolthole' in north Cyprus.

There can be no more fitting dedication of this book than to those spunky, indomitable pioneer settlers who were to find their precarious paradise in the White Highlands of Kenya to be but a tantalizing fantasy.

Never again will there be the same of their ilk. It was a glorious era of great endeavour and exciting promise, of testing hardship and joyous individualism.

Those who knew them understand only too well just how much their industry, enterprise and resoluteness during half a century contributed so decisively to making Kenya the envy of other emergent colonial territories.

Contents

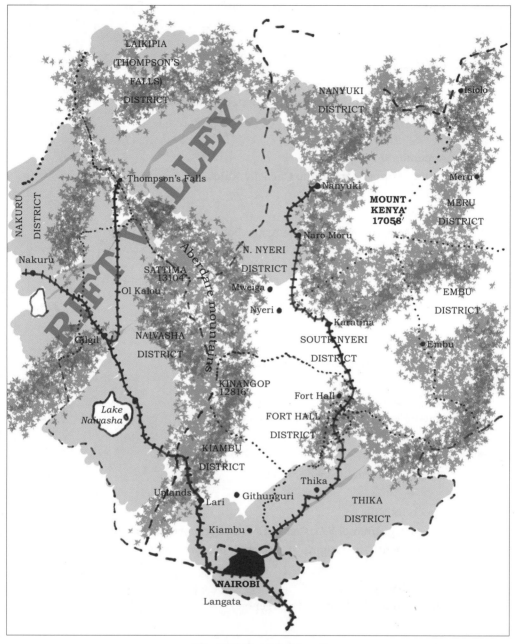

The White Highlands

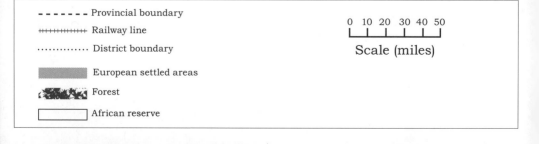

- - - - - - Provincial boundary
++++++++++ Railway line
············· District boundary
█████ European settled areas
✿✿✿✿✿ Forest
□ African reserve

0 10 20 30 40 50
Scale (miles)

Author's note

Not unusually, books such as this, having a strong autobiographical or memoir element, are a post-retirement undertaking; a desultory leisure activity to counteract cerebral atrophy, or even, sadly, to assuage the ennui that can so often become an unwelcome concomitant of senior citizenship. Doubtless, too, are those hopefully submitted manuscripts that are the culmination of literary aspiration long repressed, while earning a living took priority.

Not so this book.

The initial draft had been furiously pounded into shape and form on a sturdy veteran Underwood during 1963 in Blantyre, Nyasaland, as and when my (not too onerous) constabulary functions allowed. (The Malawi emergency was then still in force but was, however, a relatively benign situation.)

Ten years had mercurially elapsed since I was sucked into the vortex of violence, fear and hatred that had swirled so devastatingly over a benighted Kenya. The experiences, events and matters that were to provide the essential material for the book may not have been dewy-fresh exactly but did have the warmth and crispness of bread not long out of the oven.

Very shortly, as the process of de-colonization everywhere gained momentum at a most bewildering rate, and, pending the next phase in my increasingly uncertain career, the several reams of typed foolscap sheets were thrust into a large manila folder. So began the long gestation of *Kenya Cowboy*.

The manuscript was to remain virtually untouched during the intervening years of dormancy, though some alterations of tense there had to be; when a character such as the exalted Jomo Kenyatta passed away then all relevant text needed to be edited, thus, an 'is' became a 'was'. The book that has at long last materialized from that initial draft is, in effect, an encapsulation of those four horrendous years during which Kenya was being stretched so painfully taut on the rack cranked by the hideous Mau Mau.

In a sense then, the reader will enter a startlingly vivid time-warp. Astonishingly it remained impervious to all that has happened in, and to, Kenya during these last five decades or so. It is to be stressed that this book is not a memoir. Indeed, to have aspired to such would have amounted to outrageous pretentiousness. It is, as the sub-title states, 'an account of'—it is my account, a contemporaneous one, of fact and fictionalized fact. There has been no need to dredge up unreliable reminiscences from the gloomy depths of a geriatric memory. I should perhaps mention also that the book was never expected to be a scholarly historical work or critique. Yet, notwithstanding, it will be found to be a revelatory, compelling and, some may say, controversial study of a segment of British colonial history long overdue for elucidation and reassessment.

So, has the book's belated debut detracted from its topicality? Quite possibly it has. On the other hand, an earlier appearance may well have provoked an unbalanced and prejudiced reaction; the greater would have been the risk of confronting an intolerant, hostile, partisan media, or those harbouring a grievance. Whereas, at this distance in time, it is possible to get an unbiased, dispassionate view, one that is less crowded and jostling.

Introduction

It should not be too difficult for those beyond their sixtieth year to remember maps of Africa that were patterned with patches of red, large and small. The same red tint filled the contours of the British Isles, of India and Burma, of Ceylon, Borneo, Sarawak and Australia, and so on, all around the globe; colonies, protectorates, dependencies, trusteeship territories and, of course, dominions.

It was, however, in Africa where the patches of red were so impressively widespread; from the Nile Delta to the Cape and the Niger to the Zambezi, they bespoke the might and extent of the British Crown.

A map of Africa today would evince nothing of the kind. The red has disappeared insofar as it would indicate a British possession. The words 'Colonial Empire' have long since been studiously avoided by advocates of democratic rights, though one may still hear them uttered occasionally by Britain's political detractors whenever it is wished to inject some venom into a scathing diatribe against the old colonial despots. One by one the subject territories became too hot to hold and were dropped (with relief?) into the fierce fires of nationalism that burned beneath them, often to be cooled with disconcerting speed by the chilly waters of economic instability.

Their cries for freedom became steadily more articulate and ominous. That magical, if somewhat elusive, inalienable right of mankind, freedom, could not be denied. Has any nation in the history of the civilized world ever had to suffer slings and arrows of its own making such as Great Britain has? How many millions in those red patches found it necessary to scream with ever-increasing hatred their demands for *Enosis*, for *Merdeke*, for *Kwacha*, for *Uhuru* and in all the other languages of the old Empire?

But invariably the myopic and unamused gentlemen in Whitehall preferred to suggest a counter-demand: prove yourselves first by a spirited display of subversive activity, revolt or, better still, by violence and terrorism. Some were not at all averse to adopting the suggestion.

One such territory, the contours of which were among the last to lose that nice red tint, is the East African nation of Kenya. In just a little more than half a century this beautiful and prosperous farming country found it possible to worry the British government into granting it full independence. How? Through a particularly abhorrent rebellion known to the world as Mau Mau, though supported to some extent by an indifferent political climate in London.

To call Mau Mau terrorism mere worry, of course, would be a classic understatement and quite ludicrous. Nevertheless, it had the desired effect *after* being subdued—for one can hardly say destroyed—and order restored. The colony proved itself in no uncertain manner and Whitehall, albeit reluctantly, submitted.

Yet people asked themselves incredulously, "Can a country whose people were capable of such barbarous behaviour as was displayed by Mau Mau freedom fighters really govern themselves?" Whether or not they could has now been answered. They are doing so with considerably more competence than many another newly emerged African nation. Moreover, the person proved in a lawfully constituted court of law to have been the architect of that atrocious terrorist organization undoubtedly played a leading role in the post-independence government of the former colony as its very adroit president.

Having myself been present in Kenya during the Mau Mau uprising, I may, in addition to having a story to tell, be able to provide one or two searchlights with which to probe the darkness that seems always to hinder the outsider, no matter what the African territory or reason for the conflict. The story I wish to narrate is essentially my own, yet I wish not to intrude to an autobiographical extent. The book will, I fear, assume more the appearance of a miscellany and I can only hope that the chapters will not be too disjointed. Many of the characters featured are not fictional; as also certain incidents and situations that I involve them in. Their names, however, where necessary, have undergone prudent changes. Perhaps I should mention at this stage, though not too sententiously, that even if this book is to be a miscellany of my own experiences in Kenya during its Mau Mau emergency, it belongs equally as creditably, or discreditably (depending on which side you were on!), to those hundreds of other *wazungus*, as the Europeans are called, who aligned themselves with the Crown in the fearful struggle against the cyclops that reared up so starkly toward the end of 1952. In particular those 'Kenya Cowboys' who grappled with the hideous Mau Mau monster quite as conscientiously and as unrelentingly as any newcomer to the country could have been expected to; and, I might add, who were denigrated most viciously by many sections of the media and community for their efforts.

The odd thing about the virulent and savage insurrection of the Wakikuyu and its allied tribes in Kenya was that it should have styled itself 'Mau Mau'. The name has no known interpretation, is not the initials of any organization or sect and had no historical or traditional significance; merely did it have a certain descriptive value-subversion, anti-Europeanism and sinister terrorism.

It was a movement inspired and encouraged by notorious African politicians with the divine 'messiah', Johnstone (Jomo) Kenyatta,[1] as its designer, skipper and navigator until in 1949 it was proscribed and disappeared underground, only to reappear late in 1952 guerilla-ized and sworn to evict the white man from Kenya's settled highlands. But how the name Mau Mau was conceived and for what purpose has remained an intriguing mystery.

What created the movement? A few educated, power-hungry and

---

[1] Kenyatta (Jomo Johnstone) b. 20 October 1901: Kenyan politician. Convicted of managing M.M. movement and sentenced to imprisonment in 1953; released April 1959 and restricted to Lodwar until April 1961, then moved to Maralal (still under restriction) until August 1961; Hon. Fellow LSE; Knight of Grace, Order of St. John of Jerusalem (1972); Hon. LL.D. (East Africa); Pubs: *Facing Mount Kenya, The land conflict, My people of Kikuyu, Harambee*.

ruthless quasi-politicians. What fertilized it? Aggrieved Kikuyu in their congested reserves. What gave it impetus? Land discontent. And what were its aims? To wrest the land by violent means from the whites who had dishonestly acquired it.

Was it a justifiable enterprise? I would say, no. The exhaustive, impartially conducted and scrupulously fair Carter Land Commission of Enquiry in the year 1933 rejected unequivocally the wild allegations of Kikuyu rabble-rousers that the land belonged to them. Was the mighty and costly force employed to put down the rebellion justified? Far be it for me to opine with any conviction or authority but all the evidence would appear to suggest yes. If only in order to have safeguarded the lives, properties and interests of those white settlers who had been invited, and, in many instances assisted, to invest in a parcel of virgin land and to farm it correctly and productively, thus ensuring that the country could develop with a stable economy based on agriculture.

Additionally, despite the obscure ideology of Mau Mau, it was a movement that was uncivilized and wholly evil. Had it been allowed full rein it would have negated entirely the great achievements and development of half a century and resulted in serious retrogression. Finally, the sentiments and the outrageous demands of Mau Mau were confined to the Wakikuyu and its allied tribes, the Meru and Embu. It was never a homogeneously inspired rebellion and was roundly condemned by the many other tribes in Kenya (except possibly for some sympathy among the Mkamba and Luo).

This book, being something of a potpourri, does not attempt to analyze the situation existing in Kenya during the years 1952 to 1956, nor is its aim to assert where any failure may have lain. Nonetheless for that, the various narratives on diverse aspects of the emergency will, the reader may discover, be analytical in themselves. Thus, may I submit that any conclusions which emerge should be regarded as coincidental. It would be preferable that they be considered a natural end product of the matter narrated, excepting that is, for those passages devoted specifically to fact or statistical information.

The fact that I was a police officer and had sworn allegiance to the British Crown has not, I sincerely hope, prejudiced my pen unduly or daubed the pages too gaudily with red, white and blue. I only became a colonial police officer out of sheer caprice and was hardly a devout lawman. Notwithstanding, it was a period in my life quite unparalleled in excitement and interest; an undeniably catalytic phase of my life. Which is one of the reasons why I was bothered by an almost irresistible urge to commit the experience to paper. It was a job I knew next to nothing of and learnt as I went along. Even so, I should emphasize that the story is undoubtedly from the standpoint of a police officer; this is inevitable—the brush tars whether we like it or not if we are working with tar.

Outstandingly the enduring pride and pleasure was to have been one of the 'supernumerary' sub-inspectors of police who converged on Kenya by the hundred to tote a gun and to crush the 'wicked insurgents'. I doubt whether a more multifarious and un-policeman-like clique of British foreign legionnaires had ever been assembled before. A truly remarkable collection of outcasts, oddities and mercenaries; their only common denominators being no communistic tendencies, no criminal convictions, of British nationality and reasonably sound health.

To illustrate just how diverse a crowd these supernumerary police were that flooded into Kenya, consider this: in February 1956 there was in the operations room at Colony Police H.Q. in Nairobi an inspector who spent most of his time pushing coloured pins into maps and compiling daily situation reports. It was announced that His Royal Highness, the Duke of Edinburgh, was to disembark the royal yacht *Britannia* at Mombasa. The inspector,[2] ex-British South Africa Police, at his own request was sent on special duty as part of the welcoming guard of honour. He was at once recognized by H.R.H. as an old school friend. It wasn't long thereafter that he relinquished his appointment to become the Duke's private secretary.

Perhaps I should mention that my reference to supernumerary

---

[2] ORR, James Bernard Vivian, CVO 1968 MVO 1962; Secretary of Medical Comm. on Accident Prevention; b. 1917 unmarried. Ed. Harrow & Gordonstoun. RMC Sandhurst, BSAP in S. Rhod. 1939–46. Ethiopia & Eritrea Police (attached) 1941–49. Kenya Police 1954–57. Private Sec. to H.R.H. Duke of Edinburgh 1957–70.

police officers relates to their being over and above the normal requirements of the Force. They were recruited specifically to thicken the ranks of commissioned officers because of the burden imposed on the Force by the State of Emergency.

Almost from the beginning we were honoured with the catty, if not entirely inappropriate, sobriquet of 'Kenya Cowboys', and, even more cattily, 'Millionaire Coppers'. The truth was, I've little doubt that, the one thousand or so of us rushed in to reinforce the constabulary with an absurd six week's training, were an embarrassing liability as police officers. Some obviously considered it as a 'Cook's Tour'. We had been inducted to smite audacious thugs without kid gloves as stingingly as was possible within the law, no more. Later those of us who felt that normal policing held some attraction found that certain opportunities were extended and the Force could be made one's chosen career.

Yet the task was carried out with boundless enthusiasm and devotion. Mau Mau was harried and order was slowly restored. Few of us were fully aware of the reasons for all the fuss, even less were we inclined to delve too deeply into the whys and wherefores. Many, I suppose, like me, felt that there was more to it than just discontent over the land but in the vague circumstances the land itself sufficed as an incentive to do what was required of us; it wasn't theirs and they were jolly well not going to have it! There were, I supposed, aggravating factors like the unkind treatment by some settlers of native labour and the shocking living conditions of Kikuyu squatters but they were all subordinated to the major grievance of land misappropriation.

The disconcerting realization has been that, although the strong counter-measures of the British government may well have quelled the bloody rebellion, they did little to cure the malady Kenya was afflicted with at the time. In fact, if anything, they exacerbated the situation by drawing so much undeserved attention to the unreasonable demands of the Wakikuyu over the land issues. The emergency in Kenya accelerated the notoriety of the tribe and, having troubled the Crown so exorbitantly (over £55 million), it felt that it had a perfectly valid right to the lion's share of those constitutional, agrarian and property benefits to be enjoyed when the country achieved full independence. Hence, having displayed its obdurate resistance to the Crown so ferociously, it soon became apparent that the tribe would need to display an equal domination of Kenya's many other tribes—who are by far each numerically inferior—with the same ruthlessness. And, indeed, during the early sixties when the emergency was but a reverberating echo around the White Highlands, we saw all too clearly how various tribes were jockeying for power, position and traditional tribal rights. There was a lamentable lack of democratic politics; moreover, those members of the Land Freedom Armies who survived became heroes and the tribe to which they belonged had no intention other than to retain its power. I know of no other tribe that has found it possible to upset the status quo either, although the Luo have been quite a force to reckon with.

On the 14 August 1961, the expansive and brooding idol of the Wakikuyu and African nationalists everywhere, Jomo Kenyatta, arrived at Gatundu in Kiambu (a Kikuyu reservation at the time) near Nyeri, having been released from restrictive detention. He was handed the keys of an expensive house built at Gatundu by the government who had banished him from public life to a remote spot far away in Kenya's arid Northern Province.

A period of eight years and nine months had elapsed from the time he was arrested and the emergency declared. Within a few days of his celebrated release, and with government officials watching anxiously his every move, he addressed his first public meeting for nearly nine years. But now he found himself confronted by two parties. Both were strong and both opposed any suggestion of a coalition with him at the helm. However, both KADU (Democratic) and KANU (National) were prepared to offer him the presidency of their respective parties. Jomo, popularly referred to as 'Jumbo', did not demur with his message, which was, "I'm still the same old Jomo you knew before." He was eventually to take over the leadership of KANU which had a predominately Kikuyu following.

Was it possible, one wondered, that the sixty-three-year-old

Kikuyu messiah had failed to appreciate that after his long years in seclusion, his former idolatrous followers were less inclined to accept his fiery and flamboyant mobster tactics? That they'd learnt to respect the value of non-violent, non-co-operation with the government over the innocuous debating floor of Legco? Many another popular and capable leader had emerged since their idol's banishment from the platform of African nationalism—leaders that were comparatively unimpeached by the incriminatory conduct of so many of Kenya's recalcitrant nationalists during the long emergency. Some, though hot-headed, were fluent and seen to have more political composure than the ageing master of subversion.

And yet, if what he hotly alleged (when furiously bombarded by a battery of pressmen outside the house at Gatundu for his views on the Land Freedom Army) was to be believed, then the long years in exile had not altered his rumbustious ideology one bit.

"I don't know about their activities," he archly replied. "I don't know what they have been doing. If they are harmful to our country I would condemn them."

It was a classic statement in the good old evasive Kenyatta tradition whenever quizzed about Mau Mau.

The British Government had no need to fret, as the years since independence have shown. As president of the fledgling nation he demonstrated a remarkable moderation, political logic and, most paradoxically, almost no bitterness towards his former adversaries. Perhaps, after all, the long sojourn in exile did mellow him.

It must not be forgotten, if it be remembered at all, that Kenyatta himself was never an active forest terrorist. He had no opportunity to become a regular guerrilla of his Land Freedom Armies. Whether or not this nationalist demagogue would have ever risen to the occasion and led his tribesmen into the forests and gorges is solely a matter for conjecture. It was fortunate for him that he was relieved of the choice, a choice it is doubtful he'd have relished. Thus, the discomforts and deprivations of the forest gangster's rigorous life he obligingly left to those he had inspired during the stormy years preceding the emergency his rascally machinations precipitated.

Could he have ever experienced regret for having been denied the opportunity to carry that same inspiration as their 'saviour' into the dark primeval forests?

Two key disciples, considerably less accomplished as either artful orators or party politicians, led the terrorist hordes out of their reserves on his behalf. The most infamous of the two was Dedan Kimathi, alias General Russia and variously styled also as 'Field Marshall Sir', 'Prime Minister' and, even more pretentiously, 'Knight Commander of the African Empire'. He was scar-faced and had the top joints of his middle left finger missing (the result of an accident with machinery while in the employ of a white settler at Ol Kalou) and long before the emergency was declared was wanted by police for murder with a price of £500 on his head.

He was to become one of the last hard-core terrorists to be accounted for and it must surely be to his dubious credit that he should have so successfully eluded security forces for four years. One by one his personal gang were caught in the enormous dragnet of pseudo-gangsters and tribal police (Kikuyus) until he was the only significant desperado left, fleeing through the thick forests and dense bamboo groves with the cunning and swiftness of a wild cat. How appropriate it was he should have been shot by one of his own tribesmen, a tribal policeman, on the morning of 21 October 1956 (coincidentally the fourth anniversary of the declaration of emergency) when mistaken for a leopard. He was wearing a suit of rudely fashioned leopard-skin clothing!

Having been nursed back to health and the lead dug out of his incredibly tough hide he was duly tried and convicted for the offence of carrying a firearm without lawful authority. Under the Emergency Regulations this was a capital offence. He was hanged in Nairobi prison on 18 February 1957. Inevitably he has become a martyr.

The other key disciple of Jomo's was Stanley Mathenge, also a Kikuyu. His status was never clearly defined but is thought to have been on a par with that of Kimathi. During Mau Mau's declining months there grew a bitter enmity between the two leaders and their respective gangs. They conducted a deadly war of their own, deep in the silent, matted forests. Mathenge was responsible for many successful raids on farms and 'squatter' lines. He was, too, just as elusive as Kimathi.

The last report on Mathenge was when seen skulking on the borders of Tanganyika halfway through 1956. He was also widely rumoured to have been executed by Kimathi's gang. The fact is he has not been seen or heard of since and is one of the very few Mau Mau hard-core aces to have unaccountably vanished. Messrs China, Kanui, Mekanika, Chui, Kimani and Ngomi, to mention a few high-ranking rebel brass, all were ticked off during the four years unremitting and systematic elimination. Stanley Mathenge, however, remains to this day a mystery.

As for the rank and file of the Land Freedom Armies, there were few that escaped the crushing might of H.M. security forces once operational momentum was gained. Yet the irrational fact is that Mau Mau terrorists became their own executioners. Their treachery became the Crown's weapon of deadliest potential. Apostasy was to become so prevalent that the entire Mau Mau organization simply disintegrated.

At the height of the emergency over 75,000 Mau Mau adherents were in detention camps, all of whom, after a few years of building roads, irrigation systems, airfields and so forth, were returned to their homes and villages.

Had they been taught a lesson? Did the 'Kenya Cowboys', the *bwana* D.C.s, and the soldier 'Johnnies' teach them the error of their ways?

What should they have done? All the killing and savagery of the Mau Mau uprising was little different from what had been going on in darkest Africa between various tribes for centuries past. It just so happened that in this twentieth century the white man happened to get himself involved too and gave it universal publicity.

Anyone who has read an account of Shaka, chief of the Zulus, will know that before the advent of the white man in Africa, an African's daily life was fraught with the most hideous and devilish ritual. Violent death was never further away than the nearest malevolent witchdoctor.

By western codes and values, everything witnessed and suffered during Kenya's emergency was primitive, insensate genocide or homicidal mania. But, what was it by a tribal African's measure? Perhaps the reader will find it possible to judge for himself in the chapters of this book.

Chapter 1
Jambo bwana! Fully attested

Nairobi, as I had allowed myself to imagine during those final grey days in England in the autumn of 1953 should have been sprawled lethargically, lawlessly and stoically on the rolling Athi River plains somewhere near the foot of Mount Kenya and in the terrifying grip of barbaric Kikuyu rebels called Mau Mau, brandishing long knives called *pangas* and wearing little more than loin cloths.

Imagination had included in the wild picture a lion or two skulking around dilapidated wooden stores and groups of untidy, chin-bewhiskered, khaki-clad settlers, teetering fearlessly out of exclusive bars, pistols on either hip and carrying shotguns for good measure.

The police would probably be stiffly military in starched drill, tight-lipped and aggressive; tensely efficient while on duty, boastful and abandoned when off. Fear and hysteria had pervaded the British colony of Kenya. Who would the dreaded Mau Mau kill next? It was going to be pretty tough, I had decided, and the sooner I cleared my head of such ghastly visions as the atrocious Lari massacre and the like, the less would be my misgivings for having applied to join the Kenya Police Force.

In reality I was soon contradicted because, for all its appearance as a frontier boom town and its unconventionality, it was, I found, an orderly, clean and thriving farmers' city. The settler even wore a tie at dinner and touched his hat to the ladies. The Africans that thronged the city streets did not appear to be particularly sullen and their cheerful greetings of '*Jambo, bwana*' sounded sincere enough; though their frightfully tattered shorts and shirts gave one the impression they were all penniless and out of work. Shops were well stocked, roads and buildings were in a good state of repair, Europeans were not seen to draw their guns every time a car backfired. However, the large numbers of British soldiers seen patrolling in vehicles belied any suggestion of normalcy.

There was scant opportunity to explore Nairobi during the brief twenty-four hours I spent in it on my arrival in the colony. I, and other recruits, were marshalled and shepherded, interviewed and kitted out. We all spent the night at one or other of the city's leading hotels. Some were bedded at the imposing New Stanley while others enjoyed the luxury of its equally imposing sister hotel on the opposite corner, The Torrs. I found myself at a tall, stately hotel farther along the palm-tree-lined Delamare Avenue (now Kenyatta Avenue) called 'The Avenue'.

The hotel advertised dancing nightly in its Flamingo bar. I remember that, together with a fellow recruit, I decided to have a look in before retiring. The lighting was so subdued that it took me fully five minutes before my eyes became accustomed to the smoky gloom. I eventually discerned one or two couples shuffling torpidly around a dance floor the size of a boxing ring to discordant strains of a three-piece band, the rude yawns of whom soon had both me and my companion exercising our jaws in sympathy. Disgusted and disillusioned and we made our exit.

What I found so astonishing on this my first night in an exciting African city was the deep hush that descended on it after ten o'clock. It was almost eerie. A strict curfew on the indigenous population most probably enhanced it. Maybe the fact that the prices of drinks in most bars were doubled after ten o'clock also something to do with it!

The following morning at Colony Police Headquarters, I stood detached and unfeeling before a bored staff officer and repeated after him the solemn oath of allegiance, during which I could hear a dubious rendering of 'Hearts of Oak' by the police band on the nearby playing fields. Thereupon it seems I became a fully attested member of the Kenya Police and was morally, if not spiritually, committed.

I was issued with a shiny new .38 Webley revolver and twelve rounds of ammunition. Any seriousness that accompanied the issue was soon dispelled by the clownish efforts of some recruits to twirl the piece of hardware around their forefingers in self-conscious parody of a Wild West gunslinger. There were photographs taken for our warrant cards, "Just to make it all legal like," said one of our cockney members. Then a visit to the paymaster where particulars were taken in respect of any home allotments we wished to make, also to nominate next of kin.

"Blimey! Don't let's take this too seriously, mate!" said our cockney friend again.

By early afternoon when we had all been collected from our respective hotels with bulging kit-bags of uniform and personal luggage we numbered about twenty. And what a multifarious bunch of recruit sub-inspectors of police we were too. Ex-R.A.F. flying officers, bank clerks, unresolved public school boys, ex-Palestine police, retired Indian army officers and, inevitably, ex-sailors. The Kenya police (during the years 1953–1960 at least) can surely have had no parallel as regards being designated a 'motley' force. Though, alas, the only designation it appeared to have earned itself in the press while I awaited confirmation of my appointment in murky, fog-bound London was that of 'millionaire coppers' or, more amusingly still, 'Kenya Cowboys'.

In actual fact the salary was in no way fabulous and neither, I soon found, was police hierarchy at all disposed to tolerate such irregularities of dress as to simulate that of cowboys, be it Kenyan or Western. It was more probably the casual and, necessarily so, ostentatious wearing of firearms that earned Kenya's expatriate police officers their popular, though nonetheless unfair, nicknames.

Having been informed in a small handbook I'd received from the Crown Agents in London that the Police Training School was at Kiganjo in Nyeri I had naturally believed it to be there that we were destined. Most other recruits in the rickety old safari truck believed likewise and it was not until we had reached the top of the breathtaking Kikuyu escarpment a few miles from Nairobi that we bothered to enquire where it was we were really headed for. We learned that it was a town called Gilgil some seventy-five miles up the Great Rift Valley. The name conveyed nothing to either my fellow officers or me. Regardless, we continued to enjoy the ride while the Reception Officer, a Mr Rogers, I recall, unflaggingly continued to point out the various features of interest to us. This he must have done, I supposed, to many other batches of prattling recruits before us. He even sounded like an official tourist guide.

There cannot be many panoramas in Africa that will engage the human eye so enchantingly as the magnificent Great Rift Valley as one commences the tortuous descent of the Kikuyu escarpment. The gasped adjectives that flew around the safari truck were ample evidence that even the most indifferent of eyes could not but appreciate the mighty splendour of it.

I viewed the undulating Ngong hills away on the left—this phenomenal natural fault in the earth's surface fills the eye until it disappears in the shimmering haze fifty miles or so to the north. A truly staggering sight, and more, when one is reminded that this fascinating geographical fault starts in the Taurus range in Asia Minor, runs under the Red Sea, down through Ethiopia and Kenya, to peter out in Mozambique. It is the basin for Kenya's chain of fabulous lakes and surpasses itself lower down the continent with Lake Nyasa (now Lake Malawi). Of unending interest to geographers and geologists alike the fault is as wide as forty miles in some places and narrows to as little as five miles at a point near Longonot, some fifty miles from Nairobi. Perhaps only as one descends the dizzy and heavily forested escarpment and views the Rift as it closes together near Longonot does one truly appreciate the full enormity and indescribable wonder of it.

As the truck sped on towards Naivasha along the extensively cultivated floor of the Great Rift Valley, the weirdly shaped volcanic crater Longonot was passed a mile or so on the left. The sight of it stimulated excited comment from all and we were given to understand by the authoritative Mr Rogers that it was still active. I chose to believe him at the time but was to repudiate his statement several months later, when, after an arduous climb up its densely vegetated slopes, I confirmed with my own eyes that the saucer-shaped hollow at the summit was covered with sparse bush and coarse grass. There were several blow holes emitting sulphurous gases which probably gave rise to the legend that the volcano was active. It is also a fact that the crater was used from time to time as a haven for itinerant Mau Mau gangs. They made full use of the warmth to be enjoyed in the vicinity of its blow holes on cold nights.

Just before entering the township of Naivasha, we gaggle of recruits were treated to our first real glimpse of unspoilt Africa in the form of giraffe, scores of them, roaming unmolested within yards of the main road. Pointing to his right across the open scrub country toward the abrupt wall of the escarpment, Mr Rogers informed us that there was a very fertile plateau on top called the Kinangop. It extended down as far as Kipipiri, a mountain that soared up 12,000 feet and which we could just discern capped by cloud farther down the Rift Valley.

The Kinangop, explained our host, was something of a Shangri-La, ideal farming country and closely settled by Europeans. I was soon to become better acquainted with that plateau.

As I gazed, by now somewhat dreamily, across the rich ranching country in the direction indicated, I thought of John Boyes, whose thrilling book *King of the Wakikuyu* I had read some years earlier, and who had been in the vanguard of those intrepid traders in this part of Africa. He had, I mused, crossed the plateau from Naivasha late in the nineteenth century with his caravans burdened with merchandise to penetrate the dark unknown forests in which the savage and warlike Kikuyu roamed. Then to return many months later equally as burdened with rich ivory and skins.

As if he had read my thoughts Mr Rogers turned and said: "And to think there is now a jeepable track all the way from this side of that range [meaning the Aberdares] to Nyeri."

A pause was welcomed in Naivasha where we were given tea at a small cosy hotel called the Bell Inn. During this break in the journey most of us began to ask just where on earth it was we were destined for.

"Where is this place called Gilgil?" we asked our Police Reserve guide.

"Not far now. About ten miles," he assured us.

Then all of a sudden we arrived. Or so Mr Rogers would have us believe.

I tumbled out of the safari truck and stood regarding what we were led to believe was the Police Training school. Among the score of us, it was probably not at all unlike occasions in the past when, as army, navy or air force personnel, we had been set down at outlandish camps and remote training establishments. Even so, judging by the expressions of incredulity on the faces of most and the ribald comments, it was obvious that a question had to be answered, namely, "Was this the P.T.S.?"

It could be a staging centre or a transit camp. We were to idle here awhile, until perhaps a course passed out at the proper training school, which we now knew to be over on the other side of the Aberdare range at Kiganjo near Nyeri, then we'd move in.

But, the many groups of Europeans, a little browner looking and harder of face than us, moving about in an organized and purposeful manner, books under their arms or carrying weapons and haversacks, soon compelled us to accept the fact we had arrived at the establishment whereat we were to undergo training.

Gilgil, altitude 6,576 feet, is seventy-five miles from Nairobi and located dead centre in the Lower Rift Valley with the Mau summit on one side, the Aberdares on the other and undulating, variegated country all around. It had a small post office, a branch of Barclays Bank that opened once a week, a police station, an hotel (more like a hostelry) and a row of Indian-owned stores called *dukas* with not one plate-glass window between them. A town familiar with hundreds of servicemen during Word War Two as a military garrison and as the Colony's Command Ammunition Depot.

The town was also important for its railway yards and the place where the lines to Kisumu and Thomson's Falls diverged. An exclusive country club, a garage and a nine-hole golf course completed this little township that served something like fifty farms over a radius of ten miles.

Most of the trainees to be seen proceeding hither and thither were wearing clumsy blue overalls and, most incongruously, peaked uniform caps; though a few wore blue berets. All wore boots topped by short puttees and were pinched in at the waist with a leather belt. This latter item of uniform did not appear to be standard and on most had been sewn a strip of looped leather into which were pushed rounds of ammunition. The regulation police holster was slung low on two straps from either the left or the right hip. The majority of holsters were modified to suit the wearer's personal taste. From the shoulder across the abdomen passed a blue lanyard to a small ring on the butt of a pistol.

It was quite an aggressive and exciting picture that we were presented with during those first few bewildering minutes.

After placing our respective loads in one of the most ill-furnished, ill-lit, dirty and barren barrack blocks I'd ever seen, some of us decided to explore the camp—a camp that had obviously changed but little since its use by the military during the war. In particular, there was a compulsive urge to lubricate our parched throats and to wash down the dust in the canteen, wherever it was. During our tentative peregrinations about the inhospitable site we were railed at and ridiculed mercilessly, so easy was it to distinguish the newcomer. He was posh, pale and apprehensive; he also wore no pistol (they had to be called pistols and not revolvers we were warned).

"You'll be sorreeee!" jeered those who had been in the school a few weeks. "Get your knees brown," shouted others.

Yet, despite this banter and the atmosphere of grimness or the feeling that it was going to be a matter of survival of the fittest, I, as perhaps my fellow recruits did also, had a strangely satisfying conviction that I was about to face a situation that was either going to make or break me. There was a delicious sense of entering the unknown, of having made an irrevocable decision to ascertain just what sort of substance I was made of. In many respects I have always likened the general appearance and atmosphere of that training depot at Gilgil to a Foreign Legion barracks in Marseilles that I had stood outside some years earlier.

The lavatory I stumbled on and hurriedly inspected. It was an unprepossessing wood and corrugated-iron structure of the utmost simplicity. A large hole, rectangular in shape had been dug and a long wooden box placed over it. In the top of the box were twelve circular holes, yes, twelve! There were no lids or any such embellishments as partitions, not even a bevelling of the wood where buttocks came into contact with it.

The smell was nauseating in the extreme. In the brief and embarrassing few seconds that I had my head poked round the sacking screen door of this masterpiece of all 'thunderboxes', I saw half a dozen persons who sat unconcernedly upon their thrones. Grunts and groans were punctuated by hollow thuds below. The buttocks of one particularly obese trainee were overflowing his meagre allocation of box and were actually touching the hips of his co-squatter. On the ground in front of each comfortable, complacent, defecating sub-inspector was a belt, holster and Webley pistol.

As I dropped the sacking and edged away from that vulgar, if amusing, sight, I heard someone utter in answer to my diffident cough, "He has decided to write to his M.P., I'll bet."

As I found my way across to the fly-infested kitchen that was screened from the adjacent parade-ground with a sheet of kavorondo matting I thought, in anguish, that from then on I would develop the habit of nocturnal motions. Needless to say I soon found myself an indifferent and quite uninhibited member of that latrine gallery. Everyone became slowly oblivious to the pong or the bare thighs, or whether it was necessary for the fourth person along to remain seated for so long without any apparent movement of his bowel, or that the redheaded fellow with the peeling red face should become even redder as he leaned further forward and strained painfully.

Before many days passed I was to become acutely aware that,

with the dubious quality of the unwholesome food set before us, it was only the most hardy trainee who did not spend several days patronizing that disgustingly communal bog with either squirters or agonizing constipation.

My most vivid impression of the school's canteen, which was the focal point of all off-duty activity, was the radio installed therein. It was oscillating in the most fearful manner when I first entered and continued to do so throughout my sojourn at the school. I could distinguish nothing intelligible to begin with and yet several rapt ears were cocked in its direction.

There was an uncouth-looking inspector sat at one of the cheap, drink-stained tables staring absently at two hand-grenades lying menacingly before him. I timorously drew his attention to the noise. He snarled, "Shut up and use yer ears for krisake, man; it's the news!"

Expensive as the set appeared, never did it emit clear, pleasant sounds during my time at the school. It was, moreover, never switched off so far as I can remember.

Together with a few others of my dazed recruits we bought beer, the popular brand being Tusker, and it was unanimously agreed that worse had been drunk. Behind the bar were two African stewards and an Irishman. The latter was attired as other trainees were and was, apparently, a member of the senior class, or 'syndicate', as they were called.

Syndicates next to pass out were expected to perform various duties in the running of the school. Though I must admit that I was to see that same Irishman behind the bar long after his syndicate had completed its training. The rumour was that he was clinging tenaciously to what must have been a rather lucrative perk and I felt obliged to believe it. However, as he was also responsible for supervising the kitchen, he wasn't envied this perk. With the myriad flies, the heat and the clouds of dust that gusted into the primitive field kitchen, he deserved whatever rewards he could extract.

To express the feeling of us new arrivals as 'excited' is an understatement. What we really experienced during that first evening in the school's canteen was a kind of fatalistic it-can't-be-as-bad-as-it-looks emotion—a sort of brave and apathetic approach towards everything that portended misery and hardship.

Yet, such was the astonishingly abandoned atmosphere during that evening in the rollicking canteen that I began to wonder if it was simply usual gauche behaviour or whether it was an attempt to combat boredom. It transpired to be neither and I came to sense the evil that was afoot, as did the other apprehensive novices at my table.

I sat, self-conscious and ever more embarrassingly new to it all. A sack had appeared, carried by a person unshaven and loud of voice, excited and a little drunk. It was dumped upon a nearby table, untied and left to the curiosity of a gibbering group that had collected around it.

We at our table made no attempt to investigate but were aware of a pathetic falsity in the explosions of laughter, the buffoonery and bravado of the 'veteran', six-weeks-old Kenya policemen circling the sack. Some passed it by nervously; others satisfied their curiosity with a drink-emboldened indifference and felt it, their mouths set in a taut smile, breathing heavily and eyes shining.

The contents of the sack were never exposed fully to view but every time it was picked up and dropped the sound was dull and resilient, as if something made of rubber, or a snake, or even a dead cat. No! too light for a cat.

Later, after the sinister sack ceased to entertain all those lean and hard-looking 'Kenya Cowboys' our small group turned its own furtive attentions to it. Feeling the outside of the grubby sack, not one of us was prepared to submit what it was accurately. Or perhaps I should say that not one of us was prepared to contradict the fantastic story that was circulating, namely, that the sack contained a pair of human hands severed at the wrist.

We were eventually obliged to sheepishly, and not a little nauseatingly, reconsider our guesses and to agree that it was just that—a pair of human hands!

They were, we discovered, the hands of a Kikuyu terrorist shot that very morning by the senior syndicate during its final training scheme (the 'scheme' was a two- or three-day patrol to seek and eliminate Mau Mau). The body of the terrorist had been in an inaccessible place and recovery was impossible. The hands therefore had been removed and brought back for fingerprinting and possible identification by the Criminal Investigation Department.

This gory, though practical, method of identifying any Mau Mau despatched deep in forests or gorges was later to be severely forbidden. Many an outraged cry of condemnation was to reach the colony from sedate and horrified humanitarians in England. So, it came to be a practice carried out covertly and at the discretion of those on the spot. The view I held at the time was that, provided always the practice was solely for the purpose of facilitating positive identification and not just a form of trophy-collecting, there was some justification for it.

Undoubtedly the syndicate of insensitive 'bush coppers' that deposited their evidence of a kill on the canteen table were to be criticized for their actions.

During those first weeks at Gilgil I learned to refer to Mau Mau terrorists as 'micks'. It was a term that came into universal usage and had derived from the cartoon character Mickey Mouse, as used by security forces when talking about Mau Mau in uncertain company or over their radios. Even settlers and officials came to favour the expression as being preferable to uttering the sinister 'Mau Mau'. It somehow demonstrated their contempt, and their stout refusal to back up from the savage terrorist gangs, to describe them lightly as 'micks'.

Those nights during December 1953 as a fledgling member of the Kenya police were uneasy and the slightest sound would awaken me. Almost nightly the stillness was shattered by the crackle of gunfire—not always very far distant either. Sometimes it would be the activities of one of the syndicates undergoing its night-ambush training. Other nights it would be a genuine security force contact with a terrorist gang in transit or while raiding a wheat store or such like.

Indeed, sleep was elusive and the hours of darkness were tense and long. But I was not regretful of the decision I had made and, despite all, my enthusiasm quickened.

Chapter 2
'Kenya Cowboys' under training

There were lectures on law and criminal procedure. We were taught how to effect an arrest and execute warrants. There was instruction on the framing of charges and what elements of same would have to be proved. The phraseology of the 'caution' administered to suspects and persons in custody was soon indelibly printed on my mind. How to take statements from witnesses was hammered into us and it was rapidly appreciated by even the most un-police-minded of us that this was one of the really important requirements of efficient police work; the ability to sort the wheat from the chaff! There were heavy-going lectures by an expert from Nairobi C.I.D. on how to take and classify fingerprint impressions. The whorls, loops and arches that he gave such a laborious dissertation on soon had my head in a 'whorl'! I was not particularly well educated in the specialist art of fingerprints at the end of his series of lectures. I did, nonetheless, listen attentively enough to remember that fingerprint impressions were always to be rolled and not pressed—a good impression being about one and a half inches wide. Instruction on the lingua franca, Swahili, took up a great deal of the curriculum and it was not long before we came to realize just how rich and expressive the language is.

Some extremely entertaining periods were devoted to practical court-room instruction held in a crumbling old whitewashed barrack room. Members of the class were nominated to play the various roles and the performances were often quite hilarious. I have in mind an afternoon when a 'drunk and disorderly' case was prosecuted. Ricky Phillips, a broad-accented, stocky Devonian was the accused. He was escorted into the building well under the influence of several Tuskers. After pleading not guilty, he conducted his own defence and burbled on and on about the importance of diverting oneself when the pressure of work was creating tension. It was a riot and, having been subjected by the mock court to various sobriety tests, he was solemnly convicted. His incoherent address in mitigation of sentence would have been held as contempt of any court. The penalty was that he take command of the syndicate at its passing-out parade the following week. Ricky's last slurred comment was, "It's a bloody shameful travesty of justice, that's what it is."

We nevertheless gained a lot of knowledge from these practical sessions on court-room procedure. Most of us also concluded that a person accused of a crime could be as guilty or as innocent as his pocket allowed. No! Not bribery; a smart lawyer to probe the flaws?

It was generally known by all members of the syndicate that few trainees at Gilgil ever failed their final exams. And not for reasons of proficiency either. The Force could ill-afford to re-circulate a student. He had to be pushed through and put out in the field as a probationary sub-inspector with all despatch. This usually meant that a few days before the exams the class instructor would hold an unscheduled question-and-answer session. There was little doubt that this was a preliminary test based on the actual examination paper that the class would get.

This was a blatant invitation to apathy, yet it was astonishing just how keen my colleagues were to assimilate the instruction on law and to pass the exams on merit. Law appeared to hold a singular fascination for most. Possibly because the very concept of applying it was so alien and such a contra-distinction to their erstwhile mode of living. Although they had applied for the vacancies advertised for officers in the Kenya Police with few reservations, they had never really believed that statutes, penal code and evidence procedure would become an integral part of the work they would be involved in. I refer, of course, to those contract (supernumerary) officers, the 'Kenya Cowboys', and not to officers appointed in the pensionable establishment. There was a world of difference between them, psychologically as well as professionally.

I, for one, was never over-eager to grapple with the legal definitions of larceny, the Judges Rules, or the difference between best, secondary and hearsay evidence, powers of arrest, entry and search, and so much else. There was always something rather stilted and ponderous about it. In the circumstances then existing in Kenya it was expecting an officer to be academic when what really mattered was to be dynamic.

At an early stage I had decided that the lingua franca, Swahili, was the most important subject. To acquire a good working knowledge of it I considered the priority talent, not a consummate understanding of the law. I, therefore, swotted Swahili while others gave their attention to the criminal code. Seldom did I miss an evening class in Swahili run by the very able and urbane Arab named Ali, whose home was on cloves-scented Zanzibar. He cared nothing for racial controversy or the mesmeric Mau Mau organization that was disrupting the life of the colony. His only insistence was that the language be learnt the correct way, meaning as it was spoken by the Swahilis themselves (a coastal tribe much influenced by Arab traders) and not the up-country, 'kitchen' Swahili. But, naturally, almost everyone new to the country seemed to prefer the impure 'kitchen' Swahili, the idea being to make oneself understood in the shortest possible time and not to impress the East African indigene with a superior knowledge of his own language.

A large portion of the course was devoted to weapon training. Particularly interesting and of infinite value was the 'shoot to live' pistol training. The fundamentals being a rapid draw, instinctive aiming and triggering fast. Forefinger exercise necessitated what was termed 'dry-pulling'. Amusing and often perilous were the evening spells that some trainees devoted to this. The metallic click-clicking of these 'dry-pulling' sessions is a sound that will forever be indissolubly associated with my traineeship in Gilgil.

The exercise was one that was encouraged by instructors and of inestimable value to the novice. I well recall two evenings when the monotonous clicking throughout the barrack block was interrupted by the roar of a discharged round followed by an awful silence until someone yelled out, "You stupid bastard, prove the f...... thing first!"

Derision and scorn bombarded the room in which the unpardonable sin had been perpetrated. Both embarrassed and shaken recruits succeeded in retrieving the bullets and kept them as souvenirs of their folly.

This matter of proving a weapon every time it was to be handled (practice, handed to someone, cleaned, etc.) other than to actually fire it was religiously adhered to if one wanted to survive and not to harm others. The maxim was "A weapon is deemed to be loaded until personally proved otherwise". Yet another maxim that was instilled into us recruits with tiresome regularity was, "NEVER point a weapon at anyone unless you are prepared to KILL him".

Inevitably there was some horseplay with firearms but, in passing I would mention that I knew of only one probationary inspector who indulged in the wilful and atrocious game known as 'Russian Roulette'. He shot a soldier dead in a local bar one night. Both he and his sporty, though equally moronic, protagonists were rather drunk at the time.

There was one aspect of weapon training that was a signal success with everyone and I always enjoyed it immensely. It was the school's jungle range. Some miles from the town in the vicinity of the Command Ammunition Depot—Mau Mau's most reliable source of ammunition during slack pre-emergency days—in thick scrub country, were positioned assorted plywood figure targets over a two-hundred-yard patrol course. An old Sten gun was used and each member of the syndicate was required to walk with great circumspection along a narrow track a few yards in front of the instructor. At intervals a target would appear and the student was expected to discharge a burst at it, then proceed warily on his way until another and another came into view. This simulated anti-terrorist patrol terminated with leaping over a small mound to empty the remainder of the magazine into a small group huddled inside an artificially constructed hide-out. The total number of hits on targets was then counted.

I would have defied any trainee 'Kenya Cowboy' to walk that jungle trail with eyes darting to right and left to spot targets/ Mau Mau and not feel the tension and excitement knot up in his stomach.

We were encouraged, somewhat fatuously I thought, to imagine that ahead of us in the bush to be patrolled were real Mau Mau terrorists. At that stage of our induction to Kenya's security forces it was not at all difficult to imagine 'micks' under one's bed at night. The only thing was, we hadn't learnt how to distinguish them from the ordinary African!

As with most strangers to the mysterious African scene, our gullibility made us splendid customers for the peddlers of alarm and despondency. The peril of horrendous Mau Mau, according to the many 'wailing willies' who assailed us, was so ubiquitous that few young trainees would even walk the dark mile from the school to town at night. The long knives were poised in every shadowy nook.

It was not surprising therefore, sitting in one's austere barrack room, feeling inadequate and vulnerable, that the dismantling of one's pistol, cleaning it and 'dry snapping' gave an odd and comforting satisfaction. Added to this eccentric feature of evening activity were those hours spent modifying holster and belt—the attachment of straps to enable the weapon to be slung lower and the removal of some leather here and there to facilitate a faster draw.

The motley assortment of gun-slinging equipment was really something to be seen and, for some obscure reason, the camp commandant appeared to countenance it. Or did he just play at Nelson? The fact remains, however, that if an officer were on either operational or special duties no one really gave a damn if he wore his pistol through a ring in his nose.

Each syndicate concluded its training syllabus with a spell of extended patrol/ambush activity called a 'scheme'. This was, in effect, a three-day safari into the forests or gorges in full operational regalia, ostensibly searching for real terrorists. I was to learn some time later that syndicate instructors even went so far as to confer with local police and military authorities to ascertain as reliably as possible what areas were most likely to contain terrorist elements.

These schemes were regarded as an instructor's *pièce de résistance* and pre-eminently the purpose was to assess the recruits' operational ability. A great deal depended upon the recruit officer's performance during the scheme as to whether he was destined for assignment to a forest post or a town station. Naturally, if his strong suit was stalking through the jungles and toting a gun then he would take the opportunity of displaying any prowess in this respect during the patrol.

On the other hand those who had decided that such a life would be purgatory would bitch and scowl from start to finish.

The scheme arranged for syndicate 19A, of which I was a member, was surely one of the most memorable occasions in the lives of all who took part, and that includes our youthful instructor. This slightly built, lean officer was of the dedicated, outdoor scouting type. During the briefing for the scheme he apprised us of a general resurgence of terrorist activity in the Ol Kalou and Oleolondo area not far from Gilgil. The operational target was to be a towering mound of earth, rock and vegetation called Kipipiri, which is actually an appendix of the Aberdare range lying northeast, some twenty miles distant from the training school. On this mountain we were invited to believe that several hard-core militant rebel gangs were ensconced.

At the briefing we were allocated certain tasks and mine was to carry one of five Sten guns. We were made to understand that the project about to be embarked on was a most ambitious one; it had been attempted by only one other syndicate. We were expected to climb and traverse the entire bulk of Kipipiri; an extremely formidable venture for untried men. Of course, at the time, not one of us cared much what the implications were. All we were interested in was that we were going to execute something of a seriously combatant nature. Moreover, as we were by then the senior syndicate no time was wasted in savouring every ounce of the glory our 'veteran' status entitled us to.

Two tins of bully beef, two packets of dates and two packets of biscuits was all the food we were advised to carry, plus two water bottles, two blankets and a spare pair of socks.

How complacent we all were during the drive out from the school in a five-tonner at three a.m., before the initial ascent to about eight thousand feet when the denser tropical greenery was encountered. I personally discovered in myself a profound liking for the lushness of the flora, and the timeless tranquillity of its stillness, the infinite variety of nature's uncultivated wonders and her wildlife. Everything was so alive, so ageless, and gave me such a strange feeling of detachment. All the pettiness and the meanness of sophisticated living fell away. The mind was allowed to unwind and regain its equilibrium. Yes, I enjoyed escaping into the gloomy labyrinths of vegetation and during the first day's climbs I picked up the glove thrown down by Mother Nature. I accepted her challenge then and thereafter.

With my sub-machine gun cocked and thrust before me, I pulled myself up seventy-degree inclines and surveyed the breathtaking views when emerging into sunny glades. I thrilled to the sight of muddy pools by the side of which the huge prints of elephant feet looked like the holes dug by children at the seashore, and regarded in awe their even more gargantuan droppings. Bamboo exploding like rifle shots in the heat of the day and buffalo butting each other on an opposite slope—this was my forte and this was Kenya at its most magnificent.

In the teeth-chattering and numbing cold of that morning in early January in the foothills of the lofty and forbidding Aberdare ranges, the twenty of us were set down with our accoutrements and weapons. The asthmatic old cattle truck turned round and was heard to grind off back to Gilgil past isolated farms and scattered African huts, their occupants sleeping still. From the nearby Kipipiri police post two African askari (native police) of the Kipsigis tribe joined us. They were our guides and had patrolled so often through the dark, dense forests and deep valleys of the 12,000-foot-high mountain that, even if they were unable to lead us to any terrorist gangs, they would ensure we ascended and descended without getting lost too often.

At the start every member of the syndicate was well braced with confidence and had been excitedly anticipating the excursion for several days past. It was to be the culmination of all previous scampering about in bush and the jungle-range exercises. Frankly, it was believed by many to be a diabolical and whimsical waste of time, and, if the syndicate instructor was a safari type anyway, then it was perhaps a little less whimsical but infinitely more diabolical. He would plan the scheme to include the maximum amount of hiking and the minimum of anti-terrorist manoeuvre.

The short march across the foothills and wadis was a fast one in order to gain the main slopes before first light. As the last of the man-high elephant grass and thorn bush was cleared, the summit of the Mau escarpment, fifteen miles across the Rift, caught alight with the first rays of the sun as it climbed up behind the Aberdare range and brought day to the Great Rift Valley. In single file and pausing at intervals the column steadily gained height.

I found myself at the head of the defile, pivoting my head slowly from right to left and back again, eyes and ears striving to penetrate the matted and all-concealing undergrowth that crowded in on the patrol. To me it was undergrowth that hid cunning terrorists by the score, all waiting the opportunity to jump out on us. The column was called to a halt to enable stragglers to catch up with a frequency that irritated me. I could hear the curses and protests of those behind and below and was not making myself at all popular, thus I was obliged to reduce the rate of climb considerably. The urge I had to put my head down, spread my weight evenly on both feet, and just keep climbing until I reached the top was overwhelming—an urge that was never to desert me during my tour of duty in Kenya and seemed intent on purging me of all civilization's deleterious effects.

The column levelled out on Kipipiri's summit just before the cruel African sun pulled the blinds down to cool us and bring a short-lived evening. I shall always readily recall the kaleidoscopic brilliance of that sunset viewed from our perch at 12,000 feet. It was of truly poetic inspiration. No wonder Mau Mau terrorists were reluctant to quit their forest domain!

As each recruit inspector cleared his small recess in the undergrowth and heather and tins of bully beef were opened to be greedily devoured, there was a subdued atmosphere of victoriousness. Shoulders were a bit sore from chafing haversack straps, faces were reddened by a remorseless sun, the stubble on chins was darkening and the polish on boots had all but disappeared. A small party sent out in search of water returned hurriedly to report having seen elephants. Alarm created by this was quickly dispelled by the reassuring words of the instructor that we would not be bothered by them if we left them alone.

Each member was told of the hour he would perform sentry duty, and three per shift was the order. Then those that could rolled up in their blankets and fitfully slept. I was not to be one of them unfortunately. The penetrating cold and damp misery of both those nights atop Kipipiri was to serve as a harsh lesson to me thereafter. I'd scornfully decided on one blanket only whereas four would have been insufficient. I had no sleep during either of the two nights and four colleagues became the beneficiaries of my neglect. Being constrained as I was to keep on the move all night to keep warm, I did their spells of sentry duty.

Summing up those first hours of our introduction to the dark 'unknown' interior of Kenya's Mau Mau-infested forests is easy. It was a pleasure, something of an outing and, except for those at the head of the column who were rather tense from peering so closely into the heavy foliage, almost everyone settled down to enjoy the air, the views and the novelty of it all. Photographs were taken and jokes were cracked. So blithe in fact was the syndicate's spirit that a catchy little ditty was composed and sung in low tones to the tune of 'It's a long way to Tipperary':

It's a long way to Kipipiri, it's a long way to go
It's a long way up Kipipiri
There's no Mau Mau there we know
With our tins of bulleee and our packs of dates
It's a long, long way to Kipipiri and it's one place I 'ates

Not surprisingly, although there was abundant evidence of Mau Mau activity here and there along the climb, no terrorists were seen, or smelt! In actual fact it would have been nothing short of a miracle had any been bumped into, so deafening was the commotion we made. This much I realized in subsequent anti-terrorist operations even if I didn't at the time.

About fifty-six hours later, after having traversed the entire length of majestic 'Kipi' and gambolled in its sundry valleys, executing a sweep or two with 'stops' situated in (believably) strategic positions, the column began to descend.

For hours we dropped through the beautiful, peaceful, verdant forests of cypress and cedar. Occasionally a bush buck was seen to scamper off, and once we stood and watched in awe a herd of buffalo grazing on an adjacent slope. A few members even swore they had spotted rhino; all were glad that none appeared at close quarters—nasty creature, rhino, in thick bush.

It was now that one began to appreciate the fatiguing effects of the patrol, which was strung out for about two hundred yards. Some members had even removed their boots to expose raw heels and toes. Eyes, instead of scanning the rocky outcrops, were dull and unseeing. Weapons were carried in a negligent manner and conversation had dried up. Men were limping, dragging their blankets behind them and asking for water that no one had. There was throughout the column a complete disregard for safety and, as far as it was concerned, Mau Mau terrorists were a fallacy, just something that had grown out of a legend surrounding the Kikuyu tribe.

No water was found on the descent and the last drops had been mopped up halfway through that blistering morning. I found myself still at the head of the serpent and was able to maintain a comforting proximity to the two guides, both of whom were quite openly amused at our condition. The sole aim of all was to reach the haven of Colonel Franklin's farm below which, a few hours after midday, was like a mirage to most.

The pathetic groups of twos and threes from syndicate 19A that straggled rather disgustingly into the yard of Randolf Franklin's farm looked more like survivors from a plane crash. Even our Kenya Police Reserve instructor—lean, hard and seasoned man that he was—did not have the manner or appearance of an officer ready to do battle with insurgents, or for that matter to educate us in the craft of jungle operations. He too was utterly exhausted.

And so the pitiful and dishevelled body of recruit coppers concluded their scheme. There could not have been many who would have opted for forest-post duties at that particular moment. Clustered around a filthy horse trough they drank greedily while African farm labourers stood and gaped in astonishment. What an uninspiring and contemptible bunch of 'Kenya Cowboys' we must have looked. Everyone was more than ready for *mingi* bottles of cold Tusker and mighty thankful that the spectacular Kipipiri was behind him. Although I did not know it at the time I was destined to spend a lot of time on that mountain; it was to become my exclusive hunting ground for many months ahead.

The following day, spruce but aching, we formed up on the ever-dusty parade ground under the nervous command of Ricky Phillips. Our instructor approached and stood before us.

"I'm pleased, and naturally proud, to inform you that no one has failed his examinations. You are all released for the remainder of the day. I'm sure you are all feeling the effects of the scheme. It was not an easy one to be sure, but will not have done you any harm. Once those blisters heal up you'll have some nice hard skin there and should not be troubled on future patrols." At this point he permitted himself a smile then continued, "I advise all of you to prepare your kit ready to move out when your postings have been promulgated."

There was much speculation on each individual's posting. All had stated a preference and a second choice. The more long-in-tooth wanted only to find a cosy niche in a town station or the Traffic Branch in Nairobi. Others, even less inclined to hunt terrorists, had nominated Mombasa, so far away and so immune from the emergency as to be in another country. Some were hoping for a forest post, a life reputed to be tough and unglamorous. My first option was for a General Service Unit. They were a branch of the Force much admired for their operational efficiency and discipline. Failing a G.S.U., I wanted Nyanza, far off to the north on the shores of beautiful Lake Victoria. However, as was the case with nearly everyone, neither choice was granted. My posting was the Lower Rift Valley Province with its headquarters at Nakuru.

Before the parade dismissed that morning the instructor bade me see him at his office at one thirty p.m.

"Hell! What have I done?" I said to my roommate Nick Pearson as he carefully eased his boots off. "They wouldn't be going to offer me Seamus O'Flanigan's job as Canteen Supervisor, would they?"

"Bloody Jesus! Not you, *rafiki*, you are too horribly incorruptible," replied Nick rather tartly.

My brief interview with Mr Curtis, the instructor, early that afternoon, left me disconsolate and angry. The circumstances that led up to my audience with him and those that immediately followed are well worth relating as they illustrate the magnitude of any incident involving negligence with firearms. As condensed as I can possibly make it, this is what it was all about.

While on the epic scheme on Kipipiri I carried a Sten gun and two magazines. As previously narrated, there had been short but vigorous exercises carried out here and there en route. A valley was selected and swept by half the syndicate while the other half were deployed as stops further up or down. It was during one such sweep while scrambling out of an exceedingly hampering patch of jungle that I dropped my spare magazine containing twenty-five rounds of 9mm ammunition. After an immediate but fruitless search the sweep was continued. Both the instructor and I were perturbed by the loss but no time could be spared for a concerted and thorough search. Any embarrassment I felt was engulfed by self-persecution; it was a black mark indeed. But just how black I was not to know until several months later when I had learned more about terrorist tactics.

The words of Mr Curtis were weighed carefully and full of sympathy: "... so you see, there is nothing for it but to retrace our steps and attempt to recover it. We will drive out early tomorrow morning with the same two guides. Don't worry now; we'll be back by midday."

I was flabbergasted, horrified in fact. There was the whole syndicate in the throes of arranging an end-of-course party and I was to punish myself on 'Kipi' again. Where on earth would I even begin to look anyway? Could I even remember the valley we were in at the time? How stupid to think it could be found. How mortifying for me.

That I was able to drag my sore and aching body up those steep slopes and down into the nettle-ridden, creeper- and bush-entangling gullies is beyond clear recollection. I knew it was a futile task to pinpoint where I had slithered and scrabbled during that first day's play at operational coppers. I made as convincing a show as possible of being purposeful during the search but even with the efforts of the instructor, which were gallant and adequate proof of his robust constitution, it was fruitless.

The real reason why a return was made, of course, was to satisfy headquarters that some positive efforts had been made to recover the magazine. If the authorities could submit that our diligent search had failed to locate it, then the chances were that Mau Mau would not spot it either. Despite the apparent preposterousness of the direction by provincial H.Q. to search for the magazine one had to remember just how closely these wily terrorists followed the movements of security forces who sallied to and fro in the forests. Ground covered by our patrol would have been scrupulously searched for any item of equipment dropped. The resting places we had used on 'Kipi' for instance had been raked over for tins, cigarette ends, matches, pieces of rag or even occasional rounds of ammunition!

Suffice it to place on record that the damned magazine was not seen again and, so far as could be ascertained from the interrogation of terrorists captured during later months, neither were they able to retrieve it. Care of arms and ammo, therefore, was of unrivalled importance. It was permissible to spit on another without compunction if it were known he had lost a firearm through negligence. (In a later chapter I shall deal more thoroughly with the subject.)

To mark the occasion of our syndicate's passing-out, a grand tippling session was indulged, though for the record it was termed 'a dance'. We all sang the little ditty that had been composed on Kipipiri, talked of 'bumping micks' and generally made fools of ourselves.

Reflexes were sluggish and movement jerky the next day. There was an air of bustle tinged with sadness as cases and kit-bags were packed. The syndicate we had quickly become so proud of was dispersing. There had been many new friendships struck and the few months together had served to mark us as a particular vintage. We were bracketed together and, as regards seniority in the Force, there were twenty of us that would be grouped at a certain level in the Staff List. On the other hand, as the majority of contract inspectors had little intention of serving for longer than one tour, such petty matters as seniority and Staff Lists did not concern us.

As fully fledged police officers, allegedly, our condensed crash course at Gilgil came to an end. Notwithstanding the conscientious efforts of the many fine instructors and staff at the school, they could no more make efficient policemen out of mechanics, retired Indian Army officers and travelling salesmen than they could build bridges on sand without a decent foundation. But there, no one really minded because the only thing that mattered was to get out and do something about curbing the unrestrained savagery of Mau Mau.

Here I would mention that as time went on and the situation in Kenya returned to normal any contract officers who showed a desire to remain in the Force were sent to the police training college at Kiganjo near Nyeri where they underwent a more thorough and comprehensive course of instruction. The Force was always acutely aware of its professional liability in carrying so many half-trained officers.

Looking more like capable and disciplined colonial police officers in our starched khaki tunics and baggy shorts with Sam Browne belts and peaked caps, we fell in outside the Adjutant's office. All departing syndicates were addressed by him and he seemed to enjoy the opportunity of giving us youngsters a little homily on our future as law-enforcement officers.

He concluded by saying, though none too seriously, "Uniform shorts are supposed to be a regulation two inches above the knee and no more. Some of you seem to prefer to display your shapely thighs and the Force does not consider it very becoming. Get rid of them and at your own expense have another pair tailored. I don't mind you behaving like cowboys but let's have you dressed like decent ones."

Two days later, after a most impersonal interview with the Assistant Commissioner of Police for the Lower Rift Valley Province at Nakuru police station, I was officially posted to a forest post—in the Gilgil area.

Chapter 3
Vulnerable settlers on a fertile plateau

Providentially I was able to see something of the Kenya settler, his way of life, habits and reaction to the advent of the Mau Mau emergency while still under training at the school in Gilgil. Students were asked a few days before Christmas if they'd like to spend their holiday on a European farm. I did not hesitate and on Christmas Eve found myself embussed with a number of others headed for the Kinangop plateau.

I recalled that this plateau had been pointed out to us while journeying up from Nairobi several weeks earlier and I was looking forward to having a closer look at it.

When the white man first began to break the fertile earth of this plateau it was indifferently occupied by nomadic Masai tribesmen for grazing their cattle. Though, oddly enough, despite alternate grazing land provided for that tribe around Narok and the Mau (not to be confused with Mau Mau) during the first decade of this century, it was not until 1948 that European settlers began to farm in earnest on the Kinangop. Now, six years later, it would have been difficult to find an acre of its arable land not being profitably worked; and it must have been all of two hundred square miles.

With the solid blue-green backcloth of the mighty Aberdare range to the east and the yawning vastness of the Rift Valley below the escarpment as its western boundary, the plateau has all the fabulous qualities of a Kathmandu in Devon.

Situated at an exhilarating 7,000 feet above sea level the air is delightfully pure though breathlessly thin.

Crops flourish richly and abundantly; the only possible feature that marred such perfection being a tendency for too much rain at one time. Also, to remind the settler that he was an interloper on the plateau, the periodic invasion by herds of elephant from the forests of the Aberdares had to be contended with.

From what I had been sombrely told, the farmers on the Kinangop, as elsewhere, were happy to welcome lonely and bored police trainees from the school as guests for short weekends. They were unabashed in their eagerness to have an extra *bunduki* (gun) around the house, not to mention the pleasure of a strange face to study, belonging to someone who could give them all the latest news on life in the Old Country, as England was sentimentally referred too.

After the ride through Naivasha and up the rugged conifer-covered face of the escarpment with its enchanting views, I debussed at a crudely constructed building surrounded by barbed wire and heavily sandbagged. It was the South Kinangop police post. Two elderly police reserve officers greeted us warmly and proceeded to read out the names of the farmers to whom we had been allocated.

'My farmer' was a Mr Wilkins who arrived after a short interval to collect me in his car. He was accompanied by his wife and small son. Our brief pause at the post was enlivened by the arrival of several Land Rovers and a five-ton truck all full to their gunwales with mountains of equipment and African regular police askari, carrying rifles and looking very purposeful The European police inspector, like his askari, was wearing a cherry-red beret announcing his particular department as that of a General Service Unit, the strong-arm men of the Force. Looking tanned, fit and full of action he strode into the post brushing a thick layer of dust off his beret saying quietly to a hefty African sergeant, "*Ngoja kidogo, Kiplangat.*"

He emerged a little later to be immediately and ardently interviewed by me and my colleagues. Our curiosity he satisfied in clipped, almost impatient tones.

"Lot of *shauries* up here, it seems. We've been told to swan around a bit, show the flag like. Wouldn't be at all surprised if the buggers are not laying up in Armstrong's gorge; there's been too much bloody *maneno* over there lately."

He then proceeded to regale us with a vivid account of a previous day's patrol and referred casually to dropping 'micks' in thick bamboo above Fey's *shamba*. Then, patting the Sterling gun slung over his shoulder, he said affectionately, "Lovely jobs these. Not much knock-down over two hundred but the rate of fire is what counts with these bastard golliwogs—they're off before you've time to shout '*Simama*', not that I'd bother to, of course. *Kwa heri*, see you around."

This fleeting prelude to my introduction to the plateau did little to allay the uneasiness growing inside me. I'd already been told a number of times that the Kinangop was a hot-bed of terrorism. By the time our hosts began to arrive we had all decided that it was the firearm we carried that was to be hospitably welcomed and not us. However, I was soon to be contradicted.

Formal, though unreserved, introductions to my host and his wife, Doris, over, I climbed into their car alongside Tommy, their son, who was in the rear. Conversational exchange was short as it was but a few minutes before we pulled up outside an invitingly attractive inn called the Brown Trout. It was one of three hotels on the Kinangop, all of which were more like small clubs. It was the Brown Trout undoubtedly that was the most popular. My host described it as "the Mecca of weekend vacationers from Nairobi", and it was famous for its excellent trout fishing in nearby streams.

It was evidently of more personal significance to the Kinangop farmers who recognized the inn as their own warm and friendly retreat.

"I thought we might have a drink before going home," confided Mr Wilkins. "It's not often that we find a chance to come here these days."

Though in his forties my host was seasoned in features only. His physique was firm and his gait springy. When he spoke it was the voice of a farmer and he wasted no words. I remember to have felt rather self-conscious because it was the first time I had been in alien company with a pistol slung on my hip and kept wondering if it was showing too much!

He bought beer and introduced me to one or two of his friends. I chatted largely to Barry, which name he bade me call him. "No discipline up here you know," he smiled, and I listened to many a caustic comment on Mau Mau and on government mismanagement. I soon discovered that among the men this was the mainstay of most conversation apart from farming and its technical problems. There was a fierce loyalty about these expatriates and had the British national anthem suddenly struck up I've little doubt they'd have all stood stiffly to attention. It was not disaffection for the Crown they expressed, but it was for the "pin-stripe and bowler-hatted asses who brayed from Westminster's benches" that they reserved their angry dialogue. To deliver a scathing diatribe on either Mau Mau or Legco tardiness did much to relieve tension. However, after almost eight years in the R.N. Fleet Air Arm I could easily empathize with their need for a good old 'whinge'.

My room-mate at the training school, Nick, entered with his host so I moved across for a word with him. We were both a trifle disappointed for we had hoped to be billeted together. He described the huge pleasure of his host to have a police officer, armed too, on his property over Christmas. The undisguised relief of his settler host led Nick to believe that he was anticipating trouble over the Yuletide period.

Looking about us we saw that practically every person in the bar carried a weapon of some description. Also significant was the fact that no person was under the influence. I left Nick with his own brave thoughts and rejoined Barry Wilkins.

I was soon convinced that I was among a people under pressure, nerves taut, untrusting, circumspect in all activity, yet seemingly unafraid. It was like being a cog in a machine the mainspring of which was fully wound the whole time. It occurred to me that the strain of living their lives as farmers with the scourge of Mau Mau creeping over the plateau was a terrible misfortune for persons who had only decided to settle on and cultivate the virgin land because the British government had encouraged them to do so.

After an hour of leisurely drinking I seated myself in Barry's car again and was driven to his farm—a modest one-thousand-acre patch!

That night after dinner I was shown to my bed situated in a small room that was an extension of the main building. Before retiring Barry gave me a conducted tour of the house and with a grim thoroughness pointed out exits, windows, safest parts and the most likely places from which an attack could be expected. His doleful commentary I shall not forget.

"... if anything happens this is where I take up my position; I have a good field of fire. Doris would remain in the bedroom there with Tommy and would use the shotgun from that window. You in your room would cover the front approaches from the window shutter. From this dining-room, if necessary ..."

I did my best to appear as redoubtable a guest as he would wish me to be.

Before I bade my host goodnight a police reservist paid the house a routine visit on his duty rounds and informed us that all was quiet on the Kinangop. He added that there was some activity expected on a Len Hobson's *shamba* and that the army had laid several ambushes. We were advised not to stray off the farm limits unless in a vehicle. Barry dispensed a double tot of brandy to this duty vigilante before he wished us a Merry Christmas and proceeded to the next farm. I remember having some doubts as to what his state of sobriety would be when he completed his rounds, if he succeeded in doing so!

How my nerves were a-jangle as I lay myself down for the night. I must have lain with my pistol in my hand for most of it. The following morning I awoke with a bit of a start at my strange surroundings and cursed myself for having been so jittery.

I concluded that it must have been the same with most people until they became fully accustomed to living with the threat of Mau Mau each night, and only then was their relief from anxiety and foreboding the result of an angry fatalism. The attitude adopted was a kind of offended contempt for the inconvenience caused them by insidious Mau Mau. There was no hysteria or histrionics about the preparations that the settler took or in the advice offered. Such advice was all strictly bona fide and one could please oneself whether or not it was heeded.

Mr and Mrs Wilkins were both most assiduous in their ministerings to my comfort and there was nothing I lacked. And yet there was so little I could do to amuse myself until later in the day when I was asked if I would like to go fishing. Tommy had gone with his mother to visit a neighbour and Barry asked if he could see me over at the store. He had a set of scales in front of him, sacks of ground maize behind him, and an African wearing a fez with a book and pencil in his hand by his side. The farm labourers were huddled nearby carrying large pots. I was enlightened by the Wilkins' houseboy who informed me that his *bwana* was issuing the weekly *posho* ration of ground maize. The fact that it was Christmas day affected the routine of the farm but little, though I was given to understand that the farm labour had the day off.

The Wilkins' household was a quiet one. Both Barry and his wife were reserved in their manners and nothing about them or their home could be described as pretentious. They were wont to rise early and retire as soon as the eight o'clock news bulletin was over. Their clothing, food, conversation and tastes were modest but discriminating. Their one overriding concern seemed to be the safety and future of young Tommy. It was patently obvious that the farm and its ceaseless toil exacted a high degree of selflessness and loyalty from them, permitting of no relaxing of their energies and resources. It was not only the greatness of their spirit that one admired but their single-mindedness of purpose too. While living under their roof I came to feel quite guilty languishing in the barren wastes of my own idleness. The Wilkins I regarded as rather typical of most Kenya settlers; they were of sterling material, dedicated, stubborn, full of faith and battling against the odds of both nature and nationalism.

After a superbly prepared Christmas dinner, that was for the most part untouched by all—"Phew! We are not used to such extravagant fare," remarked Doris Wilkins after the pudding— Barry turned to his son.

"Well now, Tom, how'd you like to join Mr Hewitt and me for some fishing, eh?"

It's no secret that I had always eschewed fishing as being the preserve of the more advanced in years. Such thoughts I addressed to Barry. "As a matter of fact I have always preferred walking if I want to relax or to think and ..."

Tommy cut me short by jumping up, shouting, "Let me bring the flies, daddy, and I'll show Mr Hewitt what I think is the best for rainbow trout."

Barry Wilkins fixed a thoughtful gaze on me and examined my indifference more closely. "Perhaps you'd prefer to look over the farm this afternoon if you're not in the mood for fishing. No good casting a line if one is not in the mood."

"Not at all. Gracious me, no," I protested. "I may not own to being an enthusiast but I'm always more than prepared to be convinced of its joys. Where's my rod?"

He grinned at his wife who in turn smiled understandingly at me. She chaffed Barry, intoning slyly, "I suppose Mr Hewitt is of a more active nature and likes to spend his leisure time more vigorously." Little was she aware just how true her words rang.

"Here you are, daddy, I could only find the Coachman and Watson's Fancy flies. They are dressed on number eight hooks."

Glancing at the little tufts of coloured feather secured to hooks in the palm of Barry's hand I tried my best to look discerning. Alas! They conveyed nothing to me.

On the short walk across my host's fields of young wheat and oats he paused often to explain the various characteristics of the crops, or to expound his theories on how best to combat the dreaded crop disease *tackal*—an extremely difficult disease to eradicate that strikes at the root of the plant.

"My opinion is that the disc share deals with it the best. It opens up the earth exposing the fungi to the atmosphere so that it doesn't thrive. A furrow share ploughs too deep, turns the earth right over and buries it again," said Barry, now every inch the dedicated farmer. I remember grunting some sort of understanding.

During the next two hours or so I ambled up and down the banks of the quiet and picturesque stream that ran through the property. Thick tufts of grass and brambles crowded in on all sides. Occasional anthills, some as high as ten feet and looking as if they were about to topple over, sprouted up in ugly contrast. I think that I was more concerned with the presence of snakes than fish.

A desultory cast here and there yielded nothing but a fascinating glinting of the spinner as I pulled it through the racing waters. Barry's efforts were equally unavailing, although he sat there on a rock contentedly puffing at his pipe and staring dreamily into the translucent depths. He was heard to mutter, now and then, "Saucy blighter" or "Blast!" between teeth clamped on pipe stem, and would reel in to the accompaniment of gay clicking from the ratchet of his reel.

My eyes roved over the beautiful landscape and swept across the even, green sea of unripe wheat that rolled up to the edge of the stream on both sides. Vivid clumps of poppies peppered the lush green adding to the eye-catching splendour of the view. In the middle distance my gaze alighted on a small thicket of towering conifers by the side of which I could just discern the top half of a farm building, the windows of which reflected the delightfully sensuous rays of the warm, late-afternoon sun.

Sloping arms with my rod I hopped across the stones to where Barry was sucking drowsily on his pipe. I asked him if the house yonder, pointing with my rod, was where my fellow recruit, Nick, was spending Christmas. Studying the direction of my outstretched arm he deliberated a moment or two.

"No, Peter. I shouldn't think so. You see, that's where the Rucks lived and since that messy affair it has been fitfully managed by a number of people just to keep things ticking over. At the moment I don't think anyone is living there."

I struggled to associate the name Ruck with something messy. He must be referring to Mau Mau, I thought. But, before I was able to phrase a suitable question and have this peaceful angler amplify his solemn statement he stood up and reeled in.

"They're not co-operating at all today. Should have brought the Teal flies I think. Come on, let's go back and have some tea."

Then to Tommy, who I could see farther downstream and who appeared to be trying unsuccessfully to dislodge a large boulder overhanging the water, "Any luck, son? If not then follow us back. Don't stay much longer and don't fall in."

I sauntered off behind Barry who re-lit his pipe and puffed until wreathed in smoke, then asked, tentatively, "Where were you when the Rucks met their nasty end?"

I decided to be perfectly frank. "Mr Wilkins, you'll forgive me but, although the name rings a bell, I just can't fix it either in time or with any particular incident. When did it occur?"

"The Ruck murders, hmm! Now let me think. I seem to recall it would have been towards the end of January this year, around the 24th maybe."

It took me but a moment to revive my memory and I supplied him with the answer. "I was serving on a Royal Naval air station near Paisley in Scotland. The only date that I recall as being significant in its connection with the emergency is 26 March—the Lari massacre happened that night, didn't it? That was a few days after my birthday. Anyway, there were so many horrible incidents that one read of. So it occurred here on the Kinangop, did it? You folk up here have really been in the storm centre."

Ex-Royal Engineer Captain B. Wilkins, as identified in a portrait on the mantel shelf of his home, looked skyward and gently tapped his teeth with the stem of his pipe. He seemed to be not unwilling to furnish me with the details and slowed his pace.

"Yes, we have had our share of the foul Mau Mau crimes up here alright. There was Eric Bowyer before the Rucks, just as beastly, if not more so. Then we had Bingley and Ferguson. Not that we have had it any worse than other settled areas of course. The killings of Meikeljohn and Gibson were shocking, awful slaughters. Then there have been the few fortunate ones—if one may permit such a word—courageous people like Mrs Rayne Simpson and her partner, Mrs Kitty Hesselburger, in their remote house near Mweiga. What a stirring story of almost unbelievable valour and spirit that was; drew gasps of admiration from all over the world, I should think. A frightful experience but they survived the savage attacks as also did Neilson and his wife."

Some of these names were not unknown to me, having read the lurid details in the English press. They were draconian crimes that had quickly made the words 'Mau Mau' synonymous with unspeakable terror; they had become the world's most horrible bogeymen.

He continued, "... and that's the dreadful part of our lives up here these days. We are fully reconciled to the hazards of farming in Kenya but it's being so bloody vulnerable, so exposed you might say, that rattles us. It's only lately that we've had so many askari around and, now that there is one of those G.S.U. outfits on call, we all feel a lot easier."

We strolled on slowly past the rippling sea of fresh crops. I tugged off an ear of unripe corn and studied it meditatively, wondering if the risks and hard labour involved were really justified by the net profit. Barry must have read my thoughts for he too reached out and plucked off an ear.

"It's a high-grade wheat up here. With the right amount of rain and sun most years it's possible to reap two harvests. Then again. nature can be damned diabolical you know. Too much rain during planting or a swarm of locusts. Yes, it's locusts that we fear most of all—voracious insects, millions of them so thick they blot out the sun. A swarm could gobble up my entire crop in a day, which was precisely what did happen during the disastrous invasion of '47 ..."

I interrupted him. "Don't they usually come down from Somaliland and the Arabian desert?"

"They do, yes, and always fly downwind. It is said that they can move fifty miles and more in a day and have been known to cover two hundred square miles. I'm happy to say that the Desert

Locust Survey teams are on the ball and are generally able to warn farmers of the direction a swarm is travelling; we then keep a sharp lookout. Stop the beggars from settling and you're alright. They are something of a delicacy with the African you know, their favourite *chakula*."

Morbid or not I was anxious to have details of Bowyer's death and of others if possible. I remembered having been told that he was murdered while in his bath and decided to tackle my host direct.

"Wasn't this fellow Bowyer attacked as he was taking his nightly bath?"

"Indeed he was, and his two Kikuyu houseboys were hacked to death in his kitchen." His voice had a sharp edge to it. He removed his pipe and breathed heavily through his nose once or twice. The memory of it obviously distressed him.

"Old Eric lived alone over there, an indifferent sort of farmer really but well liked and respected. He was generous and kind. Used to run a little *duka* for his labour and never had a harsh word for them. It was some of his squatter labour that found him first. They had either known that something had happened or were probably suspicious to see the light on. Again, they could even have wanted to make enquiries about the two houseboys who had failed to return to their huts that night. Anyway, they entered and found Eric lying in what appeared to be a bath of blood. His naked body was slashed all over and, as one army officer who went to the scene described it, he looked as if he'd fallen in front of a combine harvester. He had been disembowelled with several thrusts of a *panga*, his entrails slopped around the bathroom. They say it was a ghastly and unforgettably sickening mess. Very few people were allowed in before he was removed. The gang responsible had plainly come from the forest. They even looted the house and rifled the safe of Eric's *duka*. Some said that the money he kept in it was the incentive for the raid. Me? I think it was sheer bloody savagery."

We were approaching the farmhouse and, looking at his watch, Barry remarked that it was another fifteen minutes or so for tea and led me onto his beautifully kept lawn in which stood a pair of sturdy, ancient silver oak trees. I saw some weathered wicker chairs under one. "We'll sit here awhile," he said.

The houseboy bounded up and relieved us of our rods and tackle. He asked expectantly, *"Wapi samaki, bwana?"* To which Barry replied with a grin that his luck was bad that day.

Stretching his legs and placing his pipe beside him Barry again took up his story. "You may know of Steenkamp, I think he's in Nairobi now, C.I.D. or something." I informed him that I didn't.

"He was assigned to the investigation—I believe he was a superintendent—the whole colony was in a terrific kafuffle and the Kinangop fairly oozed with police askari. The Black Watch moved in too, and more *mkubwas* than I care to remember. There were hundreds of arrests. I lost about a dozen of my Kukes. It was amazing just how many labour lines were implicated, if arrests were any criterion, that is. Seems the only people who didn't know of the gang's presence at the forest edge were we *wazungus*. It was exactly the same with the Rucks too; information was completely negative. Anyway, believe it or not, justice was observed some six months later and, had it not been for a brief paragraph in *The Standard* to the effect that eleven Kikuyu terrorists had been hanged in Nairobi Central, we wouldn't have known now. As usual the mammoth efforts of the prosecutor were hampered by the subtleties of British criminal procedure, but he triumphed—or did he merely outwit the defence? God! The age it takes, *and* the conniving, before justice is done."

Testily he knocked his pipe against his shoe and picked at the bowl, then straightened up and said, calmly, "Ready, lad? Let's have some of those mince pies we couldn't demolish at lunch-time. I'm talking too much here."

In the large parlour of the house were three small occasional tables by the open windows. On them was set out an appetizing assortment of cakes, sandwiches, mince pies and Christmas cake. Mrs Wilkins sat before a tray of tea cups with the pot in her hand. She looked up as we entered. "I was beginning to think that it would have been nicer to have tea on the lawn, it's so stuffy in here really. Still, come over here, Peter, and sit by the window. Sugar?"

"Please. Two. I'm absolutely ready for a nice cup of tea."

As I sat down I glanced through the window in time to see Tommy appear from the track through the wheat field. He was trailing his rod behind him and whistling.

"Seems as if Tommy has had enough fishing too," I said. "Must say, though, that he's not difficult to please. Likes the open spaces, does he?"

Fair-haired and slightly built, Doris Wilkins stood up and looked over my head through the window, then, pivoting briskly, she faced her husband. I could see that her usually serene expression had changed to one of annoyance. When she spoke it was a rebuke.

"Barry, for goodness sake! How often have I asked you not to leave that boy alone at the river. I know it is not far away but it can happen so quickly and silently. You know that children are the easiest victims for them. Dear, oh, dear! You are impossible really."

He declined to comment or to excuse the breach of security he knew he was guilty of. I felt that he was acutely aware he had committed an unpardonably negligent act. But then, as I saw it, Barry was not at all unlike everyone else; it was so difficult to accept that Mau Mau were lurking everywhere and just awaiting a chance to pounce. He knew that he had distressed his wife and that whatever he said now could only exacerbate her deep maternal concern for the safety of her boy. I did what I could to save the situation from deteriorating into a minor domestic crisis by grabbing a plate of sandwiches and pushing them, first before her, and then setting them down on the table before him. Then Tommy hove in sight through the door, still trailing his rod over his shoulder. His delighted gurgles when he saw the tempting spread of confection soon assuaged Mrs Wilkins' ill-humour.

On Boxing Day morning I awoke to the sound of a car.

The sun was climbing and I realized that I was still covered with a blanket and was uncomfortably hot. I threw off the bedding and looked at my watch—five past eight. I was surprised and had thought it to be later. I lay listening to the activity outside. A car door slammed, a tractor was droning in the distance, a peahen warbled not far off in the wheat, there was a metallic noise from the direction of the workshop. Then I heard Barry shout for breakfast: "*Chakula! Lete chakula.*"

I felt wonderfully refreshed and had slept soundly. I recall chiding myself for having lain so taut and restive the previous night. What a pity I had not joined Barry who, as he had intimated at dinner yesterday, had gone to the dam early in order to carry out some repairs to it.

The Wilkins' dog, Major, whimpered and scuffed outside the bedroom door. Taking the hint I climbed out of bed and pulled on a gown and slippers, slung a towel over my shoulder and made my way to the bathroom. Ten minutes later I joined Barry and Doris Wilkins at the breakfast table. They were earnestly engaged in conversation, in which I was immediately included once I had sat down and addressed my grapefruit.

From the talk I understood that the unoccupied house of a European had been burnt down during the night. Barry recapitulated in full for my benefit.

He had not been to the dam after all but instead had driven over to the South Kinangop police post to obtain details of the incident. It was not a house really but a wooden fishing lodge situated on the bank of the Turasha River below the escarpment some six miles from Gilgil. It was the property of a European civil servant in Nairobi, Hazledene being his name I think. Its contents of blankets, cooking utensils, tinned food, paraffin and the like, were all made off with. The building was then fired and the blaze lit the dark sky to announce yet another case of arson that was unlikely to be solved in a hurry. Police from Hermann's Post were following up tracks that were headed for the Kariandusi area.

"I don't know what the local police intend doing about those fishing huts on the Turasha," concluded Barry, "but they'd better get around to them pretty soon otherwise they'll all go up in smoke."

I volunteered, somewhat lamely, "The owners will have to clear out every bit of useful property and hope to reduce the incentive for attacks on them." This sounded most unconvincing so I added, "If not it will mean that a guard will have to be put on each one." (It seems there were about ten such huts tucked away along the Turasha River.)

Dabbing his lips with a napkin Barry pushed back his chair and crossed his legs. He said, thoughtfully, "Might as well ambush them as they are and see if the 'micks' will swallow the bait."

The incident was in some respects quite significant because some months later those same fishing huts and lodges were to be a sore headache for me. They were to fall within my area of operations and responsibility. Several others became the object of jubilant Mau Mau raids. It transpired that security forces were able to do nothing to protect them. If a building was unoccupied it inevitably became fuel for the bonfire of a terrorists' war dance some night.

While enjoying the Wilkins' hospitality over that Yuletide of 1953, I most probably did what many others of my kind did—listened a great deal with a deferential ear to the yarning and commentaries of any settler who had the time to bend my ear. And if the yarns and commentaries were not forthcoming then I would question astutely on the periphery of any matter I sought enlightenment on.

However, there was barely a vestige of bombast about either Barry or his wife. Their reticence I found to be a difficult barrier to my inquisitiveness. Towards the end of my short stay I came to realize that there existed a sort of treaty in the house. It applied to any conversation on the emergency—it was taboo. In fact, I was later to discover that such was the case in the households of more than a few settlers—it was the will of the womenfolk that the rule be rigidly imposed. They had become heartily sick of listening to their husbands, sons and brothers discoursing unendingly on the Mau Mau emergency and its allied topics. It was apparent at any social function, too, that the women were constantly on their guard against allowing conversation to gravitate to such monopolistic, though nonetheless popular, topics. They had become intolerant in a bored, as well as an antipathetic, way. They rebelled at the depressing lack-lustre conversation and sought to enrich it. And who could blame them?

So it was, then, that apart from an isolated occasion or two, such as when Barry loosened his tongue to relate the Bowyer assassination, I experienced a disappointing dearth of story-telling while his guest.

Yet it was not necessary for me to trek far in order to compensate for the scarcity of verbal grazing in the Wilkins' pastures. Fifteen minutes drive to the Brown Trout was guaranteed to satisfy my appetite because there, as with other clubs and hotel bars, a form of sex apartheid was practised. The males assembled in the region of the bar and the opposite gender either sat discreetly detached or strayed outside to gossip gaily among themselves. It was indeed most unusual to find a group of men who, while enjoying a sundowner, permitted the interloping of females. Thus, talk of the emergency and Mau Mau could proceed unrestricted by soggy female sentiment.

At about six in the evening of Boxing Day, it was to the Brown Trout that I drove with Barry and his family. It was a warm, clear evening and most folk were outside sitting or standing on the lawn. Dazzled, I watched the huge gold and red conflagration of sun as it raced earthward, igniting the puffs of cloud hovering above the Mau summit as it passed them. The great orb of blood-red beauty plummeted out of sight even as I watched, leaving the sky above illuminated by an enchanting, ever-changing pattern of glorious colour. Turning my head to the right the sight was equally as inspiring. A thick bank of heavy cloud that hung menacingly over Mount Kinangop, the highest peak of the Aberdare range, slowly became infused with a warm glow that grew in intensity until it was quite impossible to believe it was the same cloud that a few moments ago had looked so ominous. "It really is red cloud," someone nearby remarked. "It must be, for the sun has gone down, hasn't it? It can't be the reflection." A splendidly poetical, no less naïve, summing-up that fitted the magic of the moment perfectly.

I remember quite clearly as I stood with Barry and others experiencing a sharp feeling of regret that I had not spent the day arduously—out in the fields on a tractor or repairing *boma* fencing, dipping cattle. Looking around me at the brown, leathery and lined features of the settlers I felt that they deserved the refreshment they were enjoying. They were not just being sociable or endeavouring to obtain some 'lift' from the liquor, but were washing down the dust of their toil and satisfying a genuine thirst. Many of them had made the evening a special occasion and would not normally have found the time to visit the inn.

As twilight deepened into night and a million crickets came out to play and sing, it suddenly became quite chilly. People started moving into the bar or pulled their jackets and cardigans on. Many could be seen making their departures. It was seven o'clock and they wanted to be back on their farms before any itinerant gangs exploited their absence to swoop down from the forests to burn and pillage.

A short, bespectacled, khaki-clad settler, with what looked to be a 9mm Beretta stuffed into his hip pocket, was tearing himself away from his friends. I heard him pleading, "Honestly, if I don't get back now the bastards will be among my *ngombis* and I don't want this Christmas ruined like the last one." He spoke for most of them.

"Did you hear about Davo Davidson, Barry?" A lean, fair-haired and rather distinguished looking person, wearing a wide-brimmed bush hat, had stepped agilely across the lawn to where we were standing.

"No. What's he done now, Ven, shaved off his beard?" returned Barry, at the same time gripping the other's extended right hand and shaking it vigorously.

I was introduced as "... one of our new police fellows", then listened to what had happened to 'Davo'. The stranger, Ven, continued: "Not exactly, Barry, but he had a close shave even so. Met Kimathi somewhere on the Chania River in the bamboo and was shot up. Quite a *shauri* it was. I'm told that he's in hospital with a couple of rounds in his guts. Had he not been wearing that bullet-proof vest of his he wouldn't have survived apparently."

Barry chuckled once or twice then looked serious. "Well! No one's doubting that Davo knows his gunmanship, but, if he persists in conducting a personal one-man war with Dedan then my advice to him would be to return to Chicago and become Al Capone's bodyguard again. The man's tough. Crazy tough!"

The conversation soon changed to farming and I withdrew into the bar to order more beer.

To digress for a moment. I knew nothing of this character Davo Davidson at that time, neither had I heard of his feats of marksmanship. But, some twelve months later I was to meet this legendary Buffalo Bill of Kenya. He had eventually decided to give up his fearless quest for the arch-terrorist leader, Dedan Kimathi, and bought a farm at Ol Kalou, not very far from a police post that I was in command of. He still sported a shaggy beard and was still adamant that it would not be removed until Kimathi had been killed—preferably by him. He would growl to his audience with an air of the utmost confidence that he had NOT discontinued his search for the elusive gangster, that his spies were still spread through the forests and that he was but awaiting information of his whereabouts and would be after him.

It was, however, never to be Davo's destiny to bring the notorious Dedan Kimathi to book. The honours for this were to be taken by a group of ordinary tribal policemen—Kikuyu themselves in fact.

Only once did I have the chance of seeing Davo's extraordinary and renowned skill with firearms. I'd heard that his trigger-work was phenomenal. He was known to be a wizard at quick-drawing and trick-shooting and often gave exciting demonstrations that left his audiences spellbound. Shooting coins out of the air, placing six rounds in a two-inch circle while firing over his shoulder with the aid of a mirror, all ambidextrous and with ease. His *pièce de résistance* was graphically described as being the shooting of six imaginary assailants as he threw himself to the ground, drawing his pistol and hitting each of the targets before completing the fall. Somewhat improbable one must agree, but there.

The exhibition that I was to witness involved the killing of a dog. Having collected provisions from Nakuru one day I was leaving the store when there was suddenly a commotion just down the street. I saw a large dog foaming at the mouth and savaging a young African child. After the crowd that had quickly gathered had recovered its wits, several men armed with sticks cordoned off the animal. It was snarling and baring a wicked set of teeth. A Land Rover then drew up and a bearded, unkempt giant of a white man walked across. In an instant he barged his way through the crowd then walked to the child, now lying motionless. As he did so the dog leapt at him. He turned with a speed and balance that belied his size, kicked out and caught the dog in mid-air. It yelped and soared on for several more yards. The right hand of this person then became a blur as it reached under the left arm of his bush jacket and withdrew with a heavy-calibre pistol. I heard only one shot fired but the dog, having hit the ground, did not stir. Blood ran from its mouth. This person was obviously known to many in the crowd. "*Mzuri, mzuri sana Bwana Davo!*" they cried.

It was no wonder Dedan Kimathi avoided him.

I returned with the recharged glasses just as the fair-haired stranger said, "Bye for now then. See you tomorrow," and stepped lightly back across the lawn to where an attractive woman was beckoning him. I assumed she was his wife.

"Who is he?" I asked Barry.

Canting his glass and quaffing half its contents first, he then replied, "You'll be seeing him again tomorrow afternoon before you return to Gilgil. I've arranged for us to have tea at his place. He has a wonderful house that nestles right at the base of the Aberdares. It was one of the earliest ever built up here and is a bit of a show place. Ven's father was among the first settlers allocated land on the plateau."

"Is Ven himself a farmer?" I asked.

"There's no denying that Ven is a very good farmer, something of the country squire type probably. However, he spends most of his time with the army nowadays. His services as a tracker are invaluable and he knows the forest above the Kinangop possibly better than anyone else. He is a natural tracker, reputed to be one of the best. He and Ken Cunningham at Thomson's Falls should team up really."

Conversation then nibbled at the subject of tracking for the next five minutes or so. We agreed that most settlers would be worth a score of soldiers and police when it came to anti-terrorist operations, the former knowing so thoroughly well the modus operandi, the haunts and the characteristics of Mau Mau.

"Any security force commander who chooses to decline the services of the local farmer-settler will go off at half-cock," observed Barry.

I was not disposed to dispute this observation of his at the time. However, although several months later I'd have still probably agreed in principle, there would have been certain very definite reservations.

Mrs Wilkins appeared between us with Tommy, who was carrying a box wrapped in gay paper. The lad joyfully explained that it was a model aeroplane kit given him by the Kinangop Farmers' Association—I seem to recall there had been a children's party at the rear of the inn. His mother, addressing nobody in particular and looking fidgety, said, "Come on, dear! Isn't it about time we made a move? It's seven-thirty."

Barry glanced quickly at me then at his watch. "Yes, Doris, I suppose we ought to make tracks. But, look here, Peter, no need for you to rush back. Why not drive back with Payne? That's him over there in the hacking jacket." He pointed with his pipe. "He passes our place. I'll ask him to drop you off. Come on over and meet him." Draining his glass Barry gave it to a passing African steward dressed in a long white *kanzo* with a red cummerbund.

It was arranged that I be driven back by Mr Michael Payne, who was staying a little longer anyway, or at least until the result of the raffle had been announced. My host, his wife and son bade me goodnight and drove off in their Peugeot.

Although Mike Payne was chattering to several of his cronies when I was introduced, he wasted no time in detaching himself, thereafter disposing himself to me wholeheartedly. He was somewhat garrulous, angularly built and with a gravelly voice—as if he drank or smoked too much, I thought. The expression in his eyes was sad and he was forever caressing the back of his head. I observed later that there was a scar about two inches long just visible through his thinning hair. The story I heard from Barry Wilkins the next day was that it had been caused by a bullet from the rifle of a tourist he, Payne, had taken out hunting game some years earlier. Payne, it seemed, had gone on safari with a wealthy tourist and his attractive wife. The wife was rather fond of big-game hunters and the trophy-seeking husband rather jealous. While she stalked Payne, he stalked the pair of them until they were located in *flagrante delicto*, and bang! bang!

Payne had lived in Kenya for eight years but had been a professional White Hunter in Tanganyika for many more years. He proceeded to ply me with questions about why I had come to Kenya and, "Did I not realize that Kenya was finished *kabisa* for the whites?" So vehemently did he speak of the colony's vacillating economy and of the multiplying Asian community's virtual monopoly on the commerce of it that I was quite convinced for weeks after my encounter with him that the colony would be annexed by India some day. He was certain, too, that Jomo Kenyatta's defence had been rigged and financed by opulent and corrupt Indian traders, then croaked on providing what was ostensibly so much authoritative data on the Asian community. (The Asian population stood at more than one hundred thousand as against forty thousand Europeans.)

"They are the suppliers. No matter how prosperous the European settler is, he must go to the Indian [*Banyan*] for his provisions, his tractors and spares, clothing and what have you."

I accepted a proffered cigarette and supplied him with a light.

"What money the farmer earns from the land will inevitably find its way to Delhi and Bombay."

I gained the impression he didn't like Indians very much.

However alarming and, at times, nonsensical his speech may have been, he was hardly given to wilful fabrication. Most of what he uttered was obviously based on a lot of fact. Before I parted from him that lovely evening on the Kinangop, I was to be considerably enlightened on a number of things.

Oddly enough, perhaps my own initiative helped too—it was Payne from whom I learned something I'd failed to from the Wilkins—the Ruck murders. It was by any standards as reliable an account as I could have wished for, especially as I was subsequently able to verify most of the details.

It is not, I think, inopportune that I recite the story in this somewhat hotchpotch chapter as I heard it in the congenial atmosphere of the Brown Trout—a place that the popular Rucks themselves used to frequent of an evening—and which I have since remoulded with information gleaned from other sources.

He did not appear in the least put out that I should have asked him to tell me all about it. As I mentioned just now, he was inclined to be a bit garrulous. So I sat and listened attentively.

"Roger Ruck and his wife, Esmé, were neither of them in any way *kali*. They were fond of the Africans and did a lot for them, especially was this so with Esmé. She was a qualified doctor and did an enormous amount of unrewarded work at the local clinics and dispensary; all unappreciated I suppose. Roger himself was, as we all thought, a bit less kindly towards the Kukes after the carve-up of his neighbour, Bowyer; even so, like most of us, he continued to employ some. The two of them were of sober habits and usually retired early. Both were seen to carry their weapons with them at all times and I can vouch for their caution, having spent many an evening with them—their pistols in their laps and their detailed inspection of doors and windows. They were, as far as I was concerned, the last folk on the Kinangop to be caught napping. Anyway, on this particular night just as they were about to retire—their six-year-old son was already in bed and asleep—the Ruck's Kikuyu groom hammered urgently on the door shouting that Mau Mau were on the farm. He said that one had been captured and Roger was asked to go quickly to see. The cunning bastards! There was, unfortunately, no reason why Roger should have doubted his groom; he'd had him for many years; he was even teaching the Ruck boy to ride—they had some fine steeds. None of the house staff actually slept on the premises and it was the Ruck's practice to dismiss them soon after dinner. Er, wait a minute, I believe he used to have one *mchunga* remain near the house—he was a bloody Kuke, too. So, Roger, completely oblivious of the peril waiting in ambush outside, grabbed his gun and went out to where he met the excited groom who was unarmed and sounded quite sincere. He followed him with eager strides but had no sooner turned the corner by the workshop when he was set upon by the gang lying in wait and struck down mercilessly. His agonized screams rent the still night and started the cattle lowing and dogs barking. Esmé heard the terrible screams of her husband and rushed out carrying the shotgun. Her body was found a few yards from the house chopped and mutilated as much as Roger's. Brave woman, she must have known that she was going to her death; she hadn't even awakened her son. The gangsters soon found him in his bed in an upstairs room and accorded him the same grisly fate as his parents. He was butchered too."

He paused for a few sips of his beer and I did likewise.

"What savage brutes!" I breathed tensely as he took up the story again.

"It is not known who it was who raised the alarm but within an hour we all knew of it and, after recovering our stunned senses, were hard on the heels of those responsible that very night. I spent most of it rounding up suspects and for many days assisted in the screening of them. God! Were we livid! But most of us felt so stupidly lame. Blame was, naturally I suppose, placed at the door of government and you have no need of me to tell you what happened the following Monday, I'm sure. It was headlines the world over and must certainly have been an unprecedented event in colonial history. [The incident referred to was the storming of Government House by irate settlers and is described later on.] But, as I say, Europeans throughout the colony were hopping mad and wanted action, and action with a capital 'A'—not just action to find the Ruck killers, but action to stamp out Mau Mau."

"And did they find the gang?" I queried.

"Not at that time. It had been in hiding for several days in a gorge on John Nimmo's farm. Colonel Nimmo, that is. It's the farm next to the Rucks'. The hide was in the centre of thick bush that had been cleared out. After the attack the gang presumably dug in high up in the forests and it took weeks to bring the swine to book. A Chief Inspector Gordon had a devil of a job up here with the investigations—worked himself to a shadow. It was about six months before the trial took place of a few of the responsible and the irony of it is that most of them escaped from prison. How on earth that fellow, Nene, took a brief like that is beyond me [Mr Holland Nene was the defending counsel], but he was no match for Crown counsel Boyle. I went along to the hearing a couple of times but there was so much technical legal argument you'd never have known it was a murder trial, until, that is, you had a good look at the accused persons."

We both lit cigarettes and sat quietly for a few moments watching those around us. The bar had thinned considerably and I could even hear the engine of the big single-cylinder generator that supplied the power for the inn's lighting.

"So that's the price they had to pay for employing Kikuyu staff is it?" I muttered.

More briskly now he went on. "Yes, I suppose it was, but shortly after this shattering and callous raid most settlers hereabouts started sending their Kukes back to the reserves. It was impossible to trust any of them really. I wonder just how many of those spunkless hoodlums who hacked at Roger and Esmé are still at large, still stalking through the forest and plundering our farms at night and oathing the labour. Christ, they make my blood boil! What have the whites done to deserve such a nightmare existence?

The bloody government builds a railway from Mombasa to Lake Victoria, discovers it has over-committed itself financially so decides to encourage settlement of these vacant highlands. [This was so, of course, the idea being to provide more justification for the building of the epic railway.] Hanging is too respectable for them. They should be tied to stakes near hyena holes like Chief Lobengula used to do. I'm sure they'd prefer such a gruesome end."

Quite a proposition I thought; an ignoble end for the 'noble savage'!

Though but briefly sketched, this dastardly incident, so typical of many perpetrated by Mau Mau, will, I feel confident, do much to convey to the reader the true dimensions of the real crisis that had become an horrendous part of the everyday lives of these plucky, if frequently maligned, British (also Dutch, German and Italian) settlers on the Kinangop, as indeed elsewhere throughout the 'White Highlands' of Kenya at that time. I never did have an opportunity to enjoy Michael Payne's company again. However, I understand he eventually returned to Tanganyika as a game warden.

The following evening I was driven into Naivasha by Barry Wilkins and rejoined other recruit inspectors who had spent Christmas on farms. Cordial farewells to our respective hosts over, we crowded into a small bus that had been hired by the training depot for the return to Gilgil, cackling animatedly.

It had been a splendid eye-opener and I felt that my few days with the Wilkins and other Kinangop farmers had been worth months at any training establishment. I had been made aware of the magnitude of the task before us, whereas before I had only been excited and keen but woefully indifferent to the wider ramifications of the subversive organization, Mau Mau. I can only liken my pragmatic attitude towards Mau Mau at that time to the comment of one of my trainee colleagues at the school when he saw his first albino African walking along the road one day. He remarked, quite seriously, "So they have white black people here. We don't have black white people in England, do we?"

A humble observation, no less naïve, and one to be equated with: "We have dissenters and rabble-rousers in England but there is no terrorism, is there?"

To be as candid as I dare would be to submit that the greater part of the security forces, and I include the police, profoundly misinterpreted the true situation until it was almost too late.

Although I partook in the vociferous gaggle of conversation during the return journey on the evening of the 27th, my thoughts were preoccupied with a fear that I had made a mistake in going to Kenya and getting myself involved in her domestic troubles. For some peculiar reason it suddenly occurred to me that I had applied for service in a Force that was helping to put down insurgents only. Reading the newspapers at home I had come to believe that Kenya was at war, that there was an enemy, a people hostile towards the Queen and her government, and that the forces of the Crown were at liberty to kill those people. I had discovered that such was not the case at all. Only a subversive organization whose manifesto was anti-white and whose aims were to bring into disaffection Her Majesty's colonial government—to make the lives of the settler insupportably difficult, to scare them and drive them away. It was my dismal destiny to have to sort out the malcontents and scold them; so I imagined!

Nevertheless, before I climbed out of the bus at the training school I was in little doubt about one thing—that the law-abiding citizens of Kenya were with their backs to the wall and needed every possible assistance. It is not at all unreasonable to say that I felt a sort of crusading spirit. This spirit tended to diminish somewhat after a few months as a sub-inspector of police, due mainly to the pettiness of much of the Force's antiquated and bureaucratic policies. Even so, I remained imbued with an enduring sense of devotion to the cause as a whole. I like to feel that my attitude was, to a greater or lesser degree, shared by most of the constabulary's inspectorate.

Especially is this suggestion given credence when one is reminded that the Commissioner of Police who succeeded Mr Michael O'Rorke in the spring of 1954, a renowned police officer named Colonel A.E. Young (later Sir Arthur), who was seconded from the City of London Police, had struggled unavailingly against perversity and dogmatism for but nine months when, even before the year was out, he relinquished his command and handed over to the quiet-mannered and confident Richard Catling (now Sir Richard).

During his fleeting period of secondment as Kenya's police commissioner, the colonel embarked on an energetic cracking-the-whip campaign and set about improving the vacillating morale of the Force. Contract and supernumerary inspectors were encouraged to accept permanent and pensionable appointments and make the Force their career. Even while large numbers of us were deliberating the merits of such an offer Colonel Young threw up his arms in despair and wasted no time in quitting the colony. It can only be concluded that he, too, found it an irksome proposition to refer to murderous gangs of lawless thugs as 'resisters', as a number of British newspapers called Mau Mau, or as 'rebels' as other sympathizers termed them.

Unfortunately, the colonel's brief sojourn did pathetically little to inspire Kenya's much-maligned Force and we were left to sit and wonder, contemptuously, just what was wrong among the top brass. Why all the feuding, fussing and funky indecisiveness?

Chapter 4

Salus populi in the White Highlands

Salus populi, or 'serving the public', is the motto of the Kenya Police but Malcolm Todd admitted that he could never stick the life on a forest post (most police posts were referred to as forest posts—it did not mean they were situated actually in the forest though many were at its edge). Unabashed he went on to bemoan the fact that ever since leaving the training school some months previously he had wanted C.I.D. work. He had been a plain-clothes man in his force in the U.K. and this was his forte.

He had arrived at the Stag Inn, Nakuru, to collect me. It was two nights since my departure from the Gilgil police training college and I was to succeed him as commander of Hermann's Post. All I knew of him was that he was a Glaswegian, a ju-jitsu enthusiast and very loquacious. In actual fact his brief sojourn on Hermann's Post was impossible to extend due to reasons of low morale among the post's askari. He simply had not endeared himself to them at all and the uneasy relationship between him and them had reached its climax a few days before my appearance.

Having returned from a patrol one evening, he had handed his Sten gun to an askari—cocked, safety catch off, magazine on, muzzle towards the askari. His finger was still in the trigger guard and as the weapon was snatched from him pressure was applied on the trigger and a burst of fire resulted in the poor askari being rushed to hospital with a round in his thigh. I was to see the fellow several months later—he was on crutches. He was permanently crippled but harboured no malice whatsoever. All he said was, "*Shauri ya mungu*." (God's will!)

The Bedford pick-up that carried Malcolm and me to the post

pulled up in the middle of a farmyard. The first thing I remember was the sound of a fierce bull bellowing loudly in a pen situated on the far side of another pen that turned out to be Hermann's Post askari quarters.

"Fantastic," I said, more to myself than to Malcolm.

But the strands of barbed wire around the pen confirmed Malcolm's droll statement. "They find the bull fun," he chuckled. "Fact is they are not happy until they have made it snort and stamp."

Alighting, we brushed the thick dust off each other. I then adjusted my nice new cap while Malcolm gave a tug on his faded beret.

"*Jambo, effendi,*" greeted a tall, handsome sergeant to Malcolm as he strode across to the askari quarters. Then to me, "*Jambo, bwana! Habari gani?*"

My pathetic command of Swahili extended to the salutations at least and I replied, somewhat self-consciously, "*Mzuri tu!*"

Malcolm ordered: "*Peleka mzigo ya bwana mgeni,*" and pointed to my few pieces of baggage.

Two scruffy looking individuals, whom I took for farm labourers but who later turned out to be special constables on the post, shouldered my suitcases and other bundles and picked their way through the mud and dung of an adjacent cattle *boma* to a brick house on the far side. I accompanied Malcolm who chose to walk around the outside.

The house that Malcolm was quartered in was ostensibly for a farm manager. As there wasn't one, Alec Hermann, the owner of the farm, had kindly placed it at the disposal of the Kenya police. It was constructed of good limestone and had a corrugated-iron roof. There was a forty-four gallon drum perched atop a brick furnace next to the house surrounded by a forest of pipes. This was the hot-water system. Several yards from the building a seventy-five-foot aerial reared up. A cable from the top of it led through the eaves of the house to a V.H.F. radio set inside.

"Constable Jimu is the one who starts up the generator for the radio; just shout '*Sitima*' when you want to open up and he will do the rest," advised Malcolm. "You'll need to keep that sheet of corrugated iron over it otherwise the rain mucks up the innards."

Pouring methylated spirit into a primus stove in order to prepare some tea, he asked, hopefully, "By the way, can I flog you this stove if you haven't got one? What about utensils? You can have this lot for a couple of quid."

There being little chance of escaping my fate, I assented. "Okay by me. How about a pressure lamp; is there one here?"

"There's one that belongs to Alec, over there. You'll be seeing him tonight when we pop down for dinner. I'm sure he has no objections to it staying here. Wants a new mantle though."

The house was a large bungalow. It had a sizeable dining-cum-sitting room, one small and one large bedroom, a bathroom and a tiny kitchen. The only room that was furnished was the small bedroom. The remainder of the house was absolutely bare except for the V.H.F. radio set that stood upon a table in the sitting room. With the exception of a dirty fly-blown map of the area near the radio set, the walls were just uninteresting expanses of whitewash.

In the morning, despite his woolly-headedness after too many schnapps with Mr Hermann at dinner the previous night, Malcolm arose early and packed his belongings. He checked the post's stock of ammunition and I signed for it. I was handed a list of the rifle numbers of each askari (Special Police Constables and N.C.O.s). The battered old Sten gun was included in this list. Then the Patrol Register, Force communications code, emergency rations and maps. Finally I was instructed in the use of the radio and the generator that supplied the power for it.

Having called up Control and reported "Nan Tare Roger", I made the acquaintance of Betty who was the operator at Control, high up on the escarpment, at Ol Mogogo. "*Jambo*, Peter! Behave yourself," she liltingly transmitted over the air.

"As you saw last night," said Malcolm, "Alec is not the happiest of settlers. He has several fierce dogs, a lot of land, Kuke squatters and budding ulcers. The only reason he tolerates us and the askari on his farm is because we keep the 'micks' away. Don't for Christ's sake go anywhere near his house at night without identifying yourself in a loud, clear voice—you'll likely get yourself shot otherwise. Anyway, you are okay for a cold beer with Alec, and his wife is a first-class cook."

Over breakfast of new-laid eggs and beans I received a snappy briefing on the farmers in the area and hoped I'd remember it all.

"... Fielding, he's the Senior Reserve Officer, is always in a flap about something. You'll know when he is in a bad mood—he'll turn up in uniform and say, 'Come on, there's a *shauri*. Where are your men?' If you join him you'll be out all day looking for a stray cow most likely. You want to look up Major Bannon—bit difficult to get on with but he's a decent old soul ... married to a coloured bint or, rather, lives with her, but watch his house staff, they are on the list for screening when the team are next in this area ... Kruger's quarry over by the railway line requires some attention— always a lot of *tembo* being brewed and he himself is seldom on the premises ... I've a feeling it's the next place to be raided ... "

And so it went. I felt as if I'd been established as a probation officer.

"Parade *tayari, effendi!*" curtly announced the over-serious Kipsigis sergeant to Malcolm.

I could see five ranks of three outside the house on the farm road swaying stiffly at attention, their rifles at the 'order'. A group of farm labourers stood nearby watching curiously.

"Carry on," answered Malcolm, then, turning to me, "Hope you like drill because you'll have to supervise it every day. Just watch this *shenzi* shower perform."

I stood a few yards off as Malcolm marched puppet-like over to the waiting parade. It was his handing-over farewell parade, though I must admit he showed little sadness. He stood and gazed at the sergeant who lifted his chest and raised his head.

"SLOooooPe Arms!" he bawled. There was a flurry of movement and the rifles eventually came to rest on their left shoulders, each man looking furtively at his neighbour, the sergeant, Malcolm and myself and, finally, at the admiring group of half-naked native mothers and their totally naked children nearby.

Having introduced me as the new *bwana,* Malcolm bid the askari *kwa heri.* Then, shaking me firmly by the hand and without a tear in his eye, said, "Careful with that Sten. Bloody temperamental things they are. So long, mate." He climbed into the waiting Bedford and was driven off, breathing deep sighs of relief I imagined.

So, there I was—an uncertain sub-inspector of police in charge of a forest post—with one sergeant and fifteen reserve constables, about one hundred and fifty square miles of Africa to look after and a score of farmsteads to maintain law and order on. Thumbing through my *Teach yourself Swahili* book I found the word for 'holiday'. I beckoned to the sergeant and he trotted across to eye me dubiously. "Everybody *siku kuu* today," I told him.

There was no doubt he understood. His face broke into a broad smile as he straightened up and saluted me twice. *"Asante sana, bwana."*

Fortunately there were no urgent affairs to deal with and I spent the remainder of the day leisurely settling in.

I was to spend seventeen months of my tour of duty in Kenya on forest posts. Hermann's Post was the first of three. I learned a tremendous amount about not only terrorism and the African askari but also about settlers and farming. I saw my first-ever calf born on Hermann's farm, shot my first berserk bull, drove my first vehicle (and subsequently passed my driving test in Naivasha), boiled my breakfast eggs in the same water I prepared for tea, learned the phonetic alphabet and became proficient in Swahili. The life was unglamorous and tiring. It demanded physical fitness and an even temper. It was a routine that did not displease me particularly and only occasionally did I ever see a senior officer. My activity was dictated by whim and fancy, premonition and hunch. At times it was unbearably frustrating, Mau Mau everywhere, their tracks followed for miles, their hideouts located, the mutilated bodies of their victims carried to an ambulance, but few positive contacts. The life was abstemious and frugal. One had to be self-sufficient, and one had to be tolerant—especially when roused from heavy sleep at a witching hour after midnight to lay an ambush on some farm that had been raided.

An officer assigned to duties on a forest post was well advised to give early attention to his relationships with those farmer settlers in his area and to look up the senior K.P.R. officer. To be accepted by their fraternity was of an importance that could not be over-stressed. There would be anything from a dozen or more farms in the post's sphere of influence and the farmers—English, Afrikaner, Italian and German—were all of different social, cultural and economic strata. Financially they were all fairly much the same and would probably have been paying off loans to the government Loans Board. Any profits were invariably ploughed back in—a new tractor or a store, for example. The inveterate practice of credit from local Asian traders was exploited by all.

The police inspector could expect to hear from his farmers a weary lament about the hard times and impecunious circumstances that hemmed them in. This alone was sufficient grist for their mills of discontent to grind on. However, should the behaviour of their local 'bobby' disenchant them in any way, this ill-humour would resolve itself into snorts of "... millionaire coppers! ... bloody *toto effendis*".

It was a fortunate post commander indeed who was not subjected to some sarcastic innuendo in respect of his opulent service to a government whose coffers were overflowing with wealth that was persistently denied the needy farmer.

I, as did my colleagues similarly employed, had to ensure that the settler farmers in my parish were satisfied I was performing duties commensurate with the mythical salary I collected each month. (As an Assistant Sub-inspector I received a starting salary of £590, rising by annual increments of £20, to £690 a year plus an overseas cost-of-living allowance payable at the rate of thirty-five per cent of basic salary. A gratuity was also payable to contract officers and was thirteen and a half per cent of basic salary.) It is to be admitted that our emoluments were satisfactory by any standards existing at the time. It is, nevertheless, as well to have pointed out that we were supernumerary and contract, meaning, we were precluded from enjoying pensionable benefits. While most of us were at a later stage offered appointments in the permanent and pensionable establishment, the tour was for most but a means to an obscure end, e.g. escape from a sharp-tongued mother-in-law and her frigid daughter!

There were in all about fifty forest posts established throughout the settled highlands of Kenya during the emergency. Their function, of necessity, placed emphasis on the para-military. They were the operational satellites of police stations situated in the main towns and had neither the facilities nor the staff for dealing with the ordinary run-of-the-mill crime and the investigation of it.

A post commander's terms of reference were terse and indissolubly bound up with militancy—to keep the settled areas as disinfected by Mau Mau terrorists as possible and eliminate them whenever the opportunity presented itself. To facilitate these cold terms the authorities had designated vast tracts of forest and moorland as 'prohibited areas'. Any person found wandering therein, if when challenged to halt he failed to do so, could be shot. Other large areas, gorges and uncultivatable terrain such as scrub-covered lava rock and swampland, were proclaimed 'restricted areas'. It was necessary for Africans to obtain permission before entering. Power to apprehend by force of arms if need be also applied.

The usual banal tasks of *kipande* (identity card) checking, curfew enforcement and raids for *tembo* were carried out along with brusque enquiries into minor assaults, thefts and the like.

We were given virtual carte blanche within the bounds of a post's area. The officer was provided with a V.H.F. radio set and could communicate with other posts and stations if, that is, the terrain was conducive to it. He could always contact the Control Station and it was part of his duty to pass sitreps at certain times. Such transmissions were called 'skeds' or (from 'schedule'). Only on a few posts would the radio be open all the time on a 'listening watch', or should there be an important operation on in the post area or its proximity. Generally the power for the radio was supplied by a small petrol-engine generator. It was ill advised to run these small installations for lengthy periods. However, as generally the power from them also provided the officer's only domestic lighting, such advice was invariably ignored.

He would have been a fortunate inspector who had any form of transportation. It was only during 1955 that sufficient vehicles were held at Divisional Headquarters to permit an issue to all posts. It was either a case of footing it or importuning the loan of a settler's *gari*. A set of maps would be acquired for the area and he'd learn how to interpret them, also to compute six-figure map references of any given point. All incident reports had to be accompanied by a map reference; they were holy and ritualistic.

His post complement has already been mentioned. They were African special police constables and collectively called 'askari'. If he were a good enough scrounger he would have augmented his armoury with a few Mills grenades and trip-flares, etc., from the quartermaster of his nearest army unit. It was, too, a matter of considerable urgency that all askari were given as much range practice as could possibly be arranged without scaring the neighbourhood too much. Sight-setting was as profound a subject as muzzle velocity—not that the latter was ever mentioned! And yet they tended and revered their rifles as they did their tummies.

In very exceptional circumstances only did forest post personnel enjoy the security and comfort of a tailor-made post. How well do I recall the period of instruction at the police training school devoted to the construction of a forest post—comprehensive minutiae of dos and don'ts that bespoke of bloody engagements with hordes of fanatical, screaming terrorists. These posts, in theory, seemed well nigh impregnable with their high barbed-wire stockades, outer perimeter of Danert wire and wide ditch planted with vicious *panjes* (pointed lengths of bamboo), not to mention sand-bagged *sangas* (firing points), and were expected to repulse the most determined of Mau Mau assaults. With a little imagination it could easily have been the North West Frontier or an Afghanistan outpost that officers assigned to a forest post were destined for.

But the ideal forest post remained a lovely pipedream, like so many other schemes for the amelioration of the rough and hazardous existence of the personnel who manned them. Sometimes when a post commander found himself in the happy position where he could obtain suitable materials gratuitously (from a generous local farmer), he would proceed along those lines he had been instructed at the school and provide for himself and his askari a decent and defensible place to occupy. Alas! all too often such useful data as had been expounded by the instructors remained as but a few pages of uninteresting hieroglyphics in an officer's tattered notebook, never to be referred to again except jokingly.

Most police forest posts were located at or near farms. The particular farm would have been selected for its strategic position or because it was in neat conformity with areas of responsibility as demarcated on maps at divisional headquarters.

A thorny and irreconcilable problem in respect of these posts sited on farms was created by the controversy that ensued among other farmers in the area who would claim that, for this and that reason, the post should have been established on their farm. Such clamorous protests were natural enough because the presence of a group of armed police personnel on a farm or its precincts was a comforting deterrent to the sporadic raids of Mau Mau. It often resulted in a preposterous tangle of loyalties wrapped in a mantle of conflicting motives whenever justification for the choice of farm was questioned. The authorities were often sorely tried when they had to convince the unlucky and covetous have-nots that nobody was playing at favourites.

Later on in the emergency when it became compulsory for all farmers to employ a number of armed stock guards (the wages of whom were subsidized by the government in maximum danger zones), and 'villagization' of all regular and squatter labour became the fundamental principle of defence and denial, most of the protests died away. There was less benefit to be enjoyed by hosting the Kenya police on your *shamba.* In fact, the pendulum soon swung in the opposite direction and farmers who had agreed most obligingly to these posts being established on their properties grew to find their presence a nuisance—their roads being chewed up by police vehicles during inclement weather; the young askari taking advantage of promiscuous *bibbies* who beckoned them into the nearby labour lines at night; buildings placed at the disposal of the police department that could be put to more profitable use. More importantly, too, our young inspector might even have allowed his relationship with his host settler to fray. By degrees, the novelty for the farmer of having a post on his farm faded. Nevertheless, their contribution to the restoration of law and order was incalculable.

Here I propose to increase the depth of focus a bit to include a brief survey of the broader situation as it then existed throughout the settled areas.

At the turn of the century, when Kenya was opened up to settlement by whites, the land they leased was inhabited by scattered groups of nomadic Masai. Being a pastoral tribe they cared little for agriculture. The areas were not favoured either by the Bantu tribes, the Wakikuyu and Wakamba, or by the Nilotic tribes farther north around Kericho, Nyanza and Kisimu. They were disinclined to quit their inherited lands, which were still very fertile, to settle elsewhere higher up and unpleasantly cold. Allied to this reason for the population vacuum that the white man filled so delightedly were two others, equally valid, if not more so.

Firstly, the Masai who were found wandering over that part of the country loosely referred to as the White Highlands were a warrior tribe and much feared by others who maintained a respectful distance. Secondly, the devastating epidemics that decimated so many of East Africa's tribes towards the end of the nineteenth century, following hard on the heels of severe drought and famine, had the effect of constricting the perimeters of the various tribal areas. Thus, when the European arrived with his plough and Winchester repeater it seemed quite apparent that the native had adequate land for generations to come and could expand comfortably within his tribal boundaries. The highlands were, to all intents and purposes, an unwanted void of fabulously fertile land. How tragically deceptive their reasoning—such myopia!

This void that the settler occupied and developed so energetically and successfully during the first few decades of this colonial era was centred around Nairobi (which had no claim to fame other than being a railhead), Kiambu, Thika and Ruiru, where such splendid coffee was, and is, grown. It then extended up the Rift Valley to the northeast as far as Lake Baringa. Settlement halted at the Uganda border in the region of Mount Elgon. South of Nairobi there was considerably less white invasion and it extended only as far as Sultan Hamid, bounded in the west by the railway and in the east by the Athi River. The entire area from Mount Elgon to Sultan Hamid was approximately two hundred miles in length—its width from Sotik in the west through Kericho to Lake Baringo being about eighty miles.

A clearer indication of the proportion of land occupied by immigrant whites in relation to indigenous occupation is provided by the following figures:

The Highlands covered an area of about 16,000 square miles and of this just over 13,000 square miles was settled by non-Africans. It was referred to as 'alienated land'. A quarter of the total area could be written off as Crown Forests in the interests of soil conservation. The indigenous population occupied an area covering 52,000 square miles, a sixteenth of which was the Kikuyu Land Unit which stretched from the Kikuyu escarpment north of Nairobi, east between the railway and the Aberdare range to Fort Hall and Embu, then around Mount Kenya to Meru and Isiolo in the north. This spacious reserve of the Kikuyu tribe was situated for the most part at an altitude of between five and seven thousand feet above sea level, an altitude at which flora and crops flourish luxuriantly and profusely. It has an annual rainfall of seldom less than thirty inches and, as industrious agriculturists, the Kikuyu were quite able to obtain substantial cash incomes from their produce at the markets of Nairobi and elsewhere. (F. D. Corfield who was commissioned by the Kenya government to conduct an in-depth enquiry into the origins and growth of Mau Mau devoted considerable attention to the contentious land issues that gave such enormous impetus to Kikuyu malcontent during the post-war years. An excerpt of his report relevant to these issues is reproduced in Appendix VIII.)

I have not the slightest intention of suggesting that the aforegoing statistics should influence one way or the other the manifold arguments that raged in Kenya over alienated land. I have merely quoted them to give some idea of how the land was divided up insofar as it affected immigrant whites.

Those districts situated within the 16,000 square miles known as the White Highlands and which felt the fullest impact of the Kikuyu uprising were concentrated roughly throughout the whole of the Lower Rift Valley (Naivasha, Nakuru, Eldama Ravine, petering out towards Eldoret), then, skirting the base of the Aberdares to Mount Kenya and Nanyuki, westward to Thomson's Falls, Rumuruti and Solai. The southern and northern extremities, although suffering the inconveniences of infected labour forces and losing cattle and wheat to roving terrorists, were not subjected to the nightly terror of formidable raids by hard-core gangs.

On the Mau escarpment, which borders on the Masai reserve, there were roomy pockets of white settlement though less likely to exacerbate the touchy passions of land-hungry Africans. This was because the pastoral Masai were apparently satisfied with the wide expanses of good cattle grazing land allotted them. It was only those sectors of the densely forested Mau that abutted the rump of the Kikuyu Land Unit that gave cause for uneasiness among the settlers farming there. Places like Narok and Nairagi-Ngare which were contiguous with Kikuyu land, and in which has occurred fairly widespread intermarriage between Masai men (whose womenfolk suffered a high rate of infertility) and Kikuyu women. Hundreds of them who would have proclaimed themselves to be Masai were, in fact, pure Kikuyu. They constituted grave sources of collaboration with Mau Mau adherents and even formed their own small terrorist cells that ranged along the heights of the Mau and became a sporadic menace to the lives and property of settlers in those areas. Such areas remained a refuge, too, for fugitive gangs to rest and reorganize in. It was, therefore, necessary for the Force to establish police posts in such areas.

The hardest hit of all settlers farming in the Highlands were those whose properties were in the proximity of forests. If it were not their herds of cattle or flocks of sheep driven off during the night—and often the day too—then their labour lines were stormed by itinerant gangs, demanding food, money and clothing. Should the hapless souls have resisted they were slashed by *pangas* or blasted with firearms. It was quite out of the question for the owner of a farmstead ever to leave it without European supervision; such inattention would have amounted to an invitation for a Mau Mau gang to descend upon it, burning, pillaging and killing to the accompaniment of wild whooping and shrill warbling.

The accomplishment of Mau Mau's ambition to oust the white settler from the land they claimed had been usurped by the dishonest dealings of a colonial power was possible only by sustaining the militant sections of its Land Freedom Armies living in the forests with food and equipment stolen from the *shambas* of the expatriate farmers. The picture then was one of numberless hard-core terrorist cells accommodated in the matted forests and seemingly bottomless gorges, feeding off the livestock, maize, wheat and other cereals of the farms spread out around and below. They attacked any poorly defended farms and destroyed those unoccupied; terrorizing the indigenous labour force and oathing the uninitiated, their object being to make such fearful and disruptive inroads upon the orderly progress of the farms as to cause their expatriate European owners to despair, pack their bags and quit. Whereupon they would jubilantly install themselves in the vacated *shambas*.

It is now a well-known fact that these Kenyan rebels came critically near to that objective. It was to cost the British government a fabulous sum (over £55 million) to weather the crisis and avert what would have amounted to an horrendous massacre had Mau Mau succeeded in overrunning the White Highlands.

And now to return to our original theme—*salus populi* in the White Highlands.

In all areas where military exercises occurred it behoved the resident police post commander to liaise closely. It was of the utmost desirability that he did so—failure to combine forces, resources and intelligence could but result in friction, consequently inefficient anti-terrorist measures, not to mention confusion that could lead to the embarrassing contingency of clashes between police and army patrols. Invariably the army units were of sufficient strength to enable them to carry out saturation exercises and to tie an area up with strategically placed ambushes. They carried out sweeps through steep gorges and in the larger tracts of forest far more frequently than any post commander with his handful of askari was able to do. It was the accepted duty of police to provide what guides the army required for its missions and sorties. All relevant information on the operational area and its terrorist pattern would be imparted, subject always, that is, to a prerogative of police to veto any particular military activity in order to conduct its own 'Special Effort' operations. Combined operations bore the label MILPOL and, with but few exceptions, police were entitled to the last word in the planning and execution of them. While such high level policy may have displeased one or two military commanders, they had to remember that no war had been declared; we were only dealing with a breakdown in law and order!

However, the majority of police personnel took a great liking to the various British army units who undertook the most complex and arduous of manoeuvres with tons of equipment in thick bush and over tortuous terrain in the most appalling conditions. I, personally, was forever amazed to see the field kitchen awaiting the troops at the end of a gruelling sweep, its oil burner roaring away beneath a huge urn of tea, and mail being distributed. Our relationships with them were, generally speaking, on the best possible felicitous level.

Earlier in this chapter I referred to the farmers and settlers that a post commander had as his neighbours and to their attitude towards him. Perhaps the inference drawn was that if a farmer was occasionally testy it was probably because he had more to lose than his local policeman. This cannot be denied. Moreover, what one had to remember was that he was usually a person of considerable stature and resourcefulness. He had seen the evil of Mau Mau spread its tentacles among his labour force and corrupt it. This consequently had hampered his progress on the farm, not to mention the perturbation caused by Africans, who had been serving him loyally for many years, suddenly disappearing overnight to join with Mau Mau forest gangs. He had to be tensely alert and ever on guard against his (hopefully) tried and trusted house staff—who were almost certain to have been Kikuyu and oathed—waiting to seize an opportunity one evening while serving dinner to produce from under their *kanzas* a *panga* or *simi* and then to unemotionally set about hacking him and his family to pieces.

The average settler was often a retired army major or brigadier, an ex-wing commander or son of a commissioner in the West Indies. Many had received educations in famous public schools and had been launched on their farming careers in Kenya with substantial capital. Police officers knew they were dealing with a European element that sat loftily, and not infrequently in grandiose disdain, on a higher rung and would seldom react submissively or humbly to any formal measures taken to correct or reprove them. Our lowly inspector needed to make absolutely certain of his ground before invading the sacred institutions so proudly built by the settler. An individualist and a pioneer, he was still battling his way through, with the forces of nature on one side of him and the African screaming for independence on the other. No bumptious upstart of a 'Cook's tour' police inspector was going to ask to see his driving licence or to arrest him for attempted murder for having hastened the departure of a cheeky garden boy with a few well-aimed shots past his head!

"You are here in case we should want you and may come when invited ... and even then you will kindly leave your notebook behind." Most of us soon got the message.

Another kind of settler, the South African Boer, or Afrikaner, was something of an enigma. His forebears had trekked up from the Transvaal in their ox-wagons in the 1880s, had cleared the land and built their shacks; they fought off the 'heathen black *munts*' and raised their families with a shotgun in one hand and a Bible in the other. They were the toughest and the most rebellious; were never, never going to quit the land cultivated with such sweat and toil, and would die rather than be pushed out. They vehemently refused to accept black domination. To them the African, all of them, was a '*munt*' who had to be kept firmly in his place at all costs. (*Munt* is a central–southern Bantu word, meaning 'man', from *waBantu*, 'people'. In this context it is used derogatively.)

On an Afrikaner's *shamba*, if an insolent tractor driver as much as questioned his *posho* ration by standing his ground, *sufuria* held demandingly before him, he may well have been knocked across the store with a mighty back-hand slap and chased off the property. A post commander was not often occasioned the bother of enquiring into complaints against natives by the Boer farmer; they simply never complained—having no time for the nebulous benefits of such complex and dilatory legal processes—"catch the nigger stealing, then take a *kiboka* to him; far more effective'"

And, the truth is, though not too unpalatable I hope, that the local inspector was usually much too preoccupied with the tasks of harrying Mau Mau to give his attentions to routine police work; thus, few objections were raised to the exercise of this preference for speedy justice by the swarthy, hard-bitten Afrikaner settler.

Nevertheless, the proposition of any form of summary punishment as meted out by this class of settler, or any others for that matter, was not regarded with indifference, as it could often lead to abuse. I must say, in spite of this, that by far the bigger percentage of South African farmers, bellicose and extreme as they may have been in their racial sentiments, were inclined to be a compassionate people, deeply religious, and would only inflict punishment in strict proportion to the misdemeanour that earned it. Those few who were by nature spiteful or bitter, and with whom one could expect this 'instant' justice to be carried to inordinate lengths, were watched closely and cautioned where necessary. Diplomacy in large dollops was the post commander's only salvation. He was lost if he failed to understand their point of view. Sometimes it was difficult not to turn a blind eye. It was not necessary for them to remind me that Kenya was their home, that in time I would return to mine but they had nowhere else to go. Their continued supremacy was their survival.

Shambas in the Highlands were of different classes, from rambling ranches to compact terraces of coffee. There were those that farmed cereals exclusively and in the harvesting season the glorious sight of five hundred acres of standing wheat, a sea of rustling gold against the lush greens of distant hills, was one not easily surpassed. On the sinister side of cereal farming were the wily and elusive 'micks' who would lay up in the middle of a *shamba* and painstakingly strip the grain from the ears and fill their smelly sacks. Alternatively, and of equally thunderous annoyance to the farmer, they would wait until the combine harvester had finished its day's work with the sacks of grain deposited in rows among the stubble to be collected later and then, as dusk fell, they would edge in and take advantage of the tempting granary.

Other farms specialized in livestock, dairy and beef. Herds of Friesians, Ayrshires and Borans, magnificent beasts, the cows with their udders distended to bursting point, were to be seen grazing placidly around the slopes of the Aberdares or far away in the *kilileswa* scrub under the watchful eye of a Masai herdsman replete with spear and goat-bag and draped with an ochre-stained blanket. Again, on the sinister side, those same herds would be approached by a hungry troop of Mau Mau as the moon rose and driven off through a gap cut in the wire fence of the *boma*. They would be driven for miles, their tails twisted cruelly, until struck down with blows of a *panga* to sever their hamstrings and throats cut. In minutes the beasts would be expertly and neatly sectioned then carried off to the gang's forest lair.

Many farms were mixed. In fact diversified farming became more popular as the emergency wore on; the wisdom being that what was lost on the roundabouts could be gained on the swings. A wattle plantation or two was included for good measure (wattle is a hard, red wood that grows tall and straight). If a farm were situated at the right altitude and with sufficient rainfall it could grow pyrethrum, a small white flower that grows close to the ground on strong plants. When picked, dried and processed it is the basic 'knock-down' constituent of powerful insecticides. Just a few acres of healthy pyrethrum could net a farmer a sum comparable to several hundred acres of cereal crops. Its primary disadvantage was that it required such a large labour force to pluck the small flowers as they blossomed—the ironic thing about the Mau Mau rebellion was that only the Kikuyu worked so hard, thus, with so many of that tribe repatriated to their reserves the cultivation of pyrethrum suffered.

But whatever the type of agrarian activity, there was always one distressing thorn that stuck in the side of the struggling settler; a thorn that caused him discomfort that was seldom, if ever, alleviated, except by his own superhuman and costly efforts—the roads—to, from and through his farm. Most were constructed of *murram* (a brittle red earth quarried in certain areas and having a clinker-like appearance). Torrential and prolonged rains reduced most roads to pot-holed, soggy stretches of marsh. Deep wheel-track ruts stranded vehicles on the ridge between, so that only a tractor could extricate them. Most of the farm roads became quite impassable during any heavy rains and farmers were continually draining and re-surfacing them. There was a tacit understanding between them that each was responsible for the maintenance of that part of the road that ran through his property. There were but a negligible few who had private roads of access. Each was dependent upon the indefatigable efforts of his neighbour. There was, furthermore, seldom any help forthcoming from the Public Works Department who only occasionally responded to the stentorian call of an irate settler and reluctantly despatched a road grader to eliminate the pot-holes and restore the camber. But the surface? Tarmac? An all-weather road? Who would pay for it?

Our post commander, long suffering wretch that he was, could generally expect his reproachful farmers to be particularly sensitive when the weather was inclement. Their ulcers became more than just twinges of discomfort as the roads deteriorated into water-filled craters. For weeks the farmer (and his parish constable!) would be isolated and unable to make any safari into town. Any that chose to make a desperate bid would need to be accompanied by a tractor. Four-wheel-drive vehicles with low gear ratios were the only reliable transport and even these would often end up helplessly bogged down, the engine screaming and sobbing its impotent fury as the infuriated driver urged it backwards and forwards, only to sink ever deeper, bucking up and down like an unbroken bronco.

Yet if, allied to his Trojan efforts to maintain the roads in a passable state of repair, a mob of die-hard terrorists should have descended during the night to clean out his wheat store, that farmer became implacable. It would have been the local Kenya Cowboy waving a red bunting in front of his eyes and prodding his enraged hide. Like a bull he would charge snorting into the police post to demand that every sack be recovered before dusk, or else ...! (Invariably a threat to write to the Commissioner!) Was it not the entire responsibility of the inspector that the store had been raided ...? Had he not been warned a dozen times that Mau Mau were awaiting an opportunity to exploit its remote situation? Ad nauseam!

God be thanked, the tempest would pass and a day or two later the luckless officer would be sitting down to a scrumptious meal in that settler's house. He would, inevitably too, have given an ear to the stock line of conversation—government incapacity, bungling and perverse refusal to heed the strident warnings of the Kenya settler years ago of the gathering storm among the Kikuyu.

Before arriving at my first forest post in the settled highlands of Kenya and finding my neighbours to be the much maligned colonial settlers, my views on them were somewhat indifferent. I had listened to, and read of, the vituperative comment directed at them with a proverbial pinch of salt. In the United Kingdom one seldom found the opportunity to converse with anyone free of preconceived or prejudiced views on the Kenya settler—"... his serried lines of servants and cheap labour ... the land he had stolen from the ignorant African ... his licentious habits, staggering from one sundowner to another and from the boudoir of one friend's wife to another's ... his exclusive clubs and his contempt for authority ..." Then, when I did find myself amidst this controversial set of colonial British stock I was strangely bemused; nothing else, just bemused.

Frankly I had decided that much of the talk I had heard concerning the ill-treatment of Africans and of the pomposity must be true. Accordingly, from the outset I endeavoured to ensure that no African, whether suspect Mau Mau, petty thief or simply a pug-nosed face that didn't fit, was knocked around in my presence. This decision of mine did not endear me unduly to my fellow whites and I must have been looked upon with grave distrust by those farmers who contended they knew so much more about the native mentality than I. Not many months were to elapse however before I was to alter my opinions, though not radically, for I did discover that there was a little justification for handling African rural workers ungently on occasions. If a *karani* had been working for the same *bwana* for a number of years and was suddenly found tampering with the mechanism of the water pump with vindictive motives, perhaps sabotage, in mind, then I could well understand his employer's all-consuming rage. He would feel inconsolably disappointed, would even deem it an affront, to be so caused such inconvenience by a native wretch whom he had done his best to feed, clothe, accommodate and even educate for so many years.

What good would it have done to call upon the law and endure the frustration of seeing the wheels of the constabulary clank into motion, slowly moving the vehicle of good old British justice until it faltered in some bog of obscure legal anomaly?

I had heard a lot of people speak of the pauper's diet of ground maize, *posho*, that native employees of settlers were expected to subsist on. Admittedly I, too, had thought such a monotonous diet to be an insult to the stomachs of any people. Yet it was not over-long before I discovered that the Kenyan indigene thrived on his *posho*, finding it quite adequate for his needs. He had little taste for the culinary refinements and elaborate dishes of the western world. A few vegetables with a huge bowl of *posho* and he was well satisfied, assuaging hunger by a sense of fullness and not by eating and digesting well a little that was nutritious and that constituted a balanced diet. Not that he eschewed other victuals completely; on the contrary, if he were given a sheep or side of beef he would have demolished all of it in one sitting!

I shall always remember the exasperating chore I had apportioning the weekly meat ration to my askari. They were encouraged to consider the rest of the week, but it was beyond them to do so. Their argument was that whether it was consumed in one day or spread over several days, the effect on the body was the same. It was inside the tummy and should logically sustain them for a week if it was a week's ration. Unfortunately such reasoning seldom proved its logic in practice.

Most settlers I found were hardly ever able to enjoy a holiday away from their *shambas*. The farthest afield that most ever strayed was to Nairobi for a weekend. A few, more prosperous, or, more likely, ill, would escape to the coast for a longer period. The beautiful golden beaches and luxurious hotels of Malindi remained for most unrealized dreams and were for tourists only. During the emergency, trips to 'magical shores with a romantic past' were even more prohibitive due to the scarcity of responsible and reliable

Europeans to manage the farm during its owner's absence. Indeed, I recall with some feeling that while among the settlers farming in Kenya I came to know many who had been promising themselves a holiday for years. How poignant it was, and how uncomfortable I felt, as they listened to the descriptions I rendered after my own short local leave at the coast. Their poorly concealed envy curtailed my enthusiastic recollections. I was constrained to reassure them: "... of course, it's far too damned expensive and so terribly hot ..." Which was not untrue either.

This enforced attachment to the farm and its surrounds did not, I regret, make the settler a very bright neighbour. Or, assuming that he arrived in Kenya a bright boy, he certainly became little brighter. His outlook and breadth of character became somewhat atrophied and the bulk of thought and expression was channelled between the congested confines of agriculture and the emergency.

This I consider to be a convenient juncture at which to sum up the odious situation in which my settler parishioners lived and worked during the emergency years. Moreover, I can think of no better way of doing so than by reproducing in full a leaflet that was circulated during 1954.

It was impossible to make light of the reasons behind the publication of this document or to underestimate the gravity of the circumstances that gave rise to its necessity. That the authorities should have ever deemed it necessary to produce and disseminate such a dramatic document among intelligent and normally courageous people was, in itself, adequate proof of the enormity of the peril which stalked this white man's precarious paradise.

The leaflet was published by the Department of Information in Nakuru for the Provincial Emergency Committee. It was entitled 'Your turn may come'. On the front page of this melancholy document was an introductory paragraph or two. It then went on to list do's and don't's. (*See* Appendix I)

It is true to say that many settlers pooh-poohed the leaflet's contents as so much alarmist propaganda. Quite a natural reaction, of course, for a community who had already been living cheek by jowl with beastly murders for several months. But the general response, be it contempt or indifference, in no way detracted from the urgency of the message it conveyed. Privately most settlers read, digested and accepted the advice. I personally found its contents to be of great value and did my utmost to practise the do's and don't's it offered. There was no room for complacency and, unfortunately, all too often one is only wiser after the event.

My Webley .38 was always a very, very close companion.

Chapter 5

Is that gun really necessary, bwana?

With candid tongue in cheek I shall now give some attention to the Achilles' heel of the Kenya settler's irreproachability—the chink in his armour, if you like. It concerned firearms.

No farmer settler living so intimately with the fauna of East Africa and its unpredictable African passions dared scorn the advantages inherent in the possession of a firearm—whether it be for despatching wild game trampling through his maize, ending the agony of a cow with an inverted uterus, or for his own personal protection when investigating a rowdy *tembo* party in his labour lines at night. He had a reputation for being familiar with firearms of all descriptions, competent in the handling of them and not at all reluctant to use them when necessary.

Somewhere in his house you could have been sure of finding a shotgun or two. Then, almost certainly, he'd have been able to show you, proudly too, a beautifully turned .300 Express or a .375 Magnum. These pieces of heavy artillery would have sufficed his needs should he have, by design or accident, encountered the larger game—rhino, buffalo or even elephant. Displayed at his hip, encased in a tatty leather holster and positioned to facilitate a quick draw would have been a .45 revolver or a .38 Smith and Wesson, or similar handgun. Sometimes it would have been more of a museum piece like an old, long-barrelled Savage Colt with an elaborately carved butt, bringing to mind the Wyatt Earps and Codys of the American West.

Whatever the make or calibre, it was always worn with the nonchalance that a banker in the city would carry his briefcase. It was this unselfconsciousness that so clearly proclaimed his familiarity with firearms, and it was rare indeed to see such weapons being played with, any more so, I regret, than being cleaned and oiled. The womenfolk were not excluded either and, somewhere on her person, a little .32 Beretta would have been nestling in lethal repose, and was quite as likely to be used with unerring confidence. I actually knew one settler's wife who habitually displayed a heavy .45 Colt on her hip and I have no doubt that many others owned, and carried, similar redoubtable shooting-irons.

These smaller pieces of artillery were to be seen lying on the table in front of their owners during mealtimes alongside the cutlery. They would be loaded with their safety catches off! It was a studied display of preparedness devoid of any hysteria that did more than anything else I ever saw to sum up the gravity of the situation created by the spectre of Mau Mau in the White Highlands. Though, I hasten to add, to have made the slightest allusion to the disloyalty of your settler host's Kikuyu house staff would have been a blatant breach of etiquette. A doubtful innuendo on the morals of his wife could not have provoked him half as much.

To hang this particular subject on its right peg I think it would perhaps be wiser were I first of all to identify it more clearly by providing a resume of the general situation as it then was in respect of firearms.

Before the emergency was declared on 20 October 1952, and the revolt against Europeans by the Kikuyu tribe evinced its full fury, it was known that disturbing numbers of firearms and thousands of rounds of ammunition were disappearing all over the colony. One glaring instance being the Command Ammunition Depot at Gilgil which reported a loss of nearly 300,000 rounds of assorted ammunition as early as 1948–49. The depot's security was disgracefully lax and the ammunition magazines were dispersed over a wide area, access to which the public could gain with little trouble. Other serious losses were reported by the K.A.R. and, unbelievably, from the Central Ordinance Depot in Nairobi.

Police in Naivasha and Gilgil succeeded in recovering large

quantities but the bulk of these losses were never accounted for. Losses of firearms brought to the attention of the police by 1953 and covering the previous five years totalled in the region of five hundred rifles, pistols and shotguns, of which but a negligible number were recovered.

The police had never been concerned over-much with firearms except when a loss or theft was reported. In such cases, the action taken amounted to seldom more than the publication of the weapon's particulars in the *Police Gazette*. A token enquiry might have been made.

Registration, permits to import, permission to possess, and all such authority under the Arms and Ammunition Ordinance was vested in the administration. Records kept were of a most desultory nature, to the point of flippancy even, and it was not until after the emergency was declared that authority for arms and ammunition passed to the police department. Another year was to elapse before a fully revised and up-to-date Firearms Ordinance was brought into force. It gave much greater power to the police and the granting of firearm certificates became subject to greatly increased circumspection. Penalties for unauthorized possession or loss through negligence were far more severe.

However, before this shocking situation was remedied during 1953 and before there came into being a special department like the Central Firearms Bureau of today, the efficient recording of the whereabouts and owners of every firearm in the colony was not only a formidable task, it was well nigh impossible. It was the habit of Kenya's settler population to own private arsenals, albeit of weapons that were seldom declared or for which they seldom bothered to apply for a permit to possess.

It was known at the beginning of the emergency that something like 52,000 firearms were owned by the civilian population. This figure represents firearms that were licensed. But what of the countless number that were unlicensed? So deplorably slack was the system that they probably amounted to a further several thousand. By the end of 1954 the total number of firearms lost or stolen had risen to an impressive and disquieting figure of 1,178, of which about two hundred and fifty were losses by security forces.

So many hundreds of firearms, registered and unregistered, were stolen from, or lost by, negligent owners—weapons that almost certainly found their way into the hands of Mau Mau terrorists or their collaborators. It was one of Mau Mau's major precepts to continually augment its armouries by exploiting the trusted positions of Kikuyu house staff. Weapons were stolen from unlocked cupboards, the glove-boxes of cars or from a cosy nook among the mothballs in the wardrobe. In most instances the cook or houseboy that pilfered it disappeared as well, only to be identified months later as a member of some forest gang.

Apart from the spirited raid by terrorists on Naivasha police station (which I shall deal with later on) on the night of 26 March 1953, when, under the leadership of that most notorious personality, Dedan Kimathi, the entire contents of its armoury were removed, I can cite no other instance where Mau Mau made any significant hauls of firearms through the assault or investment of police or military installations. If they were not stolen from careless civilians then they were taken from security force personnel who were ambushed and killed; usually when alone and in remote parts. Some owners, however, to their undying shame, succumbed to bribery.

As well advanced in the emergency as September 1954 terrorists were still succeeding in replenishing their diminishing stocks by kind permission of the government's constipated security measures. I still remember the perturbation I felt when sitting in my police post one night scribbling down a priority flash radio message from colony headquarters to all stations and posts.

It was Friday, 17 September 1954 and at 2040 hours a well-armed gang of terrorists had attacked the prison camp at Lukenia in Athi Road, Nairobi. Two Greener guns, two rifles and a pistol plus a few hundred rounds of ammunition were stolen. One hundred and eighty prisoners were also released. To round off their busy evening they managed to pick up a short-wave radio set too, though one wonders what they intended doing with it. Having convulsed for so long after the shock of the attack on Naivasha police station the previous year, and thinking that it had been a lesson to all, one may well imagine how the settler threw up his arms and groaned in despair. He himself, of course, was in no way exonerated and was still far from being an exemplar of security-mindedness.

So the eye of the law came to regard more severely the question of firearms lost through negligence or possessed unlawfully. Loss of arms became a crime worse than treason in the circumstances, even police personnel were obliged to sign orders to the effect that their personal issue of a firearm would be chained to their beds at night. During the waking hours they were to be always on their person. Any loss, whether army, police or civilian, became the subject of a searching enquiry.

Settlers, and other civilian residents, who were the main cause of official apprehension, were made to appreciate the shameful consequences of permitting firearms to fall into the hands of Mau Mau by the introduction of the revised Firearms Ordinance late in 1953. It rendered offenders liable to a fine of two hundred pounds or six months imprisonment, or both. Such severity was of absolute necessity when one was made aware of the staggering losses that continued even after the emergency was declared, and the defence that one was overpowered and dispossessed by force was not always held to be valid either. One had to justify that it was necessary for him to carry a firearm. There had to be very substantial reasons.

Among those settlers in their vulnerable isolation up-country there was rarely any dispute—they needed a weapon near at hand—one at least; but hundreds of others living in Nairobi or Mombasa were expected to hand their weapons in for safe-keeping or destruction, thereafter to avoid the shadows!

Having, I hope, now identified the peg of this particular subject with the aforegoing assessment I will proceed to examine it further insofar as it affected the rural police officer and the settler citizen he served.

Expectedly, there was to be heard a unanimous wail of protest by the white population upon the enactment of such a stringent and restrictive ordinance. It was tantamount to criticism directed solely at them. But, the wail was only the bleat of a lamb lost in the labyrinths of martial fastnesses. It was the settler's *cri de coeur* but it went unheeded.

I found that a most unenviable task was that of ensuring those firearms possessed by the farmers in my area were not only in a serviceable condition and necessarily possessed but were also secure from theft. If security of any weapon was lax or indifferent its owner was politely advised to hand it in for safe-keeping by police or, better still, stored away, well greased, at the Command Ammunition Depot. To facilitate this task the government declared a general amnesty during July and August 1954. During this period any unregistered firearm could be handed in without fear of prosecution. The response was heartening and it was slowly realized by most that, logically, a man could only satisfactorily look after one weapon. There had to be excellent reasons why he should be entitled to possess more than one.

Once this edict, unpopular as it may have been, was absorbed by the civilian community and was showing positive results, it only remained to ensure that the farmer and others took unimpeachable care of those weapons they were allowed to keep. Being so familiar with guns literally strewn all over the place, it constituted a terrific strain on the self-discipline and unbridled spirit to be forever reminding themselves to lock the gun away or carry it on their person.

The only way in which the police officer could diplomatically ascertain whether or not the owner of a firearm was disregarding the harsh laws was by discreet observation. Was he carrying the particular shooting-piece he was known to own? If he were not, he would be approached.

"Morning, Mr Roberts, I see you go around unarmed these days. Have you sold your Browning?"

If a person was a constant offender then the matter would be pursued. Should he be a drunkard as well as negligent, then, doubtless, any weapon would have been confiscated.

It was not often, thank goodness, necessary to draw their attention to the high penalties that could be imposed for offences against the Firearms Ordinance for loss through negligence. Most white settlers found that the stigma of a conviction for such an offence far outweighed the pecuniary hardship of a heavy fine. The vast majority, I happily record, were quite amenable and were prepared to co-operate. All that was generally needed was to encourage them to be doubly aware of their firearm's prodigious significance. People who led secure, sophisticated lives in England and elsewhere would forget their umbrellas, spectacles and cigarette lighters. In Kenya firearms were every bit as commonplace and were just as apt to be mislaid.

As stated earlier in this short chapter no settler dared scorn the advantages of owning a suitable firearm, but it was a heavy burden during the emergency. It was ownership at a premium in anxiety.

Chapter 6

How to eliminate elusive 'micks'

During March and April of 1953, the first stormy year of the emergency in Kenya, in the South Nyeri reserve stock thefts were occurring with an alarming frequency and almost nightly cattle were driven off from *bomas*. Follow-up patrols had been generally unavailing, worse in fact. One K.A.R. patrol, while tracking a gang of Mau Mau rustlers, had been ambushed and in the ensuing running battle was badly shot up. It was apparent that a large and well-armed gang was operating in the area.

On the night of Sunday, 12 April yet another successful raid was perpetrated on an unguarded cattle *boma* in Location 12 of the South Nyeri reserve. A determined patrol of the Kenya Regiment followed up at first light. The patrol comprised six Europeans and eight Africans; a sergeant by the name of Hunter was in command.

They tracked deep into thick forest over undulating ground until, at dusk on the 13th, a decision was made to return. At this point a suspect native was sighted and followed. After a short distance he entered a hut—the hut was, in fact, the Priory Forest Station, which was no longer being used—and the patrol surrounded the clearing in which it stood.

Having called upon the suspect to come out several times without any response, the second sergeant of the patrol, a young Kenyan white named Baillon, went forward with an African tracker. He was observed to try the door and then put his shoulder to it. Immediately several pistol shots were heard from within the hut and Baillon fell wounded with a bullet through his mouth.

The remainder of the patrol broke cover and bounded forward

towards the hut. They were straightaway exposed to the withering fire of an ambush from either side of the clearing. Three fatal casualties, all European, were suffered before the patrol recovered from the surprise and took cover again. Sergeant Hunter managed to assist his seriously wounded colleague, Baillon, from the scene but he later died of his wounds. The survivors withdrew, though they were unable to return to the area until the following morning when, minus boots, belts and weapons, the three bodies of those shot were recovered.

That lamentable incident was to become an object lesson for many a recruit undergoing his anti-terrorist training in Kenya. It was not a common type of incident, so uncommon in fact as to be of no great consequence when discussing the risks taken by follow-up patrols. Nevertheless, security forces were often exposed to the hazards of ambush and could not afford to eschew caution. While it is true to say that patrols did proceed with due regard for the chance encounter with an aggressive and armed gang, it is more true to say that any stealth or wariness exercised was pre-eminently in order to effect contact with an unsuspecting gang, not to avoid it.

Of all casualties inflicted on security forces—comparative figures are provided in a later chapter—the greater proportion were occasioned in circumstances where superior terrorist numbers assaulted poorly defended stations and posts or attacked lone armed askari.

The incident narrated is significant in that the four fatalities were the first European security force casualties of the emergency, six months after it was declared. There can be no doubt that the valorous Kenya Regiment was to hit back with implacable fury throughout later months and soon avenged the tragic affair. If honour of first European casualties on active duty is to be awarded the KENREG, then so also is the honour for the longest sustained period of duty against Mau Mau. So many other famous British regiments came and went during the long five years but the stout-hearted KENREG were in the field from beginning to end.

❖❖❖

Referring to forest post personnel of the Kenya police, to whom this chapter is largely devoted, the element of risk was seldom considered big enough to inhibit their unremitting search for Mau Mau terrorists in the thickest of tangled jungle and deepest of gorges. But the locating of actual gangs was a game of chance with the odds stacked against them. Moreover, bumping into a gang while actually on patrol or during a follow-up operation, was even more remotely destined to occur.

Wily 'micks' had to be continually harried, their sources of food denied them, their access to farm labour lines and wheat stores sealed, and their cunningly situated hideouts located and destroyed. They had to be moved on, out of your area, anywhere. It was no good feeling chagrin or defeat if killing figures were low, or even negative. What mattered was that Mau Mau gangs be prevented from becoming too comfortably ensconced.

There was a compulsive effort by all forest post commanders to improve upon their contact/kill efficiency wherever possible. Constant training and a high standard of discipline among his askari would eventually result in a creditable performance when the quarry was located and the tactical behaviour of the patrol suited the occasion. But perfected operational standards were best left to the army or the police Special Effort units trained specifically in contact/kill efficiency methods.

So often had substantial numbers of security force personnel contacted hard-core forest gangs and failed to record any casualties that our post commander quickly grew to appreciate that it was much more a matter of luck and propitious circumstance for results to be efficacious. There simply wasn't the time to evolve the polished tactics necessary to attain the 'elimination' rate desired.

So the primary task was to purge one's area and maintain it so. The young inspector had to ensure that his farmers and their staff could go about their normal and lawful activity on the *shamba* in peace, that their losses through Mau Mau were kept to a minimum, and any inconvenience they were caused was not caused with impunity.

There was seldom the opportunity to apprehend terrorists. To do so would have required that a gang's presence in the area be cultivated, encouraged in fact, until the moment ripened for the pounce and kill. No, the inspector had, unfortunately, no choice other than to resist the glory of warming up to a positive contact. His job was to harass the thugs out of his parish into someone else's or, preferably, back into the inhospitable forests. It was frustrating, it was galling, but that was his priority task.

On the other hand it was not all passivity, not by a long way. Quite often it would become blatantly evident that some smug gang (normally with an average strength of twenty) was accommodated in some ravine or rocky ridge and, the circumstances being as auspicious as they would ever be, a sortie would be planned. With the area narrowed down to workable proportions a small patrol would slip into the immediate vicinity, well before first light, equipped to remain operational for two, or possibly three, days and nights. This would be the logical duration because if the patrol spotted no confirmatory sign of Mau Mau presence or sighted no lone terrorists then it could be quite sure its own presence had been either detected or sensed. The weird prophetic dreams that many gang leaders (who were often witchdoctors) alleged they had to protect and forewarn their members were a serious obstacle to anti-terrorist operations and could send a gang sprinting long before any military or police patrol was sighted.

Having entered the area it would be a game of cat and mouse. Should preparatory observations have accurately charted the probable locality of the hide, the patrol could easily have alighted bang on top of it. If occupied, then those within would be routed; if empty, it would need to be ambushed.

The latter was generally a hopeless gamble as it was a hundred-to-one chance that the gang would ever set foot near the hide again. During its cautious and painstaking approach, it would have been certain to detect some infinitesimal clue of an alien body; Mau Mau bush-craft and ability to interpret the minutest disturbance of grass or soil was absolutely phenomenal. In an instant the wary 'mick' could decide whether the being that made the mark or disturbance was friend or foe. There was a method, or better still, code, of movement and passage through the forest when in the vicinity of the hide that was practised by Mau Mau and which defied imitation by all except the esoteric.

This meant usually that for real success someone in the security force patrol would need to have had some measure of recent contact with the guerrillas, educated in the arts and guile of the hard-core gangster's life. Later on this led to a wider application of just these principles, and the concept of pseudo-gangsters was evolved, but more on this later.

Ambushing a gang's hideout then was usually ruled out, unless one had a very strong hunch or definite reason for believing that unsuspecting members would return. Even so it must be emphasized that such re-entry unaware to a vacated hideout was more often than not dependent upon an astonishingly well-organized feature of Mau Mau structure—the *posta*.

These were the hollow trunks of trees, empty beehives, crevasses in rocks, etc., used by terrorists for their letters and messages. They were immediately abandoned at the slightest suspicion of discovery by security forces and a gang's entire safety could depend on the secrecy and highly discerning manner in which individual members used these artfully located *postas*.

Normally they were used only on occasions of considerable importance, such as to warn detached members that the hideout was 'hot' or had been abandoned for some reason. The brief message would advise absent or transit members on where and when to rendezvous.

Needless to say the knowledge of a *posta's* location was absolutely priceless to police and army commanders. Once known, the tactical use of them had to be every bit as astute and even more discerning than that of the gang who established and used them. The intelligent cultivation of, and skilful interference with, a known gang *posta* was a vital factor in anti-terrorist operations and, allied to pseudo-gangsterism, was to become an instrument of incomparable worth, responsible, in fact, for the wiping out of many a large gang in the forests.

From a surprisingly early stage in the emergency police had

been awake to the employment of *postas* by Mau Mau and would always endeavour as a matter of urgency to extract information on their whereabouts from captured or surrendered terrorists. It was the surrender of a Mau Mau leader in the top echelon halfway through January 1954 that intensified *posta* activity by security forces. General China astonished us all when he relinquished the struggle and opted instead for the more secure, if not always comfortable, life alongside a Special Branch officer named Ian Henderson, perhaps the only officer in the Force who could speak Kikuyu. (General China—his bush pseudonym—was formally a signals corporal in the King's African Rifles. After the emergency he became a member of parliament and was awarded the Order of the Burning Spear.) Between the two of them, under the inspired direction of Assistant Commissioner John Prendergast, an ambitious scheme was embarked upon whereby active forest Mau Mau were called upon to surrender through the medium of the *postas* and 'sky-shouting' (taped messages by Henderson and China amplified from aircraft flying low over the forests). The scheme was never much of a success but there is little doubt it was the precursor of pseudo-gangs.

It is mentioned earlier in this chapter that security forces, in particular forest post personnel, sought always to improve upon their contact/kill performance. Caution the reader I must, however, that patrols were, despite their hungry weapons and overwrought patience, almost in duty bound to capture Mau Mau terrorists alive whenever possible. To have blazed away at a sitting duck would not only have reduced the quasi-warfare to monstrous murder but the most valuable thing was not another dead 'mick', but information.

To have disdained this essential would have been idiotic. Information of the whereabouts of other half-crazed rebels was the greatest asset. After a cup of tea and a cigarette the capturee would be chatted up in earnest (and without pontificating!) as to the error of his ways. With few exceptions, and little compunction he would then lead a patrol into the hideout of his comrades at dawn the following day.

If police or military came to possess a captured terrorist, or for that matter a surrenderee, he had to be used while still red-hot— before the stench of rotten meat and fat had faded from his rags; before civilized surroundings had sent the lice scampering from his body; before the wide, expressionless stare disappeared from his eyes; before he ceased looking and behaving like an animal. If he was not exploited immediately for operational purposes, then the chances of a gang being successfully stalked in the camp he'd last occupied would be thinner than those of winning the treble chance on the football pools.

Routine checks of known terrorist hideouts were considered to be a rather futile and energy-dissipating part of a forest post's operational programme. They were, of course, indispensable for the solitary and simple reason that gang members would occasionally re-occupy old hides.

I know that our police patrols would cling to the almost fanatical hope that a terrorist might be resting up inside, in transit or sometimes nursing his wounds. Therefore, we would halt at a discreet distance and allow the best tracker, a lithe light-skinned Samburu tribesman, to square the approaches to pick up some speck of evidence suggesting that a sly individual was around. Whether any evidence found purported to lead to or from the hide, or equally if nothing at all was detected, the patrol would squat in motionless observation for an hour or so. Should nothing transpire the hide would be entered and examined. Any indication that it was still being used would result in a more elaborately arranged ambush later. It was then necessary to go to infinite pains to obliterate every sign of the patrol's visitation before departing.

From the time I took up duties on my first forest post in a fever of enthusiasm and inspired with heroic visions, I was exclusively set upon creating havoc among any Mau Mau foolhardy enough to steal into my area. To encounter them became an obsession and I would lie awake at night planning and scheming ways of achieving this. Such a life became dangerously frustrating, if not downright loathsome, as the number of patrols mounted in their thwarted consistency. A year passed and I was able to chalk up a hundred patrols of one sort or another; there had been fatiguing ambushes by the score and excursions into the gloomy forests and gorges time without number; I had located numerous hideouts, some vacated but seconds before my arrival; there had been actual contacts though always in unpropitious circumstances; with my askari I had raced breathlessly to blazing farmhouses and labour lines just in time to glimpse the perpetrators slip back into the dark forest; ingenious game traps and cunningly concealed food stores were discovered; passive Mau Mau elements in Kikuyu squatter camps were apprehended for supplying the militant wings ... and so much else besides, but, as regards positive contacts where I and my crew could eliminate hard-core terrorists, I was obliged to bide my time until I was no longer in command of a forest post but skippered a Tracker Combat Team instead—as we shall see.

As the months rolled oppressively by without coming to grips with the will-o'-the-wisp terrorists, nothing was more likely to cause despondency than to learn from intelligence summaries of heavy Mau Mau casualties almost daily. Yet their strength remained, seemingly, undiminished. In one week alone during those first months I spent on forest posts, fifty-eight were eliminated by security forces here and there, either killed or captured. The evidence of their impudent, ubiquitous presence throughout the length and breadth of my area was abundant; the villainous brutes were even known to sit and watch us from their eyries high up on Kipipiri. Alas, as for a group of them composing an inelegant cameo study in the aperture sight of my 9mm Sterling automatic and me pulling the trigger to take a lethal picture, that was the perquisite of others; such as Field Intelligence Officers and their Special Effort groups who seldom acted unless it was an objective certainty. Nudging the elusive terrorist into the eager arms of other security forces was the responsibility, albeit an important one, of our post commander and his askari.

And yet, if the picture presented is one of disconsolation, then I have little difficulty in redressing the harmony of it. For instance, there were few things I enjoyed more than to set off with a few askari in the early morning mists, past groups of quaint African *rondavels* with the smoke seeping through their grass roofs from the fire within. There were the mad chases through the *kilileshwa* scrub after small dik-dik or impala until a lucky shot brought one down. And always entertaining (to a point) were the Sunday-morning inspections of labour lines, searching, or rather sniffing, for illicit *tembo*. There was the ineffable beauty, peace and poetry of cascading water through narrow declivities and the invitingly cool, lucid pools. I revelled too, in the lush variegated flora that, from a distance, made giant gorges look only half their actual size. The changing landscape of the farms and the variety of climate, never uncomfortably cold, all stimulated the senses and salved the tired mind. Such a pity it was that all this was overshadowed by the spectre of Mau Mau.

I recall an evening when I returned weary from having tracked grains of wheat for about twenty miles until I had ventured too far for safety outside my own area (the grains had fallen from sacks carried off by a gang that had raided a nearby granary). Sitting outside my austere quarters I wondered about the particular hideout that I and my askari had stumbled upon that afternoon. It was a shallow cave, the front of which was screened by bush and overhanging creeper behind a ledge a few feet above the racing waters of the Turasha River. So well concealed was it that none but the most diligent of searchers would have located it. I was fairly certain that a patrol of the Black Watch Regiment had discovered it some months previously after a terrorist gang had used it while leisurely laying bold plans to raid and plunder the Carnelly farm house (which they subsequently did, too).

That afternoon I had seen irrevocable evidence that the cave was being used by terrorists in transit. There were the remains of a meal, fresh fire embers, naked foot prints, bits of old rag, fresh cut wood and strippings of bark. In short, all the usual minutiae clues of Mau Mau visitation, including even a sack of maize.

So it was, then, a practical hideout, almost inaccessible, nicely sheltered and reasonably cosy. It was going to be my horrible misfortune to have to check it periodically.

"What was the damned use? Why the hell should they jeer at me?" I thought in anguish.

An unusually profound weariness assailed me on that particular evening. Damnable Mau Mau appeared to be mocking me. They had me chasing all over the district in circles until I was giddy. Well, I decided, it was one hideout for which I would not endure cold, tense nights lying alongside the track leading to it in the damp, musty, ant-ridden vegetation.

It was especially galling to have tracked so tenaciously the gang who had lifted several sacks of wheat from a store on Gordon's farm without making contact with it. I was convinced that the sacks would have been carried without pause by the sinewy, half-starved vagabonds right up onto the desolate moorlands of the Aberdare range. Was it not time I hit back? But how?

The distant crump and reverberations of a muffled explosion suddenly leapt across the *shamba* from the dark shape of Kipipiri. As the night was so still it startled me; what could it be? A delayed-action bomb from the recent Lancaster bombing raids? A blind mortar fired by the KA.R. last week that a wild animal had now just stumbled across? An ambush sprung and a grenade tossed? A booby-trap laid by an irate farmer at his wit's end? ... Booby-trap! Yes, that was it, a booby-trap! Why not? What could be easier or more efficacious?

"Hmm," I reflected moodily, "instructions from the C-in-C and the Commissioner were strictly that under no circumstances were security forces to set booby-traps."

I was well aware of the endless speculation there was at the time concerning this desperate stratagem by frustrated police officers engaged on anti-terrorist duties. Officialdom had hinted repeatedly that we were NOT at war—merely were we putting down a subversive uprising and, plainly, it was an anti-terrorist measure that was very much open to the most diabolical abuse once sanctioned officially, even if only tacitly.

Through dint of sheer desperation, caution is occasionally thrown to the devil. Ruthless conclusions, however tempered by objectiveness they may be, are arrived at. Surely then, if booby-traps were resorted to then those responsible were motivated not by malice but by expediency.

Before lying down to sleep that night I had made up my mind; booby-trap it would have to be, regardless ...! I was responsible for the area and knew that no persons except me and my post personnel were allowed in the gorge concerned. It was gazetted as a restricted area and permission was required by the local *watu* before they could enter to collect firewood or honey. Any military forces or other security forces would obtain authority from my district H.Q. in Naivasha before entering and I would be advised accordingly.

My agitated mind could not escape the fact that a sack of maize had been seen in that cave, obviously put there during the past few days, too. Something drastic had to be done about it or I'd become a raving lunatic.

The following afternoon I returned with several askari to the top of the gorge above the cave. In a haversack I carried a Mill's hand grenade. A noisy and conspicuous show was made of carrying out the sack of maize—no easy task either up an entangling sixty-degree slope of some five hundred feet—which ensured distraction of attention from the extra few minutes that I spent inside the cave.

Around the lethal object that I carefully withdrew from the haversack I tied a single piece of string. Then, having primed it with a two-second detonator, I removed the pin which I pocketed. Gently releasing my grip on the lever, which my fingers held captive, I relaxed as it held in position against the pressure of the spring under the top of it. I then scooped out a fairly deep hollow in the embers of the fireplace, set the grenade at the bottom of it and covered it over again. Having achieved this, I then took a small twig and traced slight impressions in the ash to fit the pattern of bird claws that were almost always seen in empty hideouts, also small indentations were made to repair a disturbed area of dew drops. With a sigh and final wrestle with my conscience I scrambled up out of the stifling and gloomy gorge and joined my askari. When informed of my nefarious act they were highly delighted.

"*Mzuri kabisa, bwana. Akili sana,*" they chortled. (Very good, very clever, *bwana*.)

That, I thought, will do the job nicely if they, as they nearly always did, lit a fire to roast maize or cook a hunk of their ill-gotten meat. The explosion would be heard by those farms in the vicinity atop the gorge who would report it to the post, thus enabling me to hurry to the scene to succour and bring out any casualties. A deplorably callous attitude perhaps but, as already stated, desperate situations often demanded desperate measures.

I awoke the next morning with little thought of this infamous arrangement or its devastating potential. After a hasty toilet I checked in at the radio room. As the post incorporated a signals station that was also the Rift Valley control station there was no necessity for me to maintain scheds. The operation of this radio equipment was most ably managed by a farmer's wife, Betty— a full-time K.P.R. member—who coped with the complicated operational dialogue and jargon with the equanimity of a trained military signals officer.

She was sat alongside her two sets when I entered to look over the log for any incidents that had been reported during the night. Between bites of her breakfast and sips of coffee she was acknowledging sitreps as they came in from the various posts. Asked by her if I'd been awakened during the night by the noise of the army five-tonners grinding up the escarpment road during the early hours, I replied that I had not.

"I didn't turn in until about one o'clock due to the hyena scare and slept rather heavily." (The hyenas had jumped the cattle *boma* during the night.) "Anyway," I continued, "what are they doing in these parts, Betty? No incidents last night, were there?"

Checking through the 'IN' tray of signals, she produced one that explained the Gloucester Regiment had a new batch of recruits they proposed to acclimatize with a sweep from Venter's down to Oliver's in the ... TURASHA!

"What!" I exclaimed in alarm and anger. "Why no warning? Why so bloody sudden?"

I paced outside the radio hut and sat on the step staring into space more anxious than I care to remember. Every second I expected to hear the distant thud of an explosion. I visualized the enquiries and, worst of all, the funerals with full military honours. The condemnation, the reports in home newspapers. And not the least of my troubled thoughts was the unsolicited victory that would result for Mau Mau.

"But they can't sweep that gorge," I moaned aloud. "They just can't!"

Betty emerged and stood behind me. She tapped me playfully on the shoulder and said: "What's worrying you, my boy? Do you think they are going to bump into your pet gang and earn the praise of we settlers up here?"

She stepped briskly back to the radio set to acknowledge a call from Ol Kalou: "... Morning Betty. Nan Tare Roger. Anything for me?"

Ol Kalou were bid to "stand by one or two", then leaning round the door she addressed me. "Go and have breakfast, Peter, and don't be so terribly, terribly keen. We shall say that you provided the info and the guides if they bump into anything."

I shuffled off leadenly into the main house where I joined Ian, the owner of the farm, who was finishing his coffee. His rugged features broke into a smile as he greeted me gaily. He was, as usual, about to streak off to his thousand and one tasks about the farm.

"Hello! You don't seem too happy this morning. Still peeved about being dragged out after those hyena?" he queried.

"No. Not at all, Ian. On the contrary, it was fun really. After all, it could have been a gang that was using the presence of the hyena as a cover." I stirred my coffee and took a sip or two. "No, Ian, I didn't mind the hyenas, rather enjoyed it, in fact. Horrible creatures, aren't they? Made me quite shiver when we caught up with the brutes loping across the *shamba*. Nice bit of tactical flanking, I thought, though I was half afraid that your fire would come in my direction once they were in your headlights. How many did we get?"

Ian said he thought four, but had not checked. "But they finished two of my best milkers," he added ruefully. "One you saw last night and another they dragged a quarter of a mile to the *boma* fence and had stripped most of it before we were alerted."

"Yes. It doesn't take the filthy beasts long with those massive jaws, does it?" I enjoined sympathetically.

He poured more coffee and while perusing some documents before him, asked me casually if I was going to join the army in their sweep.

"Join them!" I blurted out. "I should have preceded them hours ago."

Ian had half stood up and was draining the last of his second cup of coffee. He sat down again and regarded me questioningly.

"Look," I appealed. "Remember what I told you last night about taking a chance with that hide in the Turasha? Well! What do you think about it now? Couldn't be a bigger chance could it?"

He elected not to reply immediately and when he did it was accompanied by a low chuckle. I thought, or rather hoped, he was going to tell me it was the Malewa and not the Turasha that the Gloucesters were to sweep. Perhaps the troops that passed through during the night were to be employed as stops. But my hopes declined as rapidly as they had risen because Ian merely suggested: "You don't think that those soldiers will discover that hide unless you or your askari go along and show them, do you? And, anyway, are they going to light a fire in it? If I were you I'd simply trot along and see their Sunray—he's probably based himself at Griffin's place—and tell him to warn his men. That's all. Failing that, say nothing of it."

"*Ndio, ndio, lakini,*" I mocked, as he patted my shoulder and departed.

119

Later on I drove to the top of the gorge above the hide where I encountered a cluster of young soldiers clad in jungle green. They were sauntering along chatting unconcernedly among themselves. I asked one of them how far the sweep by their companions below had progressed and a point some hundred yards or so downstream was indicated. I sat down and waited for an hour until I deemed the excited recruits to have almost completed their little exercise. I then prepared to descend into the cave. My mind had resolved to effect recovery of the grenade and not to concern myself with booby-traps any more. They were simply not worth the anxiety or consequences, adverse or otherwise.

Taking two of my askari with me I slithered and swung down the precipitous side of the gorge. The askari I instructed to remain close by me for fear that soldiers might still be hovering in the vicinity. Some were reputed to have a flair for popping off at anything black and resembling a human being.

Entering the cave I saw straightaway that it had been visited by the army patrol. The impressions of their boots were abundant. Even the fireplace ashes had been disturbed. I remember silently praising the diligence and thoroughness of their searching. Recruits were invariably more enthusiastic anyway, but, "How would they be when they have done the same arduous thing twenty times and more?" I thought, mournfully.

Cautiously groping beneath the powdery ash my fingers closed over the hard metal object. I could not actually feel the string. I encircled the bomb with all fingers and thumb. Drawing it out I blew off the ash ... the string was still in position and the lever was positioned comfortably in the fleshy part of my hand between index finger and thumb. I don't think I would have really been much surprised had I heard it ticking or, ghastly thought, to have even heard the sharp crack as its detonator cap exploded—which would have left me exactly two seconds to be rid of it!

So, there it was. All neat, safe, intact and really very like an insignificant toy. But, what a nuisance! What to do with it? There was nowhere in the immediate vicinity that was sufficiently clear of bush to ensure my hasty retreat. No matter where I threw it I was restricted to a downward throw towards the stream outside and it was sure to be arrested in flight by tree or creeper and fall short. I therefore climbed back up to where my two askari were waiting, curious and expectant, on a small ledge over the cave.

The string was severed and I leaned over as far as I could, released the troublesome object and threw myself back. I did not hear the crack of its detonator cap but saw the lever fly away. It seemed an age that I lay face down before the roar of its lethal contents leapt across the gorge to bounce back and forth in ever-diminishing rumbles.

Dust rose, I and my askari rose. Our hearts commenced to beat again. We all laughed rather self-consciously and descended to examine the now disordered hideout. The explosion had achieved no useful purpose whatever. The foliage around the entrance was seared and blackened but, so far as the cave's amenities to terrorists in search of shelter and concealment were concerned, the exercise could adequately be described as worthless. However, the object had not, of course, been to destroy the hideout but to eliminate the dastardly, nasty, smelly, predatory humans, rotten with the infectious scourge of Mau Mau, who used it during their iniquitous nocturnal marauding.

So much then for the folly of resorting to booby-traps. Barely a week passed without some incident of consequence or interest in the life of the police officer on a forest post. One or two worthy of note and amplification I propose to narrate later on. At this juncture, however, by way of rounding off this chapter, I suggest that few descriptions or anecdotes could serve better to illustrate his general life and times than to reproduce a random selection of entries culled from a diary I tried hard to maintain. The robustness, unpredictability and tone of life is, I believe, imparted by the clipped log of daily events. There is every reason to suppose that they would be very typical as regards the lives of the majority of inspectors who discharged their duties in rural areas of the

White Highlands with a handful of special constables. The diary excerpts are for the year 1954:

Friday 26 March

... all's well. Nothing strenuous done, no outstanding problems (except how to catch Mau Mau) ... had more askari arrive making my total now eighteen. Just a comfortable number. Am pleased with the efforts to elaborate on the post. Compliments received from several quarters. Tomorrow we embark on a three-day patrol into the northern sector. News from Nairobi is that penalties for neglect of firearms have been increased. Shall have to set an exemplary standard now!

27 March

After a fairly eventful patrol that involved the chase of a suspect terrorist (and during the course of which I lost two askari) we arrived at destination C. It is the *shamba* from which we operate while in the area. Mr C. is a bachelor farmer of some prominence, his habits frugal, his company entertaining to a point. He evokes my admiration, being a person of sixty-five years, still very fit and upright, with some thirty years experience in this country.

29 March

Sleep last night, for some unaccountable reason, was fitful, but I was quite refreshed by 0700 hours and we made our departure from G's ... two askari still had not returned so set off without them. Patrolling with blankets rolled up and draped over one's shoulders is as near flagellation as one can get in the heat of the day. The return was made at a killing pace, why I don't really know! Probably peeved that there was nothing of a suspicious nature to lie up on.

30 March

Have just returned from a night patrol and am thoroughly enjoying a cup of hot cocoa made with cream (the buxom wife of the Afrikaner, T, must be a fan of mine for she now provides me with cream almost daily!), nourishing compensation after a slow, tense patrol on a moonlit night. It is my intention to institute a series of well-planned night ambushes in an effort to sight the gang that is moving around here, not possible either unless there is some moon. It's an indescribably wretched task trying to lead a patrol along uncertain tracks to ambush positions on a pitch-black African night. An allegation received of rape against one of my askari; a Kuke *bibby* is the victim. Did she or didn't she consent?

25 April

Looking back from the 28th to insert a jotting or two in the blanks. A 'mick' captured after the ambush recorded opposite, I had brought to the post. He was transported in the Chev, cowed, wide-eyed and stinking. The instant I pulled up he was pounced on by the askari who then commenced to beat him most mercilessly. It was a very unpleasant moment or two I had trying to separate the hate that constant seeking has generated in me for these filthy gangsters from the natural compassion I'd feel for anyone being beaten up so unrestrainedly. Why I wasn't compelled by my own detestation of Mau Mau to strike him myself I just cannot fathom. Merely did I experience an awkward discomfort and found myself doing my utmost to conquer a welling-up of stupid pity.

3 May

The weather is awful! Really Scottish in its misty, damp drizzle. Worst of all is the mud created. It all but isolates us; the roads are impassable. Ambushes have been put out every night on all cattle *bomas* in the area. They are a tiring and tedious business—total darkness makes it a great strain on one's eyes—but they must be continued in an attempt to trap M.M. when hungry and coming off the mountain for food ... there is news again of my being supplied with a *gari*. Such to me is now a myth.

7 May

Today has been very hot for the most part. Visited Sattimer police post (also on the slopes of Kipipiri) and met the inspector there. He is a one-tour bod like me and has one hell of a grievance. His post is appalling; they all sleep in tents. Furthermore, like many others, he is at loggerheads with the local settlers—they like to dictate, he won't permit it. Had an awful ambush session tonight; poured with rain, scrambling and sliding in inky darkness.

13 May

More indefiniteness from H.Q. The G.S.U. platoon that has been assisting me has returned on orders to Gilgil. All the plans I had are now destroyed. A cinema (mobile) that was due to visit this area to boost low morale failed to turn up ... All my arrangements spoilt and, with no transport, I had to walk three miles to the farm it was going to give the performance at and notify the *watu* of its cancellation. Yes, it's not M.M. or the routine on this post that will wear me out, it's the obscurity of purpose and the rashness of decisions of those above me that bind my enthusiasm.

7 June

Have heard that two Europeans were murdered at Nyeri on the 5th; don't know yet whether they are settlers or security forces. The reports roll in, the forces go out, the directives become more indistinct, the results less and less heartening and the emergency slides sluggishly on and ever more ugly. Individuals like myself are endeavouring and tolerating, but the zeal is gradually evaporating under the arid and barren influence of unsuitable superiors and petty inadequacies. The latest from my host farmer is that I do not address him as Michael anymore. It must be 'sir' or 'Mr H.' ... he can forget the former right away!

12 June

Lots of rain, too much of it. Farmers are bedevilled by the worry over late planting ... it is wise that I avoid crossing them just now.

15 June

Again the alarm rings mockingly at 0600 hours. We were operational by 0640 hours in conjunction with a Black Watch mortar platoon. The observation groups saw nothing at all but a patrol found a hideout that had just been vacated. An ambush at night made the operation an extremely long and tiring one.

20 June

I made out yesterday's entry rather prematurely because in the wee hours we were out at the rush. Rifle fire and a ruddy glow from a *shamba* about two miles away had us going up the road at a steady trot (no bloody *gari*). There was the usual confusion—burning huts, bodies running around naked; lots of shouting and a marked absence of M.M. when we arrived. They'd done their business well and had simply vanished. One native shot with a .303 in his guts was found lying groaning. I pushed back the viscera that bulged outside like a little balloon and fastened an old belt tightly around his abdomen. We were unable to have him moved to Nakuru until this morning ... Labour Officer and O.I.C. Naivasha arrived during the day to have a *baraza* with the labour who were all threatening to pack up and *kwenda* ...

6 July

Yesterday's entry was missed for a very good reason—I wasn't here last night. In fact from noon yesterday until late this afternoon patrolling activity has left me gasping. With a few askari I followed a wheat (grains) trail from F's store that took us to a food store with sacks of grain nicely stacked away in a hollow on a jungly slope just on the Ol Kalou border. A most pleasing reward after such an arduous patrol. An ambush was laid hoping to nab the bastards in the act of removing it ... the sour note is that we spent a perfectly abominable night freezing in my mud-bound *gari*.

23 July

Mau Mau to Barker's! A timely and most commendably sharp turnout by my post scotched their intentions to commit arson and murder ... chased them into the edge of the forest and opened fire on one or two stragglers. If only the stupid, cowering, dithering labour had drawn our attention as we tore past their huts we might have inflicted heavy casualties. Not much sleep.

24 July

Sequel to last night's raid was the tracking, and most successfully too, of the gang right over the stark and forbidding mass, Kipipiri. Lack of food and blankets compelled the abandonment, not to mention the inevitable and torrential rain. I returned quite wet and fatigued.

22 August

After staying the night at the farm of Mr L., I returned here at 1100 hours this morning. Very, very disappointing to have bumped into those four micks and lost them. My temporary partner Dick returned from his 48-hours leave—seems to have enjoyed it. There is much thunder and bad weather about. No mail yet. Perhaps I, too, should take a 48-hour in Nairobi; it's winding me up too much here. I'm gaining too much momentum.

11 September

"*Effendi! Effendi!*" hoarsely yells the corporal. "*Iko mutu karibu kufa.*" Here, or rather, there, I was about to start my supper and the corporal informs me that a man is almost dead. In point of fact he had been beaten up and was unconscious not through the beating though, but through DRINK—the bastard. I was some three hours rounding up his equally drunk assailants. God! This *tembo* is a vicious brew.

19 September

A lay-in today till 0745 hours. Indulgent and torpid creature am I! A neighbour, the implacable, irascible Col. F. hove to halfway through the morning (on a Sunday too). Among other things he caustically bellowed, "... and get this drunkenness cleared up." In amazement, unfeigned, I asked him, where? He indicated H's labour lines. Here? Under my very nose? Am I credited with no sense of duty? True, drink was there; true, two of his house staff had been found staggering, but ... oh! ... it just doesn't bear writing about. The man is bombastically impossible. Tomorrow I am clearing off for a two-day op in the Ndutura ... wonderful!

28 September

Been out since yesterday morning bashing around a section of my area hitherto unbashed. Spent a cruel period at the bottom of the Manunga gorge. If M.M. care to reside therein they have my full approval and greatest sympathy. One unforgivable event today was the leaving of my Lanchester at the place where we slept last night. I was caused untold fear and cringed at the thought of the consequences. I'd have been kicked out of the colony or at least ostracized, should I have not recovered it. My relief was overwhelming when, after a frenetic return, I saw it propped against the tree exactly as I'd left it ... miraculous! It had been available for the taking for an hour and a half. I'm now pretty satisfied there are no micks in that area.

13 October

Another post success to record, not to mention all the night patrols of late. I took a look into a gully near the Kasariga gorge and, voila!—cattle remains a day old and a plethora of good tracks. Five had been slaughtered and the remains of all we recovered. Then, just at dusk, we bumped into a gang of six terrs, ostensibly returning to carry off the meat. We opened up on them until they scampered into the bush, and what a lot of damned bush there was. I'm certain that casualties were inflicted.

25 October

Mr Leakey (the Nairobi anthropologist) has been found in circumstances that suggest he was buried alive by M.M. How atrocious! How ghastly! I am boiling with rage (Leakey was abducted from his home after his wife had been strangled). Three miles from here last night a formidably armed gang launched a determined attack on a farm; it wrought havoc and caused considerable bloodshed. I've just returned from another ambush, sodden and shivering (is there a wetter place anywhere?). Time is 0045 hours. Am I a fool to be so involved?

3 November

A farmer just beyond Dawson's on the edge of the Kinangop yesterday commenced to harvest his volunteer wheat. By nightfall he'd taken off twenty sacks and, silly fellow, left them on the *shamba*. They were nowhere to be seen this morning. M.M. had certainly not been slow. By 1600 hours I had discovered where several of the sacks had been hidden and have just returned from a futile ambush of them. Where are the remainder? I wouldn't be at all surprised if they have not been carried all the way to the top of Mount Kenya!

4 November

There is a distant thud of heavy bombs (Lincoln bomber sorties) on the Aberdare range which means that terrs will flood this area in no time at all. Where do they come from? Why are we always several steps behind? Where do they vanish to? It is virtually their war as they dictate the terms. Only when they make a slip do we catch them ... more reliable info is what I want.

It must be true to some extent that life on a forest post was a potent panacea for all those trifling anxieties, deficiencies in social stature, disappointments and frustrations of the ordinary everyday lives common to most of us in towns and cities. Life was unfettered and unregulated. It was at last possible to exercise some initiative; moreover, the hidden characteristic of the hard-bitten warrior was exposed and allowed some recognition.

A palpable glory, leavened with dash and savoured the more with physical fitness; such was the distinction an officer known as a 'bundu basher' was allowed to enjoy; nothing more.

Chapter 7

The tempo quickens: the massacre at Lari and the sack of a police station

In an earlier chapter mention was made of the unrest and furious outcry of the settler community that seethed in the wake of the Ruck atrocity. I seriously doubt whether any colonial citizenry had ever before acted in such an ominous and Bolshevistic manner or have come so close to outright anarchy (in more recent times the French *colons* in Algeria went a step further in their disillusionment at the policies of the 'Grand General'). I am certain that the event I am about to narrate has been conveniently forgotten, or at best seldom referred to, by many of the politicians and high officials of the day. We cannot, however, afford to have it excluded from any chronicle relating to the Mau Mau emergency.

May I emphasize that the following account is not quoted from any official source. My aim is only to record the most consistently authentic account I have learnt of. Should the reader seek ratification, however, I am confident he will find little discrepancy.

During the afternoon of Monday, 27 January 1953, just two days after the Ruck murders, over a thousand Europeans, comprised mostly of irate settler farmers from areas more seriously affected by the omnipresent Mau Mau, marched to and congregated outside Government House in Nairobi. Sir Evelyn Baring, the Governor of Kenya, was at home and in private consultation with Mr Michael Blundell (later knighted, became a Kenyan citizen and chairman of East African Breweries), the leader of the European elected members of the Legislative Council, and members of the Executive Council. The white mob had no set purpose and was for the most part, if noisy, quite orderly. They shouted for His Excellency but he declined to appear. They grew restive and surged ever nearer to the inviolate sanctum of Her Majesty's illustrious representative in Kenya. The agitated throng of settlers yelled demands that something be done to rid the colony of pestilential Mau Mau.

A cordon of apprehensive African police askari was the Governor's last and only line of defence from the outraged mob; a mob protesting that after nine murders of European settlers it would tolerate no more.

It is known that the Sultan of Zanzibar was a distinguished guest of the Governor at the time, which did not help matters at all but His Excellency steadfastly refused to accede to an appearance before the mob in such undignified circumstances and, very soon, the line of nonplussed native police was broken through and the aggrieved settlers were hammering at the massive doors of Kenya's Buckingham Palace.

It was the grace of God, and the fortuitous intervention of Mr Michael Blundell who desperately harangued them, that prevented an ugly riot. He made wild, impromptu promises of mobilization and of the appointment of a supreme military commander. His exhortations won the day and, apart from the unsavoury skirmish in the beautiful grounds of Sir Evelyn's magnificent residence, there was no lasting damage to the reputation of the Crown or the prestige of His Excellency, a self-possessed personage if ever there was one—later to become Lord Howick of Glendale. (Tragically this celebrated Peer and Servant of the Crown died in March 1973 aged sixty-nine following a fall down a rock face on his Northumberland estate near Alnwick.)

It is interesting to note that the crowd was shouting demands for "rule from Nairobi and not from London". The passions of the European community were as articulate for the colony's secession as were the Africans for *Uhuru*.

The aforegoing incident is no personal reminiscence of mine for it happened before I made my inconspicuous appearance. Nonetheless, the underlying causes of that momentous storming of Government House had not been eliminated entirely when I arrived.

❖❖❖

Mobilization gained momentum rapidly during the first few months of 1953. The Black Watch Regiment, which had been flown in from the Middle East at the declaration of the State of Emergency in October the previous year, was garrisoned at Gilgil and spread its tentacles in company and platoon form over the settled areas and into the forests and gorges. The Lancashire Fusiliers, bivouacked on the south shore of Lake Naivasha, ranged across the Kinangop plateau, west to the Mau escarpment and south to Longonot and Kijabi. The Kenya Regiment expanded its ranks and grew in strength and stature—a fine force, its members, many Kenyan-born, were of a high calibre. Their assignment was the infected locations round Mount Kenya and the eastern slopes of the Aberdare range, scouting up as far as Thompson's Falls.

The King's African Rifles, under its sterling leadership of British regular officers, entered in countless defiles the heavy blanket of lush greenery that covered the Aberdare range along its forty-mile length, forever harrying the terrorists, forbidding them to become comfortably ensconced. The police and police reservists increased in numbers beyond the wildest dreams of the commissioner, Mr Michael O'Rorke. Here, there and everywhere, disseminating the influence, if not the full weight, of the law in every nook and cranny where Mau Mau were rife and lawlessness caused anxiety—the Kikuyu Land Unit, Naro Moro, Rumuruti and Thomson's Falls, Sabatia and Njoro, down through Nakuru, Ol Kalou, Gilgil, Naivasha and the Kinangop to such far-flung places as the Uasin Gishu and, in the south, Narok.

From the cadre of the Force issued the small cells comprising a European inspector with a handful of special police askari to become known as forest posts, policing areas that hitherto had seldom seen a policeman. Even the Kikuyu themselves began to play their part in ever-multiplying formations. Loyal tribesmen were sworn in and called Homeguards. They were made largely responsible for their own locations, issued with shotguns or spears, armbands and green berets; and what a terrible toll Mau

Mau took of them. Face to face with their own progeny these loyal Kikuyu subjects, from the very beginning such a strange contradiction in mentality to the militant Mau Mau elements of their tribe, were the easiest and most hotly pursued quarry of terrorists. In a rebellion that was to develop into something more the nature of a civil war it was the Kikuyu loyalists themselves whose casualties ran into four figures. Suffice it to say that during the years 1955 and 1956 the bodies of no less than one and a half thousand Kikuyu were recovered from shallow graves throughout the Kikuyu reserves, all murdered, throats cut or strangled, and all, ostensibly, traitors to the cause of the Land Freedom Armies of the 'saviour', Jomo Kenyatta. And, one may well ask, how many old scores were settled under the guise of Mau Mau? Never an easy assessment to make when primitive societies wage a bloody campaign against an oppressor.

And yet, in the midst of all this frenetic mobilization, the mass arrests, screening, curfews and counter-revolutionary activity, there occurred, just two months after the maniacal slaughter of the Ruck family, two events that sent the population reeling. They were hefty blows to the colony's solar-plexus that stunned and nauseated. And not only in Kenya either. I, for one, had been stunned and nauseated, too, when I read of them in peaceful Scotland where I was serving at a Royal Naval air station.

Both events happened on the night of 26 March 1953.

Whether or not they were planned to occur simultaneously is difficult to say. They did, nevertheless, assert with confounding suddenness the power and potential of Mau Mau. Security forces were made to appreciate with sickening clarity, possibly for the first time, the true capacity of this insurgent tribe for planned terrorization. From the Director of Operations, Major-General W.R.N. Hinde, CBE, DSO, to the humble *duka wallah* there was an incredible gasp of disbelief as the brutal facts trickled through.

One of the events showed how exposed and defenceless the Kikuyu loyalists were; the other revealed how lax police security was. Of the two the former was to cause the gravest anxiety for, although it was possible with discipline and improved methods to rectify slack security arrangements, it was considered an impossibly huge task to guarantee protection for the lives of over a million Kikuyu.

The first of these staggering events took place at about ten p.m. on Thursday, 26 March 1953 at Naivasha. There was some moon and it was a delightfully clear night. It was a slumberous township at any time and on this particular night was as placid and inoffensive as the graceful flamingos on Lake Naivasha a few miles away—the only sounds distinguishable above the chorus of cicadas being a train shunting at the railway sidings, a lorry descending the escarpment in low gear and the generator of the police station thumping away. The cosy Bell Inn was empty except for a couple of off-duty police inspectors huddled at the bar ogling the soft, ample curves of the proprietor's daughter. In the distance the delirious beat of a drum bespoke a wild *tembo* party.

At the police station an African sub-inspector dozed in the Duty Officer's room; in the sandbagged emplacements dozed African sentries; in the watchtower another inalert sentry, his searchlight also. The barbed-wire perimeter was incomplete and no one had been in any hurry to perfect the station's defences. (Mau Mau, they had decided, only bothered to attack small isolated posts!) Within the compound of the station on the other side of a few strands of barbed wire was a detention block in which lay, fitfully sleeping, about one hundred and fifty detainees and Mau Mau suspects. Nearby, lolling against the wall of the District Officer's *rondavel*, was another askari, rifle slung over his shoulder, his thankless duty being a roving patrol within the station's perimeter. In the Charge Office a young constable sat scribbling an entry in the Occurrence Book in respect of a prisoner by his side. He thought he heard a vehicle clatter to a halt somewhere near the main gate but paid no attention. Those days lorries were rumbling in and out all the time. He never finished the entry in the Occurrence Book because a sharp *panga* bit deeply into his skull and spilled out his brains. Blood splattered over the book before him and poured over the cement floor to mingle with that of the prisoner who grunted, gurgled and fell lifeless, a wide gash in his neck.

From across the station yard the startled shouts of a sentry followed by a rifle shot were the first sounds that indicated all was not well. Soon there were screams and further shots, the sound of many running feet from the direction of the District Officer's compound. From the station armoury were noises of doors being battered, a few shots, rattling of chains and of rifles being thrown, dragged and dropped. The shouts and whoops in a Kikuyu tongue were laced with sharp orders and terrified shrieks. After about ten minutes a vehicle, now inside the compound, was heard to start up, rev furiously and rattle off at speed along the road to the escarpment. It was later found abandoned several miles away. In the rear was a constable's fez, some rounds of ammunition, torn case files, a rifle magazine and a bloody *panga*.

By the time any response to the rape of the station was observed and cars started to arrive from which taut Europeans leapt, guns in hand, the station was quiet again. Only the noise of the generator throbbed indifferently on. Then an African woman over by the District Office started whimpering, it soon grew to a high-pitched wailing. The first on the scene rushed across, sweating and breathing heavily, still ignorant of the monstrous nature of the occurrence, fingers tremulous on the triggers of their pistols.

They recoiled from what they saw in the pale moonlight—the mutilated and decapitated body of a constable and not far away another lying prostrate in a pool of blood. Having recovered from this gory sight, and realizing that the attack was over, they proceeded cautiously to tour the ravished station still reeking with the smell of cordite. Their gasps became ever louder and longer as they went, until their discovery of the ransacked armoury drew the most anguished groans. Their horrified astonishment was soon converted into radio signals that flashed out to alert the Rift Valley Province; not that there was much that could be achieved.

The full facts the following day were gloomy and disquieting. Over one hundred and fifty prisoners released, half a dozen police constables slaughtered, their weapons seized, and, most frightful of all, forty-seven precision weapons (twenty of them automatics) and almost four thousand rounds of ammunition stolen from the armoury that had been burst asunder.

What an inexcusable boost to Mau Mau and, in particular, the prestige and following of Dedan Kimathi, who was responsible for the organization and execution of the audacious raid. The repercussions were incalculable—the ranks of the Land Freedom Armies swelled by many of the freed prisoners and the formidable equipping of the forest gangs with the seized artillery. Naivasha bowed in shame and the whole colony was alive to the dreadful consequences. Inevitably it was the Kenya police that came in for the most stinging criticism—due largely to the fact that no European officer had been on duty at the station.

Had this been all that happened on that fateful night in March it might have been possible for the authorities wryly to laugh it off and accept the scandalous episode as an object lesson, after which the usual severe reprimands could have been meted out where necessary.

But, while Dedan and his woolly-haired boys were whooping it up delightedly at Naivasha police station, a frightful massacre of unprecedented ferocity was going on in the lurid light of burning huts not far from Uplands in the Lari reserve (part of the Kikuyu Land Unit).

The victims were loyal subjects under the benign jurisdiction of Chief Makemei, Kikuyus all of them. The inhabitants of Lari had long since been regarded as anti-Mau Mau and had denounced the evil secret society. Whereupon orders were issued from the callous Mau Mau administrators in Nairobi as hundreds of its subscribers from miles around converged on the sleeping village to descend in a frenzy of killing indescribably savage.

Only *pangas* and other wicked knives were used for the orgy of butchering; no firearms at all. The grass huts were fired whether the occupants were inside or out, such being their ghastly choice that they either burned to death inside the raging infernos or were hacked to death as they ran out screaming.

There were very few spared the revolting thoroughness of the horrendous maniacal attack, not even Chief Luka who lived peacefully on the Lari ridge. One can only wonder how the brutes were able to distinguish the loyalist victims from their own heaving masses. The scenes of sickening slaughter looked upon by dazed survivors and tight-lipped officials at dawn next day were grisly beyond words. There was absolutely no parallel for the unmitigated fury of such inhuman havoc. It was quite impossible to comprehend that any member of the human race could be motivated by such a pitch of genocidal hatred or be so utterly pitiless.

Fires were still smouldering, the acrid smoke being gratefully inhaled by the awed and silent crowd who retched from the stench of so much carnage. The corpses lay strewn in every conceivable position, mutilated, grotesque and revolting. Pregnant women had been slit open, their embryo young torn from their wombs, cut in two and thrown back onto their dismembered parents. (Two thirds of the victims were women and children.) Heads, arms and legs were scattered in gory profusion, just nondescript fleshy objects that were stared at in puzzlement. In the smouldering ruins of the huts could be seen the blackened and cracked remains of those who perished within, their distorted limbs and bloated trunks hideously unreal, yet resembling closely enough a human form for onlookers to grunt in disgust and turn abruptly from the horrible sight.

In addition to the vicious slashes that shredded the bodies, some displayed small incisions in the side of the neck, the edges of which were swollen, but on the hard earth beneath the corpses was surprisingly little blood congealing. Odd? Not really! The blindly ecstatic blood-lusting mob was not merely content to spill the blood of its helpless victims; it was drunk until thirsts were slaked. Bestial? Not even animals indulge in such a welter of senseless slaughter.

Adding to the macabre scene and perhaps by far its most gruesome feature was the piteous moaning and occasional screams of those lying wounded. Most were beyond medical aid and had to writhe in agony with their bowels strung out or a limb hanging on by a thread of flesh. The merciful injection of morphine rushed from hospitals and clinics relieved their agony somewhat but they expired just the same.

Notwithstanding the unenviable efforts of police and medics it was quite impossible to arrive at an accurate figure of the death toll. It would have required a team of surgeons to match up and piece together the grisly mess of human remains scattered far and wide. The figure was officially put above a hundred but could not possibly have taken into account the many bodies that were but ashes along with those of sheep, goats and dogs. Which was which? Who could say? Who wanted to say? And, to round off Lari's night of the long knives, the butchers despatched several hundred head of cattle.

No wonder the face of every decent citizen was tense and drawn for days after. The atrocity dulled the senses. Adult men and women walked around for weeks after, bewildered, and asking silly questions like: "Have any of those responsible been caught yet?"

And, you may well ask, was the stupendous crime ever matched with justice? The facts regarding the titanic trial held at Uplands I found to have been conveniently forgotten by those who knew. The initial round-up of suspects had been spirited enough, if somewhat indiscriminate, and several hundreds were caged at Uplands police station where the investigators steadily, albeit laboriously, conducted identification parades.

When, however, the positive identification of an accused person is to be the foundation of the case for the Crown and the shocked survivors making the identifications were, at the time of the crime, solely concerned with self-preservation, God help the prosecutor.

British courts have been evolved to equate crime and justice with the subtleties of evidence procedure and 'reasonable doubt'. Of course, with diligent investigation the prosecutor is invariably provided with some cogent evidence with which to prove the charge. But, where the perpetrators at Lari numbered themselves a thousand or more, was one Kikuyu any more distinct from another on that ignoble night? How many were found guilty? Out of one hundred and ninety tried, about half were convicted, and, by the time I arrived in Kenya, six months after the massacre, none had been executed, yet all had appealed to the Supreme Court!

Such dilatory processes of British justice became the impassioned theme of a motion by the leader of the European elected members of the Legislative Council on 8 October. The motion was directed at the urgent need to speed up the processes of law and it condemned existing methods as being no deterrent in a primitive society. The motion was supported by Mr Humphrey Slade, another elected member. In his speech Mr Michael Blundell said:

"Unless we can convince the great majority of our people that the processes of our law are as effective and as swift against the wrongdoers as the old tribal sanctions, we are going to have a great danger in front of us."

Mr H. Slade, supporting the motion during the same debate, said, inter alia:

"... better, surely, be honest and cut away some of the trimmings in order to satisfy all that there is still justice of some kind, because that is what we must preserve."

The reader will, I feel sure, now have some conception of the tremendous difficulties that beset the forces of law and order in Kenya. It was this inability to overcome or to compensate for these difficulties in bringing offenders to justice speedily that vexed the settler population so bitterly. So far as I can recall the chasm that yawned between the white settler and the government was never fully bridged on this issue by any subsequent turning of the tide—which was attributed to the quantity of materials and personnel and not to the quality of politics or practicability of the colony's laws.

Perhaps Lord Justice Denning in February 1955 unwittingly

provided us with as adequate a summary as one could find anywhere in respect of the invidious situation that Kenyans were confronted with. During a judgement he delivered on the Nyali Bridge Tolls appeal (Nyali is a suburb of Mombasa), he said:

"Just as with the English oak, so with the English common law: one could not transplant it to the African continent and expect it to remain the tough character which it had in England. It had many principles of manifest justice and good sense which could be applied with advantage to peoples of every race and colour all the world over, but it had also many refinements, subtleties and technicalities which were not suited to other folk. These off-shoots must be cut away. In those far off lands the people must have a law which they can understand and which they would respect."

So be it! The pity is that his words went unheeded.

It behoves me to conclude this rather dramatic chapter with a brief account of another high drama in the desperate struggle, Mau Mau versus Settler. I want particularly to quote it for it illustrates so splendidly the indomitable spirit and courage displayed so casually by the ordinary men and women of British stock who decided to make their homes and livelihoods in Kenya's fertile highlands.

The drama was acted out in a farmhouse situated on the lower eastern slopes of the Aberdare forest range, some eight miles north west of Mweiga. It was occupied by two women who had teamed up some years previously and had successfully farmed the land around them. They were Mrs Kitty Hessleburger and Mrs Rayne Simpson. Both were in their thirties and lived alone. Like most settlers they usually took a hot bath after listening to the news, then retired. On 2 January 1953, the same month as the Ruck murders and so many other sensational happenings, they had finished dinner and had switched on the radio for the news. The only other occupant of the house was a Boxer dog. Both women had pistols handy and had trained themselves to use the weapons competently. A paraffin pressure lamp burned brightly on the table.

Having brought in the hot water for the bath the houseboy departed in an unnatural manner, not saying, as he usually did, "*Bath tayari sasa*" or "*Kwa heri*". Mrs Hessleburger was at once on guard and went so far as to push off the safety catch of her pistol. Almost immediately the open doorway leading to the kitchen framed the savage figures of several Kikuyu carrying *pangas* and spears. They threw themselves into the room with murderous expressions on their black faces, hideous and glistening in the glare of the lamp. The most fortuitous thing was that Mrs Hessleburger had but to point her gun and pull its trigger. This she did and the first of the Mau Mau brutes collapsed at her feet, his *panga* having grazed her waist. Mrs Simpson, who had not had the same premonition as her companion, was unable to take off the safety catch of her gun in time. The next wide-eyed, stinking terrorist had taken her by the throat and was throttling the life out of her when Mrs Hessleburger fired her next shot and neatly dropped him. He crawled off to die on the back step. Yet another of the would-be assassins bolted into the bathroom when he saw the strength of the opposition and locked the door.

By now Mrs Simpson was also firing steadily into the shadows of a sultry African night after the fleeing gang. Not to be outdone our gallant women reloaded and shot their way into the bathroom, alas! only to find that the beast had jumped through the window and scurried off, terrified, to join his fellow gangsters, now in full retreat. A trail of blood bore testimony to the efficacy of the counter-action.

One unfortunate aspect of this amazing adventure is that both their devoted Boxer dog and cook were killed. The former by a mis-aimed *panga* blow, the latter shot when mistaken as one of the gang (which was probably not far off the truth, either).

There can be no doubt that such valour and coolness was an

inspiration to settlers everywhere, no less than it was a sharp reminder to terrorists of the devastating reception they could expect by attacking such intrepid women on isolated farms. It was by no manner of means the only such act of bravery during the emergency displayed by European women, but was certainly most gratifying in that, not only did they successfully drive off a formidable Mau Mau gang, but accounted for three dead and possibly others wounded.

Their only laconic comment later when interviewed was that they had felt the need of a cup of *chai* and described the nightmare incident as "quite a *shauri*". I was reliably informed that both women continued farming at Mweiga and were not bothered again.

When one imagines the setting—lonely farmhouse with no other dwellings within miles, on the edge of the dark forests, no menfolk around, no telephone or other form of communication, a filthy terrorist dead in the sitting room, another crumpled up on the back step, the cook boy lifeless, not to mention the poor Boxer, then to sit taut and listening, grasping their re-loaded pistols, until the rockets they had fired off were investigated by their nearest neighbours who appeared and confirmed what had unbelievably happened—then one could only accord the two women the greatest admiration and unstinted praise.

Chapter 8

From running battles at dusk to simple
assassination

My diary entry for Tuesday, 28 December 1954, which was
ecclesiastically shown as 'Innocents' Day', starts with:

> From about 1730 hours today until nightfall I was engaged in
> a running battle (literally) with some forty or more Mau Mau. I
> had only six askari with me all of whom I adjudged as having
> behaved in the most meritorious manner. It was just before
> 1700 hours that I learned of the burning of a settler's house
> some five miles away ...

The entry refers to a conspicuously momentous incident and
should merit some expansion.

It was two days to New Year's Eve and most settlers in my area
were doing their best to capture some of the gaiety and festive
atmosphere that would be prevailing in the 'old country'. One
or two of the larger spreads had announced that they would be
throwing 'sundowners'. These would be on an extravagant scale
and other settlers and their families were expected to gravitate
to them—it being impractical for every farm to organize its own
party if it was to be a successful convivial gathering—provided
they took along a 'drink' contribution!

In my post area most settlers were going down the escarpment to
invade 'Pop' Rodew's place. He was a retired army major, suffered gall
bladder trouble and trusted his Kukes as he would his barber with
a razor. He was testy but generous, overbearing but wise, hospitable
but fussy. Reputed to be more affluent than his settler colleagues, he
had influence and worries and was always a candidate for ulcers.

We had all been invited to his lovely ranch-style house that nestled at the foot of the forested escarpment with its beautiful clear rushing stream that wound through the property within sight and sound. Poor old benign 'Pop' Rodew never knew just how many Mau Mau took advantage of that nice clear running water, or of his obliging Kuke houseboy, or of the boundless faith he had in the loyalty of his labour line. Yet he was greatly respected. I, as the local policeman, admired him because, even though he was deceived by his treacherous Kikuyu staff, he still knew far more about them than ever I would. He would, moreover, have rather died at their dastardly hands than submit to the embarrassment of a public denouncement of them. But there, I am digressing unduly.

Just a few more hours of the old year to shuffle past. I'd had my new Land Rover but three days. It was still revered by my men and me and was the finest New Year gift we could have wished for. It reduced our walking time by two thirds and gave us a wider, more efficient coverage. Within a very short time of its issue to my post we were able to prove irrefutably the huge advantage of a vehicle to our operational efficiency.

I'd just returned from a *shamba* at the far end of my sector where some investigations had been conducted into the arsenical poisoning of a cow (such cases were quite common) and, as I was about to enter the farmhouse for a late lunch, my sergeant intercepted me, breathless and excited.

"*Effendi. Nyumba ya Bwana Carnelly naungua.*" He was pointing to the north from whence I had just come and sure enough I saw a column of billowing smoke in the direction of Carnelly's *shamba.*

Rapid instructions were issued and I leapt into the signals hut wherein sat Betty, cucumber cool, busy compiling her sitrep log, her radios humming patiently.

"Betty," I hollered, "I believe there's trouble over at Carnelly's or possibly Oliver's. There's a lot of *moshi* that way and the sergeant informs me a house is on fire."

Bidding all stations to "wait out" she emerged to confirm the report of smoke; then said: "I think Les Carnelly is in Gilgil, I saw him pass through this morning. Anne and the children must be there. You'd better hurry, Peter. I'll call up Nakuru tower and ask if any 'Vultures' are available."

"Yes, do that. I'll take a pack-set with me just in case I'm in range."

She brought one out to me saying, "This one should have good batteries."

"Thanks, Betty, I'm not going to the scene, it's too late. I will cut across Venter's *shamba* and try to head them off—if there's anyone to head off, that is. Will give you a sitrep as soon as I can."

My sergeant and four constables were already in the Land Rover and I was handed my Sterling gun and two magazines. We then moved, God, how we moved along the rutted and potholed roads! The dust cloud behind followed like a curious, devoted streamer; an integral part of the vehicle almost. At Venter's farm turn-off we met a group of agitated and frightened natives.

"*Mau Mau*," they gasped. "*Nyumba ya Bwana Carnelly.*" Thus confirming the urgency of our mission.

I questioned them rapidly and sufficiently to learn that two settlers, Venter and Buckley, were already on their way to the scene. But, more importantly, the gang had finished its mischief and had departed in the direction of the Cezoroni gorge. This supported my earlier rapid appraisal of the situation and I was, accordingly, able to put into practice those tactical sentiments I had for some time advocated; namely, that it was useless to hustle to the scene of the crime if one is after the perpetrators. Make up one's mind where they will most likely head for, then detour and intercept. This is exactly what I intended doing on this occasion.

A hundred yards farther on I turned left onto a narrow track and careered along the edge of Venter's immense acreage of lush, golden wheat, quite six feet high. The track snaked this way and that, rose and fell, until we rushed past Bennett's dam with a herd of cattle drinking placidly at its edge. A little beyond I glimpsed a combine harvester, a silent, weird monster, just where its operators had abandoned it when they heard of the attack on Carnelly's house. A small dik-dik scampered off into the wheat; such a sight on a normal day would have enticed us all off on an exhilarating chase to augment the askaris' always inadequate meat ration and to improve upon my own economy.

Climbing now in second gear, the engine screaming robustly, we continued along the fringe of the *shamba*, then, clearing the shallow end of the right fork of the Cezoroni gorge, we hurtled on into uncleared *kikileshwa* scrub country. I'd seen Africans collecting their *kuni* often in the area and the stumps of this hardy bush could, I felt, have flourished even in the arid Kalahari Desert.

Then, quite suddenly, we were up high enough to see the wooden, thatched Carnelly farmhouse blazing fiercely over on our right some two miles away. Ahead of us the bush was thicker and presented a serious obstacle to continued progress in our *gari*. We were now between the Cezoroni and the escarpment, an area that for months past had been used sporadically by itinerant gangs in which to lie up. It was central, watered by a couple of lazy springs and its topography was such that Mau Mau were afforded easy escape, whether into the shadowy depths of the gorge or the congested slopes of the escarpment. It was an area that I and my men had operated in often, sleeping under a sheet of canvas at night, watching and waiting during the day, and with minor successes too.

"*Naonakana! Huko!*" roared my sergeant. And there they were, too. About four hundred yards ahead of us. Fifteen? Twenty? Thirty? Difficult to say at that distance. All seemed to be carrying something and were strung out. They might have been a troop of colobus monkeys or, more likely, a group of disgruntled squatter labourers absconding with their *bwana's* belongings. Anything really but Mau Mau. I just couldn't believe my eyes—after all the months of searching, abortive contacts, duff information, fruitless ambushes, the patience and hoping—praying, in fact. And there they were, four hundred yards from us. Probably General Ngomi's gang; notorious, murderous and always one hideout away.

To close more in the Land Rover was impossible. Already its front bumper had served commendably well as a bulldozer, flattening scores of stout stumps and bushes. My five askari were calmly berserk; safety catches of their rifles pushed forward, bolts drawn back to slam a round into the breach of each. As usual they paid not the slightest attention whatever to range estimation and sight setting. This much I hastily observed as I opened up the radio pack-set and called Control.

Betty's well modulated tones acknowledged and I obtained operational clearance. Having informed her that we were in sight of the gang, giving direction, intention and requirements, I remained open just long enough to receive her encouraging "Good luck!" plus the advice that a spotter plane, 'Vulture Black', was on its way. Then, abandoning both radio and vehicle, pursuit was commenced at the double.

Direction—toward the escarpment above Mentsmith's below the Malewa Bridge.

Intention—to close, drive and harass and to make contact if possible.

Requirements—army stops deployed anywhere below the escarpment between Cambell's and Cezoroni's cheese factory.

We would drive them; the military could spot and kill. And kill it had to be. This was it! This was the outstanding, momentous, never-to-be-repeated contact and pursuit of the whole bloody emergency. Every hope, prayer and frustrated plan was epitomized in this skirmish. So often before had we arrived too late and so many times had darkness assisted their successful dispersal.

Darkness! The time was nearly 1800 hours. Darkness? This was precisely the galling factor we were up against on this very occasion. The bastards had timed the raid with their usual sagacity. It was already growing dusk as the sun began to dip low over the Mau hills as fiery as our tempers. If they could elude us for another half an hour they'd be free from our clutches. This nest of terrorists, triumphant and well rewarded so far, were burdened with loot. We closed fast but they were favoured by being so much nearer the yawning drop of the escarpment. Not quite as sheer or deep in this particular sector but every bit as hampering and restrictive to free passage with entangling bush and creeper.

Barely five minutes had elapsed when a Piper-Pacer spotter plane appeared from nowhere. So preoccupied was I in keeping the gang in sight that I glanced skyward only when it whooshed weaving and dodging from below the escarpment. It seemed almost to be picking its way in and out of the taller trees, then, zooming up steeply, it levelled out in full view of us and the bounding gangsters. Wheeling on a wing tip it sank down again to skim over the tousled heads of our quarry for a second confirmatory look. It swooped so low that we thought for a horrible moment or two that it had crashed, then realized that its pilot had only dipped below the escarpment again.

Here I would explain that having had to abandon the pack-set was a most vexing and regrettable state of operational affairs. I was quite powerless to exploit the daring and skill of the spotter plane's pilot who could have transmitted to me his accurate observations as to gang direction, numbers or how they were splitting up.

It was this tactic of splitting up which they employed when hard-pushed that was so infuriating. And now, despite the surprise we had given them, they were already employing this highly effective and simple tactical manoeuvre. We were insufficient in numbers to counter such tactics by following every splinter of the gang. We could only hope to continue our wild pursuit of the largest group still within view and, at the same time of course, run the serious risk of ambush by those who had gone to earth or who might detour to our rear. Disintegration of my patrol, however, was to be zealously avoided.

Our dash was headlong and breathless. We were now relying almost entirely on the spotter plane's fantastic stunt-flying to guide us—when it dived steep and low we knew he was scaring and harassing the gang. Once, just before they scuttled down the escarpment, the plane dived low and dropped a smoke marker near them. It also ignited the dry grass and, by the time we arrived, panting and pouring with sweat, there was a considerable blaze. It was here that the first real signs of the gang's passage were seen in the form of abandoned booty—large bundles of clothing, a gramophone, even a sewing machine, were scattered along their line of flight. They had obviously had a fright and wanted to quicken their pace.

The pilot of this K.P.R. Airwing spotter plane, Mr Pakenham-Walsh as I recall, was so much in command of the whole situation from his versatile perch above that he was able to provide Control with a graphic commentary of the episode. The first job he had undertaken was to drop a message tied to a red streamer just in front of us (it gave us a bit of a scare because we thought he'd mistaken us for gangsters and was lobbing a grenade or something onto us!). It was a scribbled, terse sentence in pencil that told us what we already knew: "Mau Mau in front headed towards Cezoroni's. Will spot for you."

It seems, as I was to learn later, that during his thrilling commentary on the chase he had credited our erratic fire with far more hits than were in fact recorded.

Darkness, as hinted, was our arch-enemy and I knew, as did our skilful aviator, that unless the military forces asked for appeared within fifteen minutes to close the trap then the encounter would be irretrievably lost. The nearer we raced to the top of the escarpment the greater became the evidence of the gang's fright with the Piper-Pacer scalping them. Huge bundles of blankets and sheets, household utensils, home-made guns, a pair of sunglasses and, of all things, a pewter beer tankard; all were jettisoned en route.

There was no time to pause to either retrieve or examine the property; all I could manage was hurriedly to scan the area as we sped past to see if any bodies were lying around. To have seen any would have been infinite encouragement. Alas, there were none! What rounds I'd fired with my Sterling gun could hardly have been accurate at two hundred and fifty yards. The fire of my askari with old S.M.L.E. rifles and wild sighting would have had but a harassing effect. And yet it was quite impossible to say how many hits might have been made.

Vulture Black appeared directly overhead again and another message dropped from it, this time scrawled on the back of an empty cigarette packet. It told me that the gang had split into two groups, one making for Cezoroni's and the other towards Ware-Austin's. God! What a dilemma and no time to ponder it. In actual fact I was to discover that they were the two main groups but that several other splinters were almost certainly as small as twos and threes and widely dispersed. Additionally, by the time we had arrived, heaving, eyes popping and limbs aching, at the top of the escarpment, it was safe to assume that we must have passed within yards of some of the gang cringing low in the thick scrub. This was, of course, the grimness of the situation—no opportunity at all to pause and search or even, for that matter, to check the pace for a breather and perhaps ease the pain in my chest and sides. But, my oath! How exciting was the chase, so unreal as to be almost theatrical.

About to plunge into the musty dense rain forest at the rim of the escarpment, I glanced quickly skyward to my left and saw the fussy little Piper-Pacer in its persistent efforts to hold the gang back awhile. I was reminded of a yapping terrier dog worrying off an intruder. That was the last I was to see of Mr Pakenham-Walsh, that magnificent man in his flying machine, for that day.

Pressing the magazine catch of my S.M.G. I removed its spent magazine and smacked home the remaining full one. Had the terrorists known just how ridiculously few in number and pathetically ill-equipped—ammunition particularly—we were, they would, surely, have stood their ground and hacked us to pieces as we started to penetrate the dark, enveloping and maddeningly entangling bush.

And then! What was that? A few yards ahead I vaguely discerned in the sepulchral gloom a group huddled together. With heart beating through aching rib cage and every nerve of my tense body twanging I expended half the precious magazine before realizing that what confronted me was just another bundle of clothing tossed aside by the terrified gangsters. Regaining my composure I cursed the confounding anti-climax. My poor askari, on the other hand, were speechless with dismay.

The pursuit was now blind and all we could do was grope and

tear through the brambles and creeper, slithering and sliding ever lower and to our left. Here and there was evidence of those who preceded us in such desperate haste—broken branches, bits of material snagged on a spiky bush, fresh slide marks and overturned stones—but no sign of the rascals themselves. There was no alternative but to press on doggedly in the general direction.

Presently the hideous jungle thinned out and we could see again. The sun had now disappeared though it was possible to see the river glinting below and a few fishing huts.

Kimedi, my sergeant, shouted behind me, urgent though fatigued. *"Huko, bwana! huko chini, karibu na daraja."*

They were, too! Way down below a small cluster of bouncing, leaping, hurdling 'micks' were about to cross the Malewa bridge.

"Christ! Where is the flaming army?" I thought in anguish. I wrenched the rifle from the sergeant's hands and took a couple of aimed shots. They were seen to pause and look over their shoulders but almost at once were off again with lengthened strides. I saw none sink to the ground; my heart, however, did.

Another cry, this time from Kiplangat on my left. *"Iko upande hii, mingi sana."*

Yes, it was another bunch of them but not *mingi sana,* about five only. They appeared to be making for the river at a different spot. I yelled back at him, *"Fuata hawa."* (Follow them.)

This meant regrettably that we were now split up.

We all continued sliding and stumbling down the steep uneven slope. For over half an hour we had been doubling over this incredibly rough country and the gruelling pace was beginning to have an effect on us. I was scarcely seeing or feeling and had very little idea left of what we were trying to achieve. A choking realization that we had lost the day overwhelmed me.

Still carrying the rifle I'd taken from the sergeant, I allowed myself to hurtle on down with massive strides that jarred my knees painfully, resigned now to just wait for something to happen. My askari, still enthusiastic, were well scattered by this time and there was little hope of co-ordinating this final sprint.

As we lost height and came within sound of the rushing torrent of the Malewa so I became completely out of touch with the situation. Over on my right I saw two askari regarding apprehensively the racing waters trying to decide where best to cross—or so I thought. Being in no mood to fuss and quite oblivious to discomfort, or even danger, I dropped down into the cold waters. As I waded across with rifle held high the water rose to my waist and pulled with alarming force. There was a moment or two of panic, and then I was scrambling up the other bank. I felt a trifle foolish when I stood up dripping and observed the two askari on my right eyeing me anxiously and far drier than I. They had forded the river at shallows several yards upstream!

We joined up and lunged forward into the sparse, but quite expansive, area of holly oak and cedar saplings with the intention of doing I knew not what. The whole object of the exercise seemed ridiculous and obscure; I felt confused and dejected. The action had now assumed a dream-like quality. So much so that when we found ourselves face to face with a line of jungle-green clad soldiers advancing cautiously out of the dusk towards us I wondered for a brief second what on earth was going on. They, too, came to an uncertain halt and looked at us and at each other dumbfounded.

The full danger of the sudden and confused merging of forces hit my tired mind with a dull thud. With calm deliberation I pulled out my whistle and blew it several times. The thought of having my askari shot up accidentally after the cruel gauntlet they had just run was a dreadful one.

I was shortly surrounded by soldiers and my own askari; the situation was bizarre indeed. A young lieutenant stepped forward and requested of me an appreciation of the situation, eyeing me oddly and looking somewhat bewildered.

"Well! As far as I'm aware they have either slipped past you or have gone to earth hereabouts," I wearily informed him, adding: "Did you not see any of them as they came down the escarpment?" realizing as I addressed him that it was futile to debate the issue where we stood.

I handed the sergeant back his rifle and took my Sterling gun in exchange. And then the most galling of sequels developed. As I stood swaying before this lieutenant I espied several figures sprinting toward the foot of Scholl's hill—a very thickly forested knoll about two hundred feet high—just one hundred yards from where we all stood. They were Mau Mau alright, but my astonishment was totally devoid of any enthusiasm. Merely did I raise my voice slightly and, attempting to introduce some inflection of excitement, announced, "There are some of them now, over there, see them? Just about to climb that hill. There are mo ..."

I had no time to complete the sentence; he and his army simply evaporated. And anyway, how were the lieutenant and his men to know that those few rebels were but a decoy and that, with night having fallen, they could slither and scamper along the sides of the dark hill all night and still wouldn't bump into them.

Unfortunately my askari, still full of momentum from their praiseworthy though, alas, unavailing chase, bounded off with the army. I last saw them and the lieutenant disappearing into the bush at the foot of the hill. Ragged rifle fire ensued and continued for a long time; the wildlife on Scholl's Hill must have suffered a very rude intrusion to be sure!

A mile or so farther on near the main Gilgil road I located an army truck and climbed in. Its driver established my identity and agreed to speed me into Gilgil. I could hear the sporadic fire and urgent shouts of the army who seemed to be having a wonderful time fighting themselves on Scholl's Hill. But, for me it was just another contact that had aborted and the buggers were able once again to display their incredible facility for Olympic athletics when capture is imminent.

That night a fairly extensive pattern of ambushes was laid, ostensibly to seal up the area until some tracking could be done at first light on the morrow. I was avidly debriefed at my H.Q. and informed that we must have caused a number of casualties. Nobody was inclined to accept my nil report of known hits. I learned that the running engagement had been observed by many people at the foot of the escarpment and it had provided them with a very entertaining evening, which only served to pique me further. Did they think we had obligingly arranged it as ad hoc open-air theatre! (*See* Appendix II)

Nevertheless for that, the whole colony was soon bristling with anger over the audacious raid on the Carnelly farm. Everyone was marvelling over the miraculous escape that Anne, Mrs Carnelly, and her two young children had had. Apparently she had pleaded for her life and, having surrendered her pistol, was left unmolested.

Next morning I returned with a patrol to the area over which the pursuit had taken place and all the abandoned property was recovered. From members of the gang captured later I learned that they did not double-back to repossess their spoils for fear of ambush—and to think there had been none at all! The gang had killed one old watchman, burnt the farmhouse and several huts, bashed up anyone they could get hold of and plundered all but the heavy contents of the farm. Reporters and photographers inundated the place throughout the following week. It was a pathetic and grim sight. The house had been devoured by the fire as completely as a haystack, only its brick chimney stood intact, rising up from the ashes and debris like a memorial obelisk.

The fact that caused the bile to rise in me when able to piece the incident together later was to learn that when my men and I passed the farm earlier that afternoon the gang had been ranged up in the wheat waiting to spring the raid. They had seen us pass and bided their time until they were satisfied we had returned to the post. The starkest and most disturbing conclusion was that the attack had been planned and launched with inside information. Carnelly's movements and, of immeasurable significance, his shotgun lying in the house, were vital disclosures acted upon by the gang. Several weeks later I was able to pin down the Mkamba employee who had been responsible for passing this intelligence to the North Kinangop's resident gang.

By the greatest providence the re-formed gang was ambushed by the army the very next night, and one of its number, shot and captured, had with him the stolen shotgun. I was able to interview him briefly and discovered that only two of their members had been hit by our fire, though many bullets had whistled past them, giving cause for some to mess their ragged pants. It seems, however, that on the whole they had been fairly well looked after by *Ngai.*

This impudent raid was, as stated, made possible through the spying of a Mkamba employee, the Carnelly's cook. This fellow's loyalty came under suspicion immediately after the raid for two reasons. Firstly, he lived in a solitary hut with his two children on the far side of a gorge from the farmhouse. Secondly, although it was known that a large gang was operating in the area he remained inexplicably unharmed and was left in peace. This strange immunity while living in such isolation was to be his downfall and he failed miserably to explain it away. By then, of course, it was too late.

Possibly the most infuriating aspect of his life on a forest post was that the inspector never knew with any degree of confidence just where he stood among the so-called loyal Africans. So many hundreds of Kikuyu, Meru and Embu tribesmen were oathed and contaminated that the only really safe course was to regard them all as potential Mau Mau terrorists. It was no good saying that if one remained on the alert with his weapons near at hand little harm would befall him. It had been proved time and time again during the emergency that it was always at the least expected moment and in the most unlikely circumstances that one came face to face with the peril of Mau Mau.

I shall never forget my own uncomfortably close encounter with this treachery and it was to serve me as a sharp reminder in personal security. It portrayed in bold, heavy lines how terribly easily one drifted into the deceptively still waters of safety only to find the unnerving rapids just around the bend. It was an experience that was the absolute epitome of an ever-present conflict between my ingrained trust and their primitive loyalty.

At the time I was bunking with a K.P.R. signals operator in a small, plain brick building on a farm at Ol Mogogo. It had three rooms—bedroom, kitchen and dining/office/restroom. I should add, perhaps, that it had long ceased to bother me what the standard of quarters were that I occupied. So long as there was a bed and reasonable protection from the elements I aspired to nothing more elegant or grandiose. My (stoical?) view being that the more comfortable a man made himself, or was made, the less he was inclined to do.

The arrangements provided at this particular police post had not been to my liking ever; the quarters of my askari were situated some three hundred yards away which I considered to be impractical and most unsatisfactory.

The young signals operator who shared the simple quarters with me was a lethargic, untidy and uninteresting, though agreeably natured chap who had been in Kenya many years. He spent most of his spare time either reading or sleeping. Whenever I arose at four-thirty a.m., which was quite often, he would ask in a horrified manner, "Where on earth are you off to at this ungodly hour?"

One night I returned from laying some trip-flares around a wheat store on a farm in my area, a store that I hoped the Land Freedom Army fanatics were about to pay a nocturnal visit. It was a little before midnight. Tired, I felt my way to the bed alongside Mervin who was fast asleep, or appeared to be. Call-outs had been so numerous of late that I didn't consider it worth undressing and bedding down snugly. Putting on pyjamas was a bedtime ritual and luxury I'd gradually dispensed with. I sank down heavily on the bed and pulled off my boots.

Placing my Sterling gun alongside on the floor, magazines in their pouch, I lit a cigarette. Strolling over to the door I then stood and gazed for a few moments over towards Wilson's *shamba*, half expecting to see the dark night sky prettied by a three-star red distress rocket that would speak of unpretty raids on labour lines or a cattle *boma*. Anxiously I thought of the trip-flares I'd placed so carefully around Colonel Ronny Devlin's wheat store and of the frightened, though, alas, safe retreat of any 'micks' that stumbled across the wires. I had sufficient men to ambush the store but had decided that the setting off of the flares, being preceded by a sharp explosion, quite harmless, would be heard by my sentry who in turn would arouse me. Together with my askari plus Devlin and his home-guardsmen, we'd make for the Sitima River which the scallywags would almost certainly ford at a particular spot en route to the Aberdare forests. Or, even more likely of success, we would pick our way stealthily to the dam below van Rensberg's maize *shamba* and there lie in wait at the track most prevalently used by 'micks' when returning to their forest lairs. In any case the wheat store itself would not be approached until first light tomorrow.

Heavens! How often had I permitted myself such hopeful thoughts and over-estimation? Stubbing out the cigarette and filling my lungs with a deep breath of the hay-scented air mingled with pungent wood smoke that wafted up from the nearby *rondavels*, I entered the dismal dwelling and flopped down on the bed. It groaned and creaked, then settled fitfully. I soon slept.

"*Bwana! Bwana! Fungua mlango. Iko Mau Mau hapa. Kuja upesi. Bwana, fungua.*" The urgent, though subdued, Swahili from outside the door jerked me into wakefulness. Dazedly, and not without considerable annoyance, I rolled off the bed and gathered up my Sterling. Visions of rounding up cattle from a raided *boma* and waiting for a count to be made before planning necessary action, formed before my leaden eyes. I had, however, learnt not to curse. It seldom did any good.

When I opened the door and thrust the snout of my gun out, three Africans confronted me. All were Kikuyu and all were domestic staff of the farm owner. They were, too, all highly trusted employees. The quietest and most intelligent of them was Daniel, the houseboy. Big and very strong, I had seldom seen him smile. Of an uncannily silent nature he seemed so detached and uninvolved with Mau Mau. When he wasn't working in the house he would be sleeping in his hut nearby. He was also known to be a staunch homeguardsman. According to Mr and Mrs Kydd, he was an indispensable domestic asset, one of the family almost and likely to become a respected retainer.

Still with that inscrutable expression and wearing a heavy army greatcoat over his long white *kanzo*, he carried a *panga* with unconcern at his side and peered at me questioningly. He was flanked by the cook, Kamau, and the house guard, whose name I wasn't certain of but never did like the look of. Both the latter carried spears and looked agitated; so much so, in fact, that it flashed through my mind that they might have been drinking.

Actually, as the seconds passed and my eyes adjusted to the dark and focused on the trio, they evinced a wicked and sinister appearance. For a brief moment I felt inexplicably ill at ease.

Daniel spoke in deep and steady, unhurried tones. "*Sisi nataka wewe, bwana, kutafuta Mau Mau karibu na store ya ngano.*"

I was being bidden to investigate the presence of some terrorists over near the wheat store. They further advised me of sounds they'd heard and of shadowy movements they'd observed.

"*Unaweza kuja sasa-hivi?*" asked Daniel, respectfully.

Yes, I was able to go with them at once, I replied, testily.

It occurred to me that it was so utterly quiet everywhere—not even the chirping of a cricket or croak of a bullfrog could I hear. Taking a couple of paces beyond the house I stood and listened intently. Why had they not gone over to the askaris' quarters to first warn my sergeant? Or why had they not even approached the sentry to seek confirmation of their suspicions before dragging me out? It was the usual thing to do. These and other questions I hastily put to myself as I looked and listened.

"*Ngoja kidogo* [wait a minute]," I said quietly, and went back into the house.

Adjusting my dress and slipping a magazine into the Sterling I bent over Mervin and spoke close to his ear, decisively. I told him that I was going to see if there were 'micks' over by the wheat store. I knew he was awake, I also knew that the excitement and possibility of shooting up a few Mau Mau could never take precedence over the overwhelmingly powerful urge he had to remain nice and comfortable right where he was. I'd never known such a torpid and sluggish youth. I could feel only scorn and left the room making more noise than was necessary. And yet I had desperately wanted his company on this occasion.

As I passed through the door I heard him mumble: "Christ, man! Don't believe them. Mau Mau on *this* farm? Never!" Whereupon he turned over, disgustingly indifferent.

My first reaction was to run across to the post and call out the corporal and some men. There was no sense in going so far as to ascertain the presence of terrorists if effective action could not be taken. But my three informants lurking in the shadows were now beckoning with imperative gestures and had begun to move off in the direction of the workshop and stores.

To reach these buildings one needed to negotiate some barbed-wire fencing—a couple of strands only—then, passing close by several huts, about thirty yards of open ground had to be crossed. I could just discern the outline of the workshop and store where the Mau Mau were alleged to be skulking, or doing what? The stillness of the night seemed to deepen and became oppressive. I allowed the three of them to precede me but soon sensed that they were disinclined to have me in rear; their pace was checked. It was Daniel who actually dropped behind me. It was a deliberate manoeuvre and of no possible consequence at this particular stage of the jaunt.

No! I simply couldn't go ahead with it. I felt horribly unsafe and helpless. To proceed with Daniel behind me carrying that wicked *panga* was absolutely out of the question if we were supposed to sidle up on lurking terrorists. I became quite tense with apprehension.

What the hell could I say to explain away my circumspect behaviour or my disbelief of their report? Was it really even necessary to give an explanation? I'd already been much too imprudent in my assent to accompany them this far. Excerpts from a security pamphlet flitted across my confused mind—'Do not go out at night with Africans, Kikuyu especially, you are not certain of. Always ensure you are covered from behind if you have to ...' etc.

In the distance, perhaps on Bollard's upper *boma,* a hyena howled. So strange that none of the occupants of the huts we passed were disturbed or alerted. Daniel, being a prominent homeguard personality, would surely have rallied them with a few soft warning calls. Why should a Mau Mau gang venture this close to a farm that had a police post sited on it? Where was the wheat store guard, too? From past experience of these guards I knew that, given a shotgun, a nice big overcoat and a whistle, they would either discharge a cartridge or blow furiously on the whistle the instant they were aware of any irregularity. The possibility that he could be lying with his throat cut did not, however, escape me.

Then suddenly I was afraid, very afraid, though remarkably unembarrassed by such a condition. My Sterling gun felt hard and protective hugged against my hip. Yet I also felt so stupidly impotent against spears and *pangas* at close quarters.

I was a police officer with wide and comprehensive powers; known to be zealous, even ruthless, when it came to hunting Mau Mau and using firearms; known too to be compassionate and helpful when the occasion warranted. But I was also probably thought to be an unsuspecting, trusting and gullible *mzungu*—also inclined to be somewhat over-enthusiastic, to take chances and to find out things for himself. This then, was one time when I should consider it most discreet, a matter of life and death, in fact, to display the same distrust and apprehension that the three Kikuyu behind me were now displaying. This was one situation when it was vital I had with me a well-tried and trusted man, one I had trained and lived with and understood, someone disciplined and dependable, like my Somali corporal. But he was asleep in the snug, smoky fug of his hut-cum-barracks with no thoughts of his *effendi* on this crazy mission.

The sinister trio I had found myself walking with through the still blackness to investigate the presence of verminous Mau Mau had every sign and every opportunity of being, not only disloyal, but barbarically murderous as well. Already I had felt that *panga* cleave my skull and that spear enter the small of my back.

"*Basi!* We shall return," I addressed them in the calmest tones my thumping heart would allow. "I do not like this *shauri mbaya* and you will walk in front of me to the house, *endelea*." I had turned to face them with a manner of such finality and authoritativeness

Above: Senior Kikuyu Chief Njiri, prime mover of the Kikuyu Home Guard. He was murdered by Mau Mau on 6 October 1952, the last of the three senior Kikuyu chiefs to be executed.

Left: A constable savagely hacked to death by Mau Mau in the charge office of Naivasha police station, 26 March 1952.

Above: The author poses outside his police 'digs' at Hermann's Post, near Gilgil, May 1954.

Left: Masai tribesmen recruited by settlers as farm guards. Issued with a shotgun and an old greatcoat they patrolled cattle *bomas*, wheat stores and squatter labour lines.

Top: A typical sign during the Emergency.

Above: General Sir George Erskine, Commander-in-Chief East Africa 1953–59, touring a settler farmer's *shamba* on the Kinangop plateau. Note the pistol slung from the lady's waist.

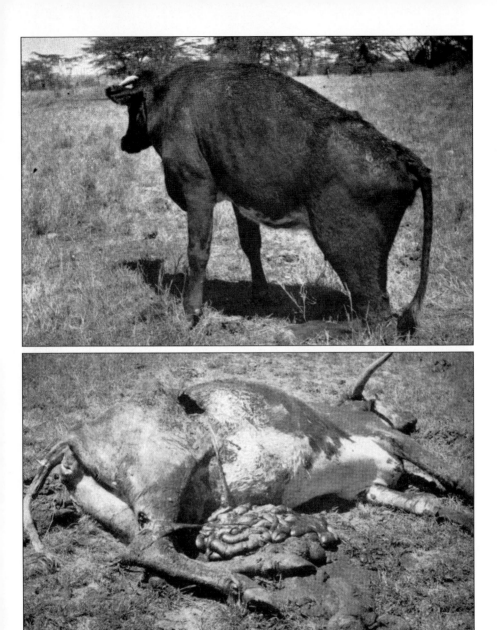

Mau Mau gangs, when thwarted in their raids on cattle *bomas*, would express their anger by cruelly disemboweling or hamstringing the animals denied them.

Above: The author by one of the gorges on the Kinangop plateau, which appears deceptively shallow. Mau Mau gangs foraging for food might elude security-force patrols for weeks ensconced in the densely vegetated bowels of such gorges. Sweeps along the roaring rivers below were both arduous and slow.

Centre: A squad of the author's askari at long last resplendent in uniforms that took many months to arrive at remote forest posts.

Bottom: In the corner of the Gilgil police station, an askari takes fingerprints off the corpse of a high-ranking Mau Mau, watched by curious onlookers.

Top: A captured Mau Mau, wounded in a fire fight with the author's patrol, is brought into the compound of Gilgil police station.

Above: Captured Mau Mau terrorists.

Top: The author (far right) with members of his Tracker Combat Team and the Gloucestershire Regiment, having successfully contacted a large terrorist gang on Mt Kipipiri. The patrol was guided to the enemy hideout by a 'turned' Mau Mau surrenderee (third from left).

Above: Following a report of stolen livestock, the author and his Tracker Combat Team attempt to track down the perpetrators. A herdsman points out spoor of the rustled cattle.

The author crouches by the remains of Mau Mau terrorists despatched a few days earlier by a security-force patrol. The hyenas and vultures have had their gory fill.

Sir Evelyn Baring GCMG, KCVO, Governor of Kenya during the Emergency. He became Lord Howick of Glendale. He died in 1973, following a fall down a rock face on his Northumberland estate.

Top: The author (left) warily views his Mau Mau capture—the self-styled 'Field Marshal' Mbaria Kanui—during Operation *Bullrush* in the Naivasha papyrus swamps, January 1956.

Above: The CO of the Glosters confers with his Sunray Minor at TAC HQ during Operation *Bullrush* in the Naivasha papyrus swamps.

A newspaper cutting depicting a framed photograph of the celebrated Mau Mau leader. Dedan Kimathi, lying manacled in a Nairobi hospital bed following his capture. Above is a home-made commemorative plaque.

Gloster mortarmen in action during Operation *Bullrush*. Mortars did not prove effective.

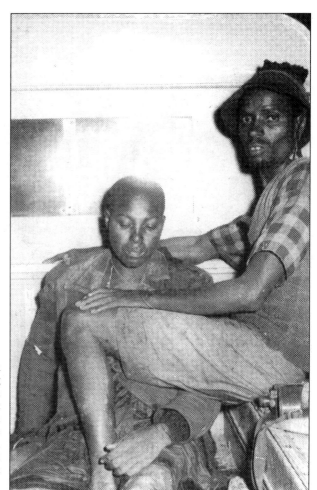

'Field Marshal' Mbaria Kanui, captured during Operation *Bullrush*. With him is his faithful forest concubine who had been shot and wounded in the thigh. He chose to stay with her in the swamps until capture rather than attempt a breakout.

'General' China stands trial at Nyeri. He had commanded all Mau Mau on Mt Kenya. The death sentence was commuted to life imprisonment as a result of his efforts to organize a general surrender.

Top: The author behind a desk. In 1956 he spent several months in the Colony Operations Room at Nairobi Police HQ.

Above: Jomo Kenyatta in 1963, with a Mau Mau leader.

Above: A jubilant Kenyatta parades through Nairobi after his swearing-in as prime minister in December 1963.

Left: Tom Mboya, a Luo, acknowledges the crowd after being elected in his KANU constituency. Widely expected to succeed Kenyatta, he was, however, assassinated in a Nairobi street in 1969. There was considerable enmity between Kenya's two largest tribes—the Kikuyu and the Luo.

'Mzee' Kenyatta, the self-styled father of the nation, had a penchant for regal ceremonial garb. He is pictured here at his swearing-in at State House, December 1963.

that my distrust of their motives must have been immediately apparent, though I had no real concern about this. Neither shame nor anger was I caused, only fear. For an instant they appeared to falter; I curled my finger around my S.M.G. They peered at me uncertainly in the gloom, then, after a hurried exchange among themselves in Kikuyu and furtive glances at the gun I poked at them with an uneasy tenseness, we all shuffled off back to my quarters where I bade them a curt goodnight.

How gigantic my relief and extreme my fatigue as I leaned against the closed door. My racing thoughts did not permit any lucid reasoning about the perilous situation I'd just been delivered from. Yet, what if there had been a gang over there and I'd lost it through over-cautiousness? Or was it nervousness? Had my three visitors been correct they were not going to have much respect for me henceforth. Word would spread slimily around the district that I was not worthy of their confidence, thus far enjoyed. Information sources would dry up, my own askari would look upon me dubiously. Furthermore, if it were reported to either Ian or Betty Kydd and happened to be included in the daily sitrep, I would have to render an explanation. To offer that I was of the opinion that the 'loyal' house staff had criminal intentions and that I was at their mercy on a dark night might be to incur their acid displeasure, to say the least of it.

And yet, as I laid myself down on the bed again fifteen minutes after the experience, I resolved to be firm in my honest conviction that I'd just been in the gravest imminent danger of my life; that my own assassination had been narrowly averted. Before falling into exhausted sleep I was convinced of the wisdom of my decision and thanked God for my timely deliverance. I do not believe that I was ever intended to return from that little nocturnal jaunt with those three Kikuyu. To emphasize this belief is the fact that, although I had advised them to go across to the post and bring out a few askari if they wished to investigate further, it transpired that they took no such action whatever.

Never again did I allow myself to be lured out into the night or to place unreserved faith in allegedly loyal Kikuyu. Several months later the houseboy, Daniel, was given a profound screening at Manyani detention camp along with other oathed terrorist adherents from my district. He had been bundled off after his name was found on the list of a local Mau Mau treasurer. To the utter dismay and grief of his employers the screening report revealed that he had been deeply implicated in Mau Mau activities, mainly on the organizational side. If it be possible to say anything at all in mitigation of his guilt he did at least agree to attend a 'confessional *baraza*' some time after and absolved himself before chiefs and District Officers by renouncing the oaths he had taken.

Needless to say, the three of them and I thereafter regarded each other with mutual suspicion. They'd muffed their chance and were not going to get another. Most important of all, their guilt had been irrevocably established when, the morning after the fallacious report to me, they made no mention of it to either their employers or to my askari. There had been no terrorists on the farm that night; the only thing that lurked in the wheat store was doom ... mine.

Chapter 9

Oathing—to make savages out of insurgents

There was a day about the middle of May during my first year on a forest post when rain had fallen steadily all morning and the damp mists of the Aberdares had descended to envelop everything. It was depressing and frustrating. It incarcerated me; all I could do was to sit by a window and through breaks in the mist study the forested slopes of Kipipiri through binoculars. It was a saturating, gloomy day that was a repeat of the previous day and the day before that.

Sitting alone in the wooden shack I had felt so bored that I'd started up the generator engine and was listening to the humdrum traffic on the air of the V.H.F. radio set. While listening to the transmissions of Vulture Red to Nakuru tower requesting clearance to land, I gazed absently through the open shutter of the window at the Ford 15 cwt. parked outside, dripping rain water and looking very forlorn. It was a square, ugly, solid mass of heavy metal. Where on earth the Kenya police had acquired the monstrosity from I couldn't imagine. How often had I bemoaned its manifold failings to my superintendent at H.Q.? There was no doubt that it was a sturdy old bus, and it was not its power that I criticized, nor its robustness—my grievance lay with its remarkable propensity for breaking down at the most unpropitious times, like while returning from an ambush six miles away at midnight in teeming rain, for instance. Or, equally infuriating, its susceptibility to the slightest patch of mud—it was quite hopeless to drive merrily through, relying on the chunky track-grip tread of its tyres; I had to stop short of the patch, put it in bottom gear, and charge it.

And there she stood in the cold, splattering rain, unperturbed and thankful to be out of commission for a spell. She had aged me ten years, and yet, how attached to her I had become, having nursed her, cooed and cajoled her when she vacillated, fussed her when she wheezed. She had protestingly borne my askari and me over some of the roughest country possible. I had serviced her myself and cleaned the rusting metal with a strange devotion. I had eliminated at least half the rattles that so obligingly heralded our approach to terrorists resting and feeding in Bwana X's labour lines at night. And how many times had I to sleep in her draughty cab after she allowed herself to become ensnared by mud, or sitting huddled up over her rapidly cooling engine cowling when the fuel had run out, praying the while that a bold gang would not elect to satisfy its curiosity. Certainly it was not her fault—the old girl was decrepit and tired—it was a shame to retain her in service. It was well past her time to be pensioned off or bequeathed to some museum.

Such idle cogitation was interrupted by Control calling on the radio: "Kipipiri from Control. Control calling Kipipiri. How do you read me? Over."

I picked up the mike and pressed its pencil switch: "Control from Kipipiri. Reading you strength five but a little distorted. How do you read me? Over."

"Kipipiri, I'm reading you quite clear, strength four. Yes, the distortion must be due to the stinking weather. How is it with you there? Over."

The mellifluous tones of our K.P.R. (W) radio operator at the Control station sited at Ol Mogogo did much to brighten the lonely and celibate lives of many an inspector on his isolated post.

"Absolutely sodden, Betty. Haven't been able to get out all day. Feel like taking a drink. Everything's quiet here. Nan Tare Roger. Anything for me? Over."

"Control to Kipipiri. Why not patrol over to see us and have a drink? We are all feeling pretty depressed too; it'd be nice to see you. Anyway, don't get drunk, you may have something on later. Harry Dawling has been on the blower and says he'd like to see you this evening. Says it's rather important and should be interesting. If you can't make it in your *gari* he says he will pick you up. What do you want to do? Control Kipipiri. Over."

"Kipipiri to Control. Roger! Roger! Betty, sounds rather intriguing. I think it'd be better if Harry collected me, I'm damned if I'm going to risk the roads in that 'wreck of a Hesperus' I've got here. Anything further? Over."

"Negative, Peter, except that you might like to know that Pape's Post shot two up on the Wanderer's track this morning. Walked straight into them at How Zebra Roger 2468 I think. Bye then. Take care! Over and out."

"Kipipiri, Control. Lucky so-and-sos, they get all the fun. Tell Harry I'll expect him about six. Cheerio. Kipipiri closing down. Out."

I ruminated: "Harry Dawling, Hmm! Wonder what he wants? I expect he has some *shauri* with his labour force again. Too much drinking going on in his lines? Must organize a raid this Sunday morning."

Bwana Mali, he was dubbed by the Africans, *mali* being the Swahili word for wealth. He'd been in the colony for something like eighteen years and had developed a prosperous farm of three thousand acres. Most of it was wheat and in the harvesting season was a spectacular sight to see. He had the biggest labour force in the whole of the Rift, bigger even than the famous Delamare estates. It was estimated to total over two hundred. And, of course, he needed such a battalion of labour with three thousand acres of wheat and oats, and a hundred and fifty of pyrethrum plus a hundred head of cattle. Then there were his pigs, wattle plantations and maize *shambas.* Indubitably Harry had made gigantic strides and Kenya, still so unexploited, was a challenge to his vigour, just as it was to those hundreds of other white settlers. With a fleet of lorries and tractors, three massive combine harvesters— they always fascinated me so—road graders and his own stone quarries, he was entitled to his claim as one of the colony's top farmers. Just the sort of successful settler at whom the covetous wrath and discontent of land-hungry Kikuyu was directed!

With his own workshops and Italian mechanics he could undertake the servicing and major repairs of all his plant and equipment. Even his power was provided by an ingenious hydro-electric unit he had designed and constructed, which harnessed the power of perennial streams that gushed down the slopes of the majestic Kipipiri, rising up mightily behind his magnificent house. There were tennis courts and stables, beautiful lawns and guest houses. Harry entertained modestly and was popular but touchy; rich but discerningly generous; patronizing but extremely capable.

Employing over two hundred Africans of mixed tribes required him to be something of a martinet and he would tolerate no back-chat or sulking. His success, as with most of the farmers, lay in the example he set. Often he could be seen out in the rain-soaked fields covered in mud alongside his workers, digging out a tractor that had sunk into a soft patch. It was he who was donating stone for construction of Kipipiri's new police post. He scathingly maintained that it was out of sheer disgust for the parsimonious authorities that he was giving the stone from his quarry. He was prepared to assist all he could for the simple reason that a centrally sited and decently constructed brick post would boost the 'dubious prestige' of the Crown in the area, and would be of great benefit to him and his neighbours. There was no doubt about it, Bwana Mali was a settler of the first water and, not surprisingly so, was famed for the high standard of fare set before his guests. A visitor was always royally received.

This was exactly the case later that bleak and damp day in May. I had arrived at Harry's 'palace', having been driven by him at a frightful speed in his Chev along roads that would have daunted the progress of a halftrack vehicle.

His wife, sitting opposite me, glanced with approval as I spooned out a second helping of spaghetti bolognese. "You will have to visit us more often, Peter; it must be pretty lonely for you in that wooden shack on Hale's place that you have to live in. Iniquitous really! Don't wait until invited, there's always an extra plate here."

I'd been likewise addressed so often by other hospitable and sympathetic settlers in the area that, although humbly grateful, I had prepared a stock answer; an answer that was, nonetheless, true. "Trouble is, Mrs Dawling, I feel rather guilty, you know, enjoying such grand food and company and never being able to return the gesture. It's all so one-sided. I shall have to invite you to be my guests at the Gilgil Hotel one night."

She murmured something about not being so silly and rang the little brass bell for the tall Kipsigis houseboy to bring the next course. It was ice-cream and delicious. As I ate it I pondered the merits of buying a refrigerator so that I, too, could stock such food-stuffs. Refrigerators? On an inspector's salary?

"Coffee, Peter?" questioned Harry, as he offered me one of his special brand of cigarettes—Markovitch. It was so typical of him to smoke only the best quality.

I took one and replied, "Please, white."

I pushed back the chair and loosened my belt to the accompaniment of a questioning chuckle from Mrs Dawling who chided: "Come now, you are not going to deceive me that we've fed you that much!"

To which I replied, though I shouldn't have done really: "Mrs Dawling! My dinner usually consists of a fried egg on toast and H.P. sauce." Her expression implied that it was a wicked shame.

Taking a long pull at my cigarette I leaned back feeling nice and contented. What a relaxing effect a good meal and a noggin of brandy can have, I thought. The Markovitch cigarettes I found were so much milder than the popular East African brand of 'Clipper' and was about to comment on it to Harry. He had, though, walked across to the radio and was switching it on. Leaving the table, I followed him into the lounge and deposited myself in a comfortable armchair.

"Now then!" commenced Harry, sinking down into the other well-worn, leather upholstered armchair by my side. "Betty probably told you on the radio that I wanted to discuss something with you.

Well, it's this. There's a lot of oathing going on in my labour camp and I think we should see if we can *kamata* them while actually at it."

"From within or without?" I enquired, with interest.

He continued: "I'm not really very certain, but I can say that a gang, probably from 'Kipi', is making regular visits to the Kuke lines. My farm guards have reported odd movements. Another thing, I can tell by their manner and their expressions that they are being 'got at'. But, most convincing of all is that two goats belonging to some Luo have gone missing over the past few nights."

"You mean that the goats have been used in a ceremony or have been stolen to feed the gang?"

Oathing was not at all unknown to me. It was a ritualistic and barbaric practice that was prevalent wherever there were Kikuyu, Embu or Meru squatter *shambas*. What surprised me was that it should be going on in Harry's lines. He was known to have such a strong, loyal section of homeguard, some of whom carried shotguns, too.

"Bit of both, I suppose," Harry replied. "They use the necessary parts for the ceremony and the remainder becomes the gang's perks, which they carry off to the forest. On the other hand, the oath administrator may very well be one of my own employees."

"Any suspicions?"

"Not exactly," he continued earnestly. "In fact, I rather think it could be one of Hugh Douglas's drivers. Fellow by the name of Musa. He's been using one of my tractors for Hugh whose own has broken down. It's collected by this Musa each morning and returned at night, but, as it's some three miles to Hugh's place, he is sleeping in my Kuke lines—he's a Kuke himself, incidentally. One of my Italian mechanics saw him returning from the direction of the pyrethrum dryer late the other evening. He's a bloody suspicious beggar and I'm going to have a word with Hugh tomorrow. Meanwhile, I thought that you might care to join me in a snap raid on the Kuke lines, night after tomorrow, together with some of your stalwarts. I want to narrow down the actual hut between now and then and will get my *nyapara* onto it—he's above all the *fatina* that goes on and I think I can trust him as well as anybody. And anyway, even if nothing comes of it, it will be a good thing to show the flag a bit, oathing or no oathing."

He lifted himself agilely out of his chair and went over to the radio again to tune it in for, I imagined, the news.

Harry's last remark—"oathing or no oathing"—made me think a bit, for it was not at all uncommon for a settler who wanted some 'showing the flag' around his labour lines to engineer it under the pretext of investigating some alleged illegal activity. However, to insinuate such was bad taste in Harry's case and I was quite prepared to do my stuff. I told him that I'd be only too pleased to string along, adding, "I wouldn't be doing my duty if I refused, now would I?"

He favoured me with a half wink, settled himself into his armchair again and said, "Good! We will tie up the arrangements tomorrow. Meantime I'll ascertain just where that blighter, Musa, has his *kitanda*, you know, where he has his bed."

Having recharged our empty glasses and supplied me with another Markovitch, we then both gave rapt attention to the news from Nairobi. The time was eight o'clock and all over the colony the settler and his family would be doing the same thing. It was most ill-considered not to stop everything in order to listen to the news. Apart from being the only touch that the majority of farmers had with the outside world, the troubles of their neighbours were always so much more dramatic than their own.

Some minutes later, having finished the usual autopsies on the various news items, I decided to tackle Harry on this matter of oathing again. It was a subject that I had only been informed on by unreliable sources here and there. I had never had the opportunity to meet anyone who had actually witnessed an oathing ceremony and, although I knew roughly what went into them and the paraphernalia employed, I was eager to have a factual and comprehensive version of the mystical and objectionable ritual. I thought that my experienced host could be encouraged to provide that version.

"Harry," I ventured, "you've been in the country a long time and know a darn sight more than I ever will of the psychology of the African and his liking for black magic. Would it bore you too much to describe briefly the evolution of this oathing that is so strong and powerful and then, perhaps, an account of its present-day form insofar as it concerns the Kikuyu?"

For some thirty seconds the sharp, but kindly, eyes of Mr Dawling studied the polished floor in front of him while his right forefinger tapped mechanically at his cigarette over an ash-tray. He began to talk, slowly at first, almost tiredly, but there was a note of authority in his voice that seemed to imply, "... you may not agree with everything I'm about to tell you but, after nearly twenty years here, I should be rather better informed than most."

Needless to say I considered it would have been impertinent of me to doubt his knowledge of the subject. That which follows is a digest of the information supplied by him. It is not a verbatim account.

"First of all you must appreciate that Kukes have always been inveterate oath-takers. Oaths are an inherent part of their tribal life and during the last half century or so, with the gales of Western civilization threatening to blow away the flimsy fabric of their tribal traditions and customs they tend to cling the more tenaciously to oathing. It's all very understandable too, because so much of a Kikuyu's personal security is dependent upon how efficiently he is able to exorcize evil spirits. Most of the evil that besets him is attributable to a bad spirit and the practice of witchcraft, sorcery and fetishes, are the surest method he knows of dispelling angry spirits. And, you'll agree, when it comes to a matter of fetishes, Western people themselves are far from being absolved. Rabbit's foot hanging in the car, St. Christopher medallions, touching wood, turning money over on seeing a new moon—dozens of them. But there, although oathing is a different sort of fetish, all are founded upon superstition. In earlier days oathing among the Kikuyu had little or no sinister connotations, no more, say, than the connotations arising from the various religious ceremonies— kneeling before a cross and invoking the spirit of Jesus, or bowing in the direction of Mecca five times a day, the sprinkling of incense among the congregation during mass, and many others. All, if controlled and healthily conceived, can do a great deal of good. A faith is a faith whether pagan or Christian, though the latter is accepted as being the more suited to this day and age. Have you ever heard of the *githathi* stone as used by the Kikuyu?"

I had and told him so. "But I've never come across anyone who has seen one."

"No! I haven't seen one either but there is no doubt that they do exist and I think it's a good spring-board for this chat of mine on oathing because a *githathi* stone was, and is, used during oath-taking. It features largely in the Kikuyu native courts that have a chief presiding. Such courts are every bit as effective, if not as judicious, as our elaborate judge and jury trial courts and the procedure is based on native law and custom. Unfortunately the hearing very often ends in a stalemate. When this happens the opposing parties are urged to seek a solution to their differences in the supernatural powers of a *githathi* stone. The magic it is invested with is profoundly feared and acknowledged by Kikuyu and is accepted as being an instrument of justice. Those who take an oath under the auspices of a *githathi* stone ceremony seldom wait for its strange omnipotent power to work and, if either party has been untruthful at the earlier proceedings, he or she would break down and admit so. The *githathi* stone has the power to kill a relative of the guilty party which means that it is they who will confess on his or her behalf if they know of the guilt and are unprepared to endure the risk. The stone is quite large and ..."

There was a point that I wished to clear up before he proceeded further, so asked, "You are saying that *githathi*-stone oathing ceremonies were not harmful or generally evil?"

"Well, the fact that the power of it could intervene and cause death, allegedly, made it an evil instrument, but the motives behind its use were really, if somewhat primitive, not malicious. It was resorted to by aggrieved parties who took the oath to settle their disputes. What followed usually was some sort of compromise."

"I see. Blackmail by the spirits, so to speak. And the stone itself?"

"Yes, well, as I said, it is quite large and has seven holes in it. They are natural holes and not man-made, which makes it something of a mystical article. During the oath-taking ceremony a certain stick is thrust seven times into each hole while muttering the oath that is being taken, or rather administered. On other occasions the stone is placed in a tree at the junction of seven branches. The number seven has a strange significance among Kikuyu and is reliably thought to represent the seven orifices of the human body."

I thought for a second on how much faith peoples of other countries placed upon numbers. I, for instance, am guilty of a pet superstition with regard to the figure three.

Harry went on. "I would say that the *githathi*-stone oath was a form of 'white magic' and a lot of it goes on among all African tribes. When disease, famine or drought descends upon their land they seek to negate the evil spirit that causes the ravaging disease or disastrous epidemic by white magic. It can take the form of a sacrificial slaughter of an animal, or the scattering of some divine powder by the tribal witchdoctor. The Kikuyu seem to have favoured the killing of a ram. It would be a ritual slaughter and its carcass hung in the vicinity of the ceremony as symbolic that the evil spirit causing the misfortune was being driven off. Such an oath taken during the ritual slaughter of a ram is called a *thenge* oath and is usually taken by the tribal authorities. This *thenge* oath has, since the emergency, been corrupted to suit the aims of Mau Mau and has assumed diabolical proportions, to the extent that it, like all other oaths among the Kikuyu now, falls into the category of 'black magic'. Dead dogs have been utilized recently and the oath attaching to the ceremony is signally vicious. It purports to be a promise of death to anyone who sells land to the *serikali*, the government, and has an unbelievably unshakeable grip on all Kukes who happen to see the dead dog wherever it may be displayed. Do you remember in October last year when a dead dog was found hanging outside the hut of my Kuke *niapara*?"

As I had not then arrived in the territory I said no.

"Of course, I am forgetting. However, it ushered in active Mau Mau infiltration into my Kuke lines and proved to me that a hell of a lot of oathing had already gone before. This particular *thenge* oath that had been administered in my lines was due to the D.C.'s eviction of some squatter labour from their *shambas* in the forest. That oath was solemn, binding and bloody repugnant. It is only under the dreaded influence of Mau Mau that oath-taking has become so inhuman and so beastly. The organizers of Mau Mau have quickly realized what a strong weapon they have with which to enforce allegiance to the movement and every concept of oath-taking has been slowly corrupted. The principles underlying the tribal usage of oaths have been flouted until they are now abhorrent to any decent, normal person. The strength of Mau Mau has grown tremendously by virtue of its exploitation of the Kikuyu's customary need and simple respect for oath-taking in times of stress."

Pausing for a moment in his narrative he allowed me to ask: "How much of a party to this wholesale oathing were the elders and leaders of the tribe during the events leading up to this emergency?"

"I'm just coming to that, Peter, but before I do let me tell you when Mau Mau oathing was first detected. During 1950 there were blatant indications that hundreds of Kikuyu, as well as Meru and Embu, were willingly being oathed into the aims and ideals of Mau Mau. Such aims, as you by now know, being to drive the white man out and to win back the land. One reason for the apparent overtness of oathing was money; the Kenya African Union, though proscribed, was operating quite audaciously under a new title, the Kikuyu Central Association, and was in need of funds. There is a charge for the administration of the oath, exorbitant, and in many cases forcefully exacted. This, quite naturally, caused discontent among many of the more moderate Kukes and their protests filtered through to official ears. The police put on some pressure and in April of the same year certain aggrieved Kukes complained to the authorities at Naivasha and a prosecution ensued. It was the first of its kind and the convictions that resulted led to the Mau Mau society being officially proscribed. However, it did not curb oathing which continued apace to the accompaniment of intimidation and beating-up. And so it went throughout that year and the next, growing uglier and more anti-European, until there was barely a Kuke anywhere who had not, either willingly or by force, been administered the sinister oath of Mau Mau."

Interrupting him, I commented, "Judging by the slow response to the 'confessional *barazas*' held on the farms in this area, there is little doubt that oathing has had an undeniably strong hold on them."

"Quite so, and it will take years before the corrosive effects can be counteracted. Probably not until the next generation. So, the inspired leader of Mau Mau, Jomo Kenyatta, achieved the solid backing of his tribe by converting to his own evil ends its old tribal custom of oath-taking, and what a degrading contradiction the present oath is to its former character and purpose. From the *Githathi* oath to the *Batuni*. Could anything be more vile or disgusting than the *Batuni* oath? I imagine that you are acquainted with the form it takes, aren't you?"

It was, I knew, the 'forest' oath and was taken by those fanatical adherents of Mau Mau that took to militant terrorism. I had learned that it was administered by gang leaders and it was to initiate the recruit as a member of the Land Freedom Army. I asked Harry, who had risen and walked across to the drink cabinet near the door: "The *Batuni* oath is the ultimate to which it is taken, is it?"

"Hmm! Who can say what other nasty oaths they will think up? There are actually two forest oaths—the other is called the *Githaki* and either one of them is the platoon oath, I'm not certain which it is. Anyway, one is administered on entering the forest and the other within his particular gang, or platoon."

To hear the groups referred to as 'platoons' was odd, but the militant cells of Mau Mau were known to borrow British army terms. In fact, it had been established by Intelligence that all terrorists were inducted into either one of three Land Freedom Armies, each being assigned to a specific zone of the White Highlands. After emptying his glass in one swallow and dabbing his lips with a large silk handkerchief, Harry settled into his chair and took up the story again.

"Bloodthirsty is hardly the word to describe the *Githaki* or *Batuni* oaths. From the description dragged out of captured 'micks' the word 'revolting' would be more appropriate. Captain Walker of the Kenya Regiment with a patrol entered a hideout a few months ago and had obviously interrupted an oath-taking ceremony. All the trappings were there in grisly detail. One of the same gang was captured the day after during the follow-up and it was possible to obtain a reasonably accurate picture of the nature of ceremony now practised. Most certainly after taking such an oath the initiate would never flinch from performing any act or crime in the furtherance of Mau Mau. No atrocity would be too despicable or obscene. He reaches the very zenith of disgust during the oathing ceremony and is thereafter considered to be as immune as the imbecile he becomes from the prickings of any conscience left in him—he becomes, let's face it, beyond redemption. This we are seeing all too clearly during recent 'confessional *barazas*', as you rightly mentioned just now. Christ, I honestly don't know why I continue to employ them."

I thought wryly, "It's because they are the best workers, surely?"

Was he going to furnish me particulars of the ceremony itself, I wondered. People spoke a lot about oathing but very few could give a convincing account of the odious ceremonies. So I decided to prompt him.

"Just what manner of stuff is employed during these ceremonies? The use of banana leaves in the shape of an arch is common knowledge, but where do they go from there?"

He pursed his lips thoughtfully, and then said: "I am not going to commit myself to any involved or hard and fast description; the oath takes so many forms and is administered in a variety of ways. I will though, explain what one may normally expect to take place." Thrusting his legs out, he sank deeper into his chair and relaxed still further.

"The arch of banana and sugar-cane leaves you know of, and is usually an indispensable prop for the ceremony. Initiates must pass through it while chanting the oath taken. These differ and I will, a bit later, let you see what an average oath is. The proceedings are conducted at night for better effect, probably in the flickering light of a low fire. There would be an animal, generally a sheep, that has been killed, and if a whole sheep is not available then at least its pubic section would be. The initiate would have carnal knowledge of the sheep or go through the motions with the appropriate separated portion of its anatomy. Most gangs have young adolescent girls with them and the initiate would quite often be expected to have public intercourse with her. In the ceremonial arena would be seen the foulest of sights—excrement, semen in gourds, menstrual discharge from the women, blood of the slaughtered beast, even such nauseating objects as a dismembered human penis. With these vomitory ingredients it would then be up to the oath administrator with his riotous and diabolical imagination, to prepare a cocktail which is drunk by the awed initiates. Even his own urine would be suitably dispensed as a revolting draught. The initiate may or may not be spared the sight of the sordid array of ingredients as, in many cases, he is obliged to lie down with his eyes covered by the eyeballs of the dead sheep, reciting the oath while doing so."

I felt it was a convenient moment to decant another measure of brandy and, excusing myself, I took my empty glass to the cabinet. My host, I was thankful to see, did not look at all bored.

"Really!" I opined. "Such extraordinary obscene behaviour among human beings is difficult to believe you know."

"Be careful my boy," he retorted. "There are varying levels of human evolution and many of these terrorists have barely reached the accepted stage of evolution as human beings before they begin to degenerate, and degenerate fast, too."

"But surely," I pressed, "there must be many Kikuyu recruited into the gangs, and who have been educated, that just couldn't stomach all that nauseating ceremony. What if they refused to have an oath administered in such a manner?"

Harry grinned as I returned with my glass. "Depends on how eager they are to continue living. Murder in the forest among gangs is a commonplace. Oathing is a periodical feature of gang life. Whenever the leader thinks that his members are getting fainthearted, or are seen to fall short of the required zeal when slashing animals or humans, he will simply arrange a ceremony. The administrator, needless to say, is given full licence within his platoon to experiment with any horrible ideas that might enter his depraved mind. Terrorists suspected of traitorous thoughts are subjected to even fouler horrors and there are cases on record which show that he would be forced to suck the penis of some Mau Mau victim. The *pièce de résistance,* for the benefit of the waverers, is cannibalism ...”

“Cannibalism?” I coughed.

“Yes, cannibalism. It’s nothing new with the Kikuyu, you know. Many were indulging in it when the white man arrived in Kenya. Sections cut from the body of a dead comrade, killed by security forces or a wild animal would be dried and carried around by the gang’s administrator of oaths. Whenever it is necessary to make an example of any particular traitor, or to boost flagging morale, the victim would be forced to eat the human flesh, having first been soaked in urine, while repeating Mau Mau oath seven times.”

I grimaced towards my obliging informant and interrupted, “I think that’s enough for one evening, if you don’t mind.”

Taking a long suck of air through clenched teeth, Harry said, very quietly, “You can see how dedicated they are to their cause, and how difficult it is for us all, faced with such mentally deranged beasts. Why on earth they have not achieved their object of massacring all us Europeans yet is beyond me.” He sighed wearily, and then snapped, “But we’ll purge the colony of these sadistic bastards. Their condition may be hopeless but ours is not. They must be cut out of Kenya as a surgeon would cut out a cancerous growth.”

“That’s the aim, Harry—agreed, but is that cancerous growth so near to Kenya’s vital organs that it would be fatal to remove it? I mean, the economy of the colony is so seriously jeopardized by the crippling cost of this emergency, and it’s going to be a long, long struggle before the battle is won. So long, in fact, that recovery may well be impossible. So many farmers packing up already.”

He was quick to reply and I detected the slightest twinge of annoyance in his voice. "You've got an interesting point there, but here is one settler who does *not* intend to abandon the colony, and I know of scores of others who feel likewise. Perhaps some other evening we shall have an opportunity of pursuing that particular line of thought."

I must humbly concede that I have lived to eat those words I spoke with regard to Kenya's economy. The emergency expenditure was so heavily subsidized by the British taxpayer that the colony was able to recoup. Her precarious economy notwithstanding, large numbers of settlers continued to quit, not that they could be accused of desertion; they despaired ... that's all.

I waited while Harry rummaged through some documents in a small writing bureau. After a moment or two he selected the one he was looking for and brought it to me. "Have a look at this before you go and you'll appreciate the more just what we are up against, if you don't know already."

"At least I know that we're up against a damned elusive foe," I dolefully remarked.

The document purported to be part of a directive to senior personnel of the security forces. He must have acquired it from one of his many army friends. He indicated with his finger the passage he wished me to read. It was headed 'The Mau Mau Oath' and underneath were listed six promises that were made within:

1. If I am sent to bring in the head of an enemy or of a European and I fail, may this oath kill me.

2. If I fail to steal anything from a European, may this oath kill me.

3. If I know of any enemy to our organization and fail to report him to my leader, may this oath kill me.

4. If I am ever sent by my leader to do something of benefit to the Kikuyu clan and I refuse, may this oath kill me.

5. If I refuse to help in driving the European from this country, may this oath kill me.

6. If I worship any leader but Jomo Kenyatta, may this oath kill me.

The reader need have no doubt that the above oath found many hundreds of innocent victims—Kikuyu and their kindred tribes who found it beyond their moral and spiritual capacity to honour the evil promises. Later in the emergency, as recorded elsewhere in this book, an uncountable number of graves were uncovered daily to reveal the mortal remains of loyal Kikuyu who had been strangled or decapitated. They were murders by the hundreds of which the police had not the slightest inkling. The oath was enforced with a terrifying and unequivocal ruthlessness. The tribe had erected a gallows for itself and the gravamen lay with Mau Mau.

Under another sub-heading 'Common Features of the Batuni Oath', I read:

1. I pledge myself to burn European crops and to kill European-owned cattle. I must steal their firearms whenever possible.
2. If I am ordered to kill I will do so, even though it be my father or my brother.
3. If I kill them I must cut off the head, gouge out the eyeballs and suck the liquid from them.
4. In particular I must kill Europeans.

What hope for persons, notwithstanding their allegiance to a revolutionary movement, who are subscribers to such disgusting oaths—oaths albeit that are administered with the same seriousness and fanaticism as they are taken?

My final moments with Harry that evening were passed citing the various atrocities that went to ratify the stranglehold that oathing, perverted oathing, had taken upon Mau Mau and its subscribers. Draconian crime on such a scale, we concluded, could indicate but one thing—diseased minds! No wonder every European went about armed. Was there not just cause?

Back at my post I bid goodnight to Harry who disappeared, skidding and sliding into the wet, black night. Then, deciding to check my askari quarters before turning in, I sloshed past the farm workshop and stores to the bull-pens that served them as such.

"*Simama! Nani wewe?*" The age-old challenge, but in Swahili, stopped me in my tracks. I was not slow in replying either for I had heard the bolt of a rifle worked menacingly and knew that there would be a round nestling up the spout of it.

"*Rafiki,*" I shouted clearly. "*Bwana yenu.*"

It was Omonjo, the only Turkana tribesman I had on the post. A friendly fellow most times, but quick-tempered.

"*Kila kitu mzuri?*" I asked. He confirmed that everything was alright.

After telling him to withdraw the round that he had put into the breach of his rifle and to apply its safety catch, I turned and picked my way slowly back to my own quarters. The roughly hewn timber shack was no better an example of a pioneer homestead than one could have seen outside of 1850 Wyoming. It had been occupied by the owner of the farm before he built a substantial brick 'mansion' for himself and his family. The last thing I did before entering, a drill I always carried out instinctively I suppose, was to look up and over towards the great, dark, indeterminate mass silhouetted against a sombre sky that was my mountain, Kipipiri. Were there any red glows of fires? Mau Mau fires? There were none. Too wet, I thought.

I found sleep difficult to court that night. Harry's lively and modestly understated monologue on oathing had so impressed me that my mind was inflated with the helium of apprehension and dread speculation on what further atrocities these disgustingly oathed creatures who called themselves Mau Mau would commit before they were purged from Kenya's ailing system. Had it not been for the earthy reality of the monotonous symphony of crickets outside that acted as an anchor on my mind I'm certain it would have floated clean out of my head, soaring up and away to leave my restless body lying in uneasy torment upon the bed.

My chaotic and kaleidoscopic thoughts gradually resolved into distinct patterns and settled down, gave a little lurch as I recalled

Harry's words about drinking human blood and eating excrement, then subsided, serene and indifferent. I was suddenly quite tired, no! weary, and shied from the prospect of spending another wretched day in my shack on the morrow. I prayed it would dawn bright and dry so that I could get out and stretch my legs.

Sleep was an elusive friend and I must have lain for several hours just thinking and remembering and wondering.

Oathing of persons who supported, or whom it was considered should support, the insurrection in Kenya was such a commonplace happening that few of us ever gave it much thought. The administration of oaths was not at all dissimilar to assassinations of loyal Kikuyus; it was simply an inherent part of Mau Mau's militant policy to enforce allegiance to its cause.

At the start of October 1952, the Kikuyu tribe had three paramount chiefs. One of them, Chief Wahuiru, had expressed the view that, "an oath taken under duress was not binding". That being so, Mau Mau hierarchy in Nairobi wasted no time in counteracting such brave and improvident sentiments. He was murdered on 9 October. Eleven days later a State of Emergency was declared. However, in order to boost sluggish recruitment Mau Mau made another turn on the screw of intimidation; Senior Chief Nderi was also eliminated. Needless to say there were few Kikuyus by the end of October prepared to openly endorse their late chief's naïve view that oaths taken under duress were not binding.

It was the assassination of the first of these loyal old Kikuyu chiefs that really confirmed the existence of Mau Mau terrorism and ushered in the holocaust that was to be the scourge of Kenya for several years to come. The facts make interesting reading and illustrate very clearly the ruthless lengths to which Mau Mau were prepared to go.

It occurred on D route, the Nairobi–Limuru road, some ten miles from the city. Wahuiru, who was the senior of the three chiefs, was returning from a meeting and was being driven by his own official driver. He observed another car following and bade the driver increase speed to prevent it from overtaking. Instinctively he felt that some peril stalked him. The following car, however, made an astute diversion and rejoined the road a short distance further on, ahead of the chief's car. Its way blocked, the chief's car pulled up short. It was approached by a cruel-looking Kikuyu wearing a leather zip jerkin who asked coldly, "Are you Chief Wahuiru?" To which the proud chief replied, unafraid, "I am."

There was no more conversation. The chief saw the glazed, expressionless eyes; saw the hand being withdrawn from the leather jerkin; then the wicked little automatic pointed towards his head. He heard the roar of it as the trigger was pulled, but no more. It was a well-aimed shot and entered his head—it's doubtful whether he heard the other two shots as they crashed into his chest. The old chief's driver was far from petrified; he ran and ran until he had put two or three *shambas* between himself and the brutal gangsters. It was some time later that he stammered his tragic story to police who then raised the alarm.

Among the many who were subsequently arrested for the crime, or for complicity in it, was another Kikuyu chief named Koinange, and his son. Both were acquitted at the trial but re-arrested outside the court and detained under the emergency regulations.

This cold-blooded assassination was the culmination of a series of violent events, including serious attacks on Europeans. Sir Evelyn Baring, who had but a few days earlier been sworn in as Governor and Commander in Chief, and who had just completed a short tour of the most troubled areas of Kikuyuland, quickly assessed the situation as critical. Shortly after, the highly successful Operation *Jock Scott* was launched in Nairobi and its environs. It was executed with bewildering surprise and swiftness and was a credit to the consummate planning that had been kept on Top Secret ice for several weeks beforehand.

More than anything else it was the assassination of Chief Wahuiru that put the colony's emergency machinery into top gear. The trial of his killers was quite a sensation. It exposed to a shattering extent the mass of maggots crawling under the guise of loyal subjects in many a highly trusted position—such as Chief Koinange, who one had expected to have been above such cheap revolutionary activity as assassination. The trial permitted the authorities possibly its first really clear glimpse of the unnerving inroads that Mau Mau had made upon decent society and stable government.

And yet, it was true to say that Operation *Jock Scott*, in its brilliant execution at midnight on 20 October 1952, resulting in the arrest and detention of hundreds of Mau Mau leaders and adherents, plus the closure of the infamous KCA/KAU central offices, had a most disrupting effect on the organization. It suffered a severe and totally unexpected setback. That Chief Wahuiru's assassins should have been found guilty and paid the supreme penalty for their crime was also a gladdening fact to record.

There must, undoubtedly, have been a dismaying number of *Uhuru* supporters that still remained unconvinced of the ruthlessness of Mau Mau's intentions. Perhaps, therefore, the assassination of the second of the three paramount chiefs caused them to do some serious rethinking.

The day following the whirlwind *Jock Scott* operation and just as everyone was hoping that the unruly elements were being put in their places, Senior Chief Nderi was virtually hacked to pieces. Let us recite the facts that displayed so chillingly Mau Mau's contempt for the new governor's sabre-rattling.

This venerable old chief had gone to the Thengenge location of Nyeri with three of his men. It was a fictitious report that had lured him there and amounted to an allegation that some of his trusted inner circle were to take a Mau Mau oath at a specially convened meeting.

He appears to have been sufficiently apprehensive enough of the veracity of the report to have first contacted a local government official and arranged for a strong police party to rendezvous with him at a place known as the Gura Fishing Camp. The brave, but imprudent, paramount chief was, alas, overconfident and decided that he would be able to handle a few hundred of his own tribesmen on his own. He proceeded without the police party.

From the moment he and his gallant little band, each armed with a rifle, arrived at the scene of the meeting the five-hundred-strong, whooping, warbling and animated mob was on massacre bent. Their *pangas* flashed ominously in the late afternoon sun as they bore down on the chief. He was much alarmed at the fearsome attitude of his subjects and felt constrained to fire a few warning shots over their bobbing heads. Such action against a simple and superstitious people, as he should have known, could have but one result—to encourage them—for their tribal spirits had turned those lethal pieces of lead to water. Thus inspired, the maddened, blood-lusting mob of Kikuyus demurred not a moment longer and surged towards its quarry. Poor, doomed Nderi, less fleet of foot than his three comrades, was soon brought down with a vicious slash of a razor-sharp *panga*. The howling, berserk rabble jostled among itself to slash and chop at his body until it was mutilated to shreds—they literally butchered him alive! His personal bodyguard was seized and torn apart by the pack as he was threshing his terrified way across the river. His remains were located long after the red-dyed waters had rushed shamefully on several miles from the scene. Only one of the party escaped to gasp the tragic details that were to stagger all sane and decent-thinking humans everywhere. Inevitably, their rifles became the highly prized trophies of their elated assassins.

So once again the forces of law and order were given a very sobering example of just how ingrained and how monstrous Mau Mau had become among Kikuyu revolutionaries. Only one of the three paramount chiefs remained, namely, Chief Njeri of Fort Hall, and, not wishing to risk further bloody human sacrifice at the pagan altar of Mau Mau, steps were immediately taken to ensure his continued safety. A cordon of soldiers was thrown around his ancestral home in Fort Hall.

The timely words of the Governor in his radio broadcast of the previous day when he gravely declared a State of Emergency throughout the colony and protectorate of Kenya now inveighed directly against the inexpressibly evil rampage of Mau Mau:

"... unfortunately, at first gradually and now swiftly, the Mau Mau crimes have increased in number, in daring and in savagery. Recently persecution of Kikuyu Christians has increased in severity, churches have been desecrated, missions have been attacked, and teachers and children in mission schools have been assaulted and threatened. At one time these crimes were committed by stealth, now one of the best-loved and most revered African chiefs in Kenya [Wahuiru] has been assassinated on the high road in broad daylight by a band of armed men ... the Government have, therefore, with the full knowledge and concurrence of the Secretary of State for the Colonies, taken drastic action in order to stop the spread of violence. This has been taken not against men who hold any particular political views, but against those who have had recourse to violent measures. This is in the interests of all ... of all Africans in those wide areas of the colony which have remained peaceful and of loyal Kikuyu who have been the main sufferers ..."

(For the full text of the Governor's message *see* Appendix IX)

Sir Evelyn's solemn declaration was soon to receive unequivocal ecclesiastic endorsement from further afield when the fearlessly outspoken and distinguished Anglican priest Trevor Huddleston had this to say in the Johannesburg *Star*:

"Mau Mau is a movement which, in its origins and its development, is wholly evil. It is the worst enemy of African progress in Kenya. It has about it all the horrors of the powers of darkness; of spiritual wickedness in high places. There can be no compromise, no common ground, between Mau Mau and the rest of the civilized world. It must be utterly destroyed if the peoples of Kenya are to live together and build up their country."

The orgy of blood-letting was to continue for a long time to come. The Land Freedom Army insurgents had been well and truly indoctrinated; henceforth they were to be regarded as psychotic gangsters. They would be hunted down as wild criminals and had, moreover, as far as angry settlers were concerned, forfeited any

185

rights to the protection of those rules embodied in the Geneva Convention.

The benign and benevolent image of the British Crown was, perforce, about to be sullied.

Chapter 10

Legal slaughter or excusable homicide?

Before the advent of Kenya in my life as one of its 'soldiers of fortune', I had seen an occasional corpse, though never torn and mangled or disfigured. And, long before I laid eyes upon my first live terrorist, the number of dead and dying I'd seen had mounted up to a score or so. In fact, shortly before my own fruitful encounter with the adversary halfway through 1955, over eighteen months after my arrival in the colony, I was beginning seriously to wonder if I would ever carve up any notches at all before every Mau Mau terrorist had been violently despatched across the Styx to Hades.

Most of these 'micks' who had met their ignoble and sanguinary end in the various clashes with security forces I saw while they were on 'display' for a few hours to the general public at my parent station.

Word of a patrol's successful contact with elusive gangsters would percolate through the African locations and weave in and out of the busy little Indian *dukas* along the dusty main street. Africans, Asians and even Europeans would eagerly speculate on the numbers involved and the chances of any bodies being recovered and brought into town. It was always debatable whether the particular encounter had occurred in terrain that would enable any fatal casualties to be recovered. In the majority of cases contact would have occurred in the green, lush, creeper-ridden depths of some stupendous gorge, or, equally as inaccessible, high up among the rocky crags and crevasses of a hazy, distant ridge. However, assuming that the bodies of any dead terrorists could be carried or dragged out to a vehicle, they would not infrequently arrive with the jubilant patrol at the nearest police station.

At the station I was attached, these bodies would be unceremoniously deposited in a corner of the station perimeter fence. The spot was next to a circle of whitewashed stones in the centre of which stood a tall flagpole; the Kenya Police flag fluttered judiciously at its head.

This macabre exhibition of dead, and occasionally dying, 'micks' became a regular feature of the unfeignedly bitter struggle against Mau Mau. Almost nervously the civilian populace would drift silently past the obscene remains. They would glance furtively down, as if something rude had caught the corner of their eye, then quickly avert their gaze. Some, more bold, would falter, turn around, and regard with blank expressions the foul objects they had deliberately walked across to gawk at.

Such stark, and to some maybe malevolent, reminders of the dire consequences to be expected from violent opposition to lawful authority became commonplace. Certainly the grisly show must have had a salutary effect upon any African who may have been contemplating a departure from his law-abiding and remunerative existence in the township or on a *shamba*. Those bundles of decaying flesh, shattered bone and malodorous rags exhibited were seldom identified by any of the spectators. Nearly always they were Kukes from over in the reserves of Fort Hall, Nyeri or Kiambu. But now and again a local settler would stop by and explosively identify one of the bundles.

"Well! Well! Well! He has been caught up with at last ... saved me the job! That's Njerogi, my old cook. He disappeared after that oath ceremony in my lines last September. The cunning bastard ... bullets were too good for him."

I remember going down to the station from my post one morning, having heard over my V.H.F. radio of an action farther across the Rift towards Eburro. A combined military and police operation had caught up with a large gang and were pushing it toward Lake Elementita (between Gilgil and Nakuru). K.P.R. spotter planes were transmitting succinct reports that the fleeing gangsters were headed for the Badlands, an area, some twelve square miles, of wicked, tortuous lava rock wherein terrorists, even if they were averse to its discomforting features, were usually unassailable once they could gain the trackless interior of it. The last situation report I heard before leaving my post was that one member of the gang had been shot dead.

On arrival at the station I saw the usual huddle of morbid sightseers near the corner of the perimeter fence. They seemed to be peering even more intently through the wire that day and I soon discovered for myself why.

What a gory mess of dead terrorist he was; and wasn't he the absolute epitome of an arch Mau Mau after months on the run? The knot of spectators were not gawking on this occasion, they were mesmerized!

I was told by the elated officer in charge of the station, the mercurial Inspector Jimmy Jamieson, that it was the body of the self-styled 'General Ngome'. This was news truly sensational. Ngome!—the terrorist leader of major notoriety and as evil as all others rolled into one. His chronicle of murder, arson, pillaging and terrorizing was known from Nakuru to Naivasha and had left us all in no doubt that until he was eliminated little progress in subduing our Rift Valley gang activity could be made.

Documents found on him plus identification by other captured terrorists soon enabled confirmation to be broadcast that it was no less a person than General Ngome, one of the top four in the Third Mberu Ngebe Army's hierarchy. It was an unexpected and long-awaited fillip to the morale of us all. Ngome was someone different and it was worth exhibiting him for the general public to view and despise. I remember that his unlamented and abrupt exit from the operational scene impressed me so vividly that back in my post that same evening I sat and scribbled an elegiac essay on him. Now, because I think that he was the epitome of his pestilential kind, I propose to include the sombre epitaph here:

"General Ngome now brought to book! What an event or is it? After a run of over two years in the bush he has organized and executed enough depredation for three lifetimes of the most recidivist criminal. Heaven knows how many times he has had me rushing about after him and his gang or sat wretchedly in ambush ... countless are the guesses I've had as to his whereabouts forever trying to anticipate what *boma* or store or labour lines he would raid next and never finding it possible. What heaps of bones have I found that were chewed by him? Or the fires still warm that were sat over by him? And the tracks I knew with such certainty he'd made that very morning? How brash the letter crudely scrawled by him addressed to the Governor and left—contemptuously brave in place of the windsock he'd removed on the Gilgil airstrip—but yards from the military camp! I had pictured him as well dressed, the best of the plunder offered him; his beard I imagined would be long, he would carry a superior type of weapon with a bandolier of ammunition over his shoulder; he'd be plump, wide-eyed and grinning; the scars on his body numerous and mute witness to his encounters with security forces. Yet ... I saw him lying there, filthy, crumpled and mutilated by Masai *simis*. His teeth were rotten and stained, lips thicker, more sensuous, more cruel than most. His hair receding but long, and arranged in the usual forest gangster's vogue. His beard was a short bushy one, jet black and neat. He wasn't big, quite short in fact. Not fat, but heavy and muscular. On his back a greatcoat, almost new and probably purloined from some settler's wardrobe, with pieces of bicycle inner tube around the wrists to keep out the chill night wind and mosquitoes. Around his neck, and almost disappearing into a deep cut that had all but decapitated him, was a necklet of multicoloured beads—the blood oozed forth from time to time and flushed over it. Another *simi* wielded by an excited Masai (naughty warriors!) had penetrated deep into his left eye, across his nose to the opposite cheek. Flies were happy in their probings ... a kneecap hanging off—another *simi* slash—and less gory, more present-day in appearance, were the neat holes in his chest, stomach and left ear. The Sten gun responsible for his demise was aimed well. Irresponsible Masai! So difficult to have him positively identified had it not been for the documents found on him. Dare people regard him with sympathy or shocked awe? Why not think of him as the wild beast he had become? One last function to perform for police record purposes was the taking of the deceased's fingerprints. The native constable whose job it was to obtain the prints was indeed a hardened fellow. His task was made the more difficult on this occasion because the rate of decomposition with Ngome seemed to be unusually rapid. The skin of his hands, fingers and legs was peeling off like flakes of old distemper from a wall to reveal a glistening white skin beneath. The piebald contrast was provoking—had that skin been all white how would I have reacted? Instead I watched, unmoved and unfeeling. He was no longer a dangerous predator."

Thus went my elegy for the late Mister Ngome! Without too much delay, usually soon after the finger impressions had been taken, and, to a lesser degree, after the curiosity of the townsfolk had been satisfied, the corpses were disposed of in the town's incinerator. Inquests consequent to these 'sudden deaths'—they were invariably termed such for judicial purposes—did not normally occasion police too much trouble. It was customary for the senior person of the group responsible for the fatality to give evidence that was recorded on oath by the coroner. If it had been possible to have the body identified, then whoever it was that did so would also give evidence accordingly. I knew of no verdict returned by a coroner that implied suspicious circumstances surrounding the death of any terrorists shot and killed by security forces.

To have an 'open' verdict returned at an inquest was so unlikely as to regard every such killing as a 'legal conclusive presumption', that is, 'that any person who so killed a terrorist did so lawfully unless the contrary be proved'. It was rather like the conclusive presumption in law that 'every man is presumed to intend the natural and probable consequences of his acts or omissions'.

It would be misleading, indeed erroneous, to say that every killing of a terrorist in Kenya was fully justified and within the law, there being so many subtle twists and interpretations of the law to take into account. Nevertheless, I can but emphasize the importance of referring to such killings as 'excusable homicide' by comparing the definition with yet another legal presumption, a well-known judicial maxim at that, namely, 'every man is presumed to be innocent until proved guilty beyond all reasonable doubt' (applicable to English law, that is). An African then, shot and killed by police or whoever, and for no question of the legality of the killing to arise, was presumed to have been a terrorist until any suggestion that he was an innocent and law-abiding citizen was proved beyond all 'reasonable doubt'.

It was rare, as rare as a hybrid pet in a royal household, that doubt as to the legality of any killing of Mau Mau terrorists ever arose. Even so, the question is an extremely interesting one and, while admitting that I was loath to exercise my mind with it at the time, I subsequently gave considerable thought to it.

The law recognizes several categories of homicide and they fall into two practical groups—those that are offences against the laws of a country (in Kenya, its Penal Code), and those that are not. In the former we have murder, manslaughter and suicide; in the latter justifiable and excusable homicide.

Could the thousands killed have conceivably been rendered justifiable or excusable by the equivocal construction of the law? Were they all genuine cases of legal homicide or were they just plain murder? One may well start at such a shocking suggestion yet it was quite extraordinary just how many confused sympathizers of African nationalism condemned Kenya's security forces as 'legal murderers'. Would it not be of some benefit, therefore, to examine some of the legal aspects from a strictly layman's point of view, albeit one that has the advantage of some personal experience as its basis. The utmost endeavour will be made to avoid ramming a suffocating dissertation on the ponderous issues involved, like suety dumpling, down the reader's throat.

Homicide—'the killing of a human by a human', and, if we are to understand the true position that existed between Mau Mau terrorists and the forces of the Crown, then a brief examination of each category of homicide is indispensable. I would mention here, too, that the Penal Code in Kenya was a slightly modified version of the English Criminal Code.

Murder is the unlawful killing of any person by another—an essential ingredient of the offence being malice (which is the same as intent). If this ingredient is absent then it could be manslaughter, which is defined in law as 'the killing of any person by another through an unlawful act or omission' (there is no malice aforethought). Thus, a man breaks into a warehouse with intent to commit a felony (an unlawful act) and ties and gags the watchman. The watchman suffocates and dies because of the gagging. Or, equally, a man drives his car recklessly down a street (an unlawful act) and knocks down a cyclist who dies as a result of the injuries he sustains. Both examples would warrant a charge of manslaughter. Suicide does not really come within the scope of this analysis but is, nevertheless, self-killing and an abortive attempt renders the person punishable in law.

We come next to 'excusable' and 'justifiable' homicide and I shall dispose of the latter without further ado by quoting the commonest example that comes most readily to mind, which is the execution of felons for capital offences. This leaves us with 'excusable' homicide and such would be the case if, during a surgical operation by a qualified medical practitioner, the patient should succumb—the integrity of the medical profession being such that, short of a blatant breach of medical prudence, it is accepted that patients do sometimes die while undergoing delicate operations.

Another pointed example of excusable homicide would be the death of a person who, while taking part in a riot that is called upon to disperse by proclamation read in the name of the Sovereign refuses to do so, is shot when police open fire to effect dispersal. It is to be noted that there is no malice or unlawful act that results in the death and the homicide is deemed to be excusable. It has been said that the acid test for most instances of homicide that bear the label 'excusable' is, 'that the evil caused be not disproportionate to the evil averted'.

Arriving now at the object of this short elementary exercise in law, what of the thousands of Mau Mau terrorists killed during the black years of Kenya's emergency? How was this welter of killing interpreted in terms of well-tried, respected and extolled British justice? What were the circumstances that placed such wholesale destruction of human life beyond the reach of criminal courts? What were the 'excusable' facts that brought the slaughter within the framework (probably) of the most incorruptible and fair judicial system in the world and satisfied the most impeccable ethics of the legal bar?

Will the answers to these questions be found acceptable, I wonder!

First, I should mention that a person killed must be under what is termed the 'King's (or Queen's) Peace' for the taking of that life to be murder. It follows, therefore, that if nations are at war it is not an offence in law to kill the enemy—within certain reprehensible limits I might add. In Kenya there was no war, neither was there any declaration of hostilities. All persons in the colony were deemed to be enjoying the 'King's Peace' (actually it became the 'Queen's Peace' when Elizabeth II took over the throne on the death of her father). What raged throughout the colony and protectorate was more the nature of a civil war, though more aptly described as a rebellion. It was a seditious movement organized and encouraged to overthrow the lawfully established government of that day, meaning the Crown, by violent means.

The enactment of Emergency Regulations, by the Governor in Council, invested in the Governor very wide and, in many respects, dictatorial powers, to enact certain other regulations that would ensure the uninterrupted supply of the necessities of life and for the continued good order of the colony. Such regulations provided for arrest and search without a warrant on almost any pretext, detention without trials, the restriction of persons to certain areas, deportation of individuals who became *persona non grata* to the administration, and so forth. The important matter of proscribing the Mau Mau organization itself had, in fact, been taken care of some time before the State of Emergency was declared. Its existence as a movement 'dangerous to the government of the colony' had been recognized and officially proscribed by the Governor during

April 1950. After which it went underground and remained, not always well concealed either, in seditious incubation.

Without wishing to plunge into the welter of interesting and uncompromising powers providing for the maintenance of public order and suppression of rebellion contained in that hallowed ordinance, the Emergency Regulations of the Governor in Council, the following excerpt is quoted insofar as it serves as our first real clue to the 'excusable homicide' we are seeking to clarify. And, clearly, it is the only form of homicide allowable.

Regulation 2(6)(a) empowered thus:

If any person ... fails to satisfy such authorized officer, police officer or member of Her Majesty's forces as to his identity or as to the purpose for which he is in the place where he is found, such ... may, *if he reasonably suspects* that person has acted or is about to act in a manner prejudicial to the public safety or preservation of peace and order, *arrest and detain him* pending enquiries.

Another regulation that was to be invoked so universally and often by security forces engaged in anti-terrorist operations was one that dealt with 'Prohibited and Restricted areas'. It, too, is pertinent to this search for justification of the thousands of insurgents so uncompromisingly despatched:

... and if any person *fails to stop when challenged* or called upon to do so by a competent authority he shall be guilty of an offence and may be arrested without warrant.

a sub-section of which continues:

... may be removed from such place or area by any competent authority *who may use all necessary force* to effect such removal ...

It is to be at once appreciated that the latitude enjoyed by security forces, which included the police, was wide. The only proviso evidently was that the soldier or policeman had to know, or to suspect, on reasonable grounds, that a person had acted, or was about to act, in a manner prejudicial to public safety, etc. And, the Mau Mau society being at that time the only proscribed organization that instigated the public emergency, its members and adherents are the persons referred to. Thereby they were liable to be apprehended without a warrant or the usual processes of the law being put into motion. The regulation states 'all necessary force' may be used to effect the arrest of any person who fails to stop when challenged to do so. This relates particularly to persons found in Prohibited or Restricted areas. *The force included the use of firearms.*

The crux of this brief analysis of the 'legal destruction' of Mau Mau terrorists is now within reach, for, with but few inevitable exceptions, where terrorists were shot and killed, they were known, or suspected, on reasonable grounds, to have been members of, or to have consorted with, that proscribed society 'prejudicial to the public safety and the preservation of peace'—Mau Mau. They were persons who, when called upon to halt, attempted to evade apprehension by fleeing, so were prevented by force of arms. Make no mistake, to have chased and captured a fleeing terrorist was rarely, if ever, possible. Could a domestic animal pursue and catch a wild animal?

To try to reconcile such powers as these, especially of detention without trial, to the Convention of Human Rights and Fundamental Freedoms, a convention to which Kenya herself subscribed, was sticky, to say the least. It is certain that some violation of rights and freedoms was unavoidable. The Charter was, unfortunately for many of Britain's undeveloped overseas territories, one that protected the individual and not the community. However, the elimination with such apparent impunity of so many Kenyans did not disturb the guardians of the Convention anything like detention without trial, or restricting the liberty of the individual; thus one can only assume that international jurists were satisfied that laws and judicial integrity were not being flouted for the expedience of colonial domination.

Inquests held by coroners would return a finding of "Death occurred while evading apprehension when ...." or something equally as neat and indisputable. No witnesses, other than the party responsible for the killing, no further enquiries and no doubt.

Why no doubt? What were the 'reasonable grounds' for suspecting the deceased to have been a Mau Mau terrorist to such an extent that a soldier, policeman or stock-guard and so on, was given the omnipotent licence to shoot and kill? How did he know that the person he was calling upon to halt was known, or suspected, to have acted in a manner prejudicial to public safety, therefore liable to arrest? That he was, in fact, either a Mau Mau or was consorting with such persons?

And it is this answer that is so necessary to complete the enquiry into 'excusable homicide'. It is, moreover, an answer impossible to put in a nutshell. Asked why he believed a man was a drug addict, a doctor might reply: "The pupils of his eyes, his somnolent behaviour, his clammy hands, the stains on his fingers, his pulse beat, and such like." He could quote positive signs and symptoms. But, to answer the question "How did you know that he was a Mau Mau terrorist?" is to attach many conditions and the reply must be, "It all depended on the circumstances."

I shall not, even so, leave the question unattempted for it is vitally important that some sort of satisfactory answer be provided. Without one the whole argument that the shooting of terrorists was within the law and 'excusable' goes up the spout of ignominy.

The answer I shall divide into two parts—'statutory' and 'visual' identification of those 'reasonably suspected persons'. With regard to the first the reader is referred to my remarks in an earlier chapter anent those vast areas throughout the settled White Highlands that were designated as prohibited or restricted. They included the Aberdares and its moorlands, the slopes of Mount Kenya, Kipipiri, the Mau escarpment and many large gorges. This greatly facilitated the onerous task of security forces and they had, in consequence, fewer scruples. Virtually anyone seen in these emergency zones could be shot on sight. I shall, nevertheless, hasten to add that if a person found in such areas made no attempt to conceal himself or to flee it was incumbent upon his seekers to capture him, not kill him. Live terrorists were an unrivalled source of information anyway! It was not necessary to satisfy oneself that they were Mau Mau; merely by being in that particular zone justified a 'reasonable suspicion' that they were 'persons who had acted, or were likely to act, in a manner prejudicial to public safety, etc.' That was 'statutory' and any homicide occasioned by a contact in such circumstances would have been excusable in law.

The second part of the answer covering 'visual' identification will take a little longer for it is not only of considerable interest but also applicable in some measure to the first part of the answer.

At this point I must plead that those who belong to the 'purist' school of thought and who insist upon absolute rigidity of form and rule when it comes to the taking of human life may be in for a disappointment. The following portrayal must be, to some, imprecise and vague. I'm afraid there is, or was, no unequivocal yardstick; the decision was always made by the man on the spot. And, to have erred in one's judgement of the accepted regalia and characteristics of a Mau Mau 'baddy' was unavoidable. Yet, perhaps I may be allowed to assert that the occasions when one did err were as infrequent as to be of little consequence when considering the huge totals involved. There was never a great deal of evidence that was incontrovertible. So much that surrounded anti-terrorist operations was inconclusive, which is why the entire campaign was so hellishly frustrating. I would even go so far as to suggest that the French in Algeria and, more recently, the Americans in Vietnam were equally as frustrated—when was a South Vietnamese a Viet Cong rebel?

The truth is, there was such a distinct, such an unmistakable, difference between active forest gangsters (the militant members of Mau Mau) and the law-abiding tribesman in Kenya that security forces, or anybody for that matter, seldom needed to hesitate over a decision. Once seen they could not be mistaken for other than what they were. Physically there is no great difference in stature or appearance between a Kikuyu and other East African tribes, except possibly that the average Kikuyu tends to be slightly shorter. Therefore, no distinction could be made by recognizing a particular Kikuyu feature. It was quite simply the actual 'Mau Mau' characteristics that allowed for any distinction. The description of an average Mau Mau terrorist must, therefore, constitute the bulk of this, the second part of the answer. In any event it should provide an intriguing portrayal quite apart from its association with the legal indemnity we seek to establish.

It was sufficient in a sense to identify gangsters by their style of hair-do, plaited in little twirls all over the head and sticking up like a porcupine's quills (not nearly so long as Rastafarians), the purpose of this being to discourage infestation by lice. It was the hallmark of a Mau Mau gangster. If an adult, he might have displayed a ragged beard, though few Africans grow long beards. Clothes as such would not have been worn; to have distinguished them as such would have meant that the wearer had recently acquired the garments during a raid on some farmhouse. What was invariably worn was a garment that had originally been a coat or jacket but had become an intricate fabric of patches. The terrorist would treasure every scrap of material and carry a small bundle around with him. Whenever he had a spare moment, which was often, he would repair his clothes by using a sharp stick to make the holes then push his thread through. After several months of wear in the forests these garments were nothing more than hundreds of colourful patches sewn together and gave the wearer a clownish appearance that, in the circumstances, was undeserved and tragi-comic. As the months passed and ran into years the forest fighters of the Land Freedom Army came to appreciate the failings of orthodox clothing and showed a preference for animal skins. Such apparel, fashioned from leopard, duiker and monkey skins, were extraordinary examples of sartorial craftsmanship—durable and practical, wind-proofed, almost impervious to the chill drizzle of the moorlands and, above all, wonderful camouflage. Among the senior Mau Mau 'staff' there were few who did not swagger around in a suit of skilfully turned-out animal-hide clothing with a cap to match. Hounded fellows that they were, once on the body they were seldom removed, except, that is, for their partial removal for calls of nature!

Our terrorist's exclusive regalia that identified him with such certainty as the desperado he was would have been further confirmed by the absence of any form of footwear. Footwear was scorned both on tactical and physical grounds. Tactical because he was the better able to obliterate his tracks in bare feet, physical because the soles of his feet were comparable in toughness to the best leather that money could buy. On the soles of his massive, splayed, calloused and cracked monstrosities of feet was skin a quarter of an inch thick and tough as an elephant's hide. He could run undaunted over rock as rough as clinker in a blacksmith's furnace and just as hot. Vicious thorns, bamboo shoots, razor-sharp elephant grass, he was impervious to it all.

Such knowledge made my colleagues and I realize more fully just where we stood whenever it came to a chase over rugged country. We knew that our boots would let us down before their bare feet troubled them.

An outstanding feature that all but shouted aloud 'I'm a Mau Mau terrorist!' was his expression. Wild and furtive, the eyes wide and swivelling unceasingly from side to side, up and down, the mouth closed to improve his already phenomenally acute sense of smell, he was forever on the mark and ready to flee and would move with short, rapid strides.

He would, more often than not, be carrying a *panga* or a firearm, be it home-made or precision. It was usual, too, to carry a sack containing his pieces of biltong, boiled wheat and old bones. I suppose that, really, the overall characteristic that was most likely to resolve any doubt as to his identity was the stark and absolute destitution of anything civilized or refined about him. From his golliwog head down past his ragamuffin clothing to his hideous feet—that one half expected to display claws—his fugitive air and, finally, his smell, the whole composite picture of primitive savagery proclaimed his nefarious calling.

But his smell! An extra word must be written about this. If every other feature of recognition were denied his hunter, then his smell would suffice. There are certain odours that are almost tangible—the faintest whiff of roast beef and we can name it, fresh tar leaves us in no doubt, a carnation flower is inimitable, garlic? Well! Need I say more? They are definite smells immediately suggestive of their origin. Well, the smell that emanated from a Mau Mau terrorist was one of those exclusive ones. Take a pile of clothes that have been worn continually for a year and on which greasy hands and bloody *pangas* have been wiped day after day, take a few lumps of putrefying meat, some old bones and really high cheeses, include a vagrant who hasn't washed his body for months, stir all their respective smells together and add a pair of humming, sweaty socks. Then, to boost the resultant stink, set it in the middle of the pure, fresh unpolluted atmosphere of a pine forest. You then have the unriddable, all-pervading and unforgettable Mau Mau terrorist's special odour. And, if one happened to have been upwind and denied the identifying characteristic of his distinctive pong, then the supersonic manner in which he took flight would have left one in no doubt whatever.

If I have expatiated somewhat in order to adduce the evidence necessary to support the contention that the killing of three or four hundred terrorists a month was 'excusable homicide', I humbly apologize. I feel certain, however, the reader will agree that such a contentious topic merited elucidation.

It is, in spite of the foregoing passages, fitting that I append a final word or two in deference to the by no means insignificant number of detractors there were of Britain's colonial policies and her overseas civil servants. I propose also to append a message that was distributed among security forces by the Commander-in-Chief relative to the questionable treatment of Mau Mau. It will go a long way toward consolidating this particular topic.

It would be dishonest to say anything other than that instances of impetuous trigger activity or brutality were bound to occur. Not every soldier or policeman was a paragon of discipline or restraint.

After months of patrolling and ambushing in foul weather against a foe as wily as Mau Mau terrorists, it was inevitable that there were operational encounters where, despite some doubt as to an individual's identity, he was deemed to be Mau Mau and, 'bang-bang', eliminated. Again, he may have been a capturee who was glowing red-hot with information as to his gang's present location and food sources, etc. Possibly his captors were inclined at times to be rather impatient in their persuasive methods to elicit such information.

The message from the C-in-C, General George Erskine, shows that such excesses were not tolerated even if they did now and then occur. (*See* Appendix III)

And in his own admonition to police personnel the Commissioner, Mr M.S. O'Rorke, had this to say (*see* Appendix IV for full version):

"We have recently seen yet another shocking case of brutal handling of two Africans in custody proved in open court against three police inspectors of South Nyeri. I would remind you all that where evidence of brutality by police officers comes to light I shall continue to have no hesitation in submitting cases to the Attorney General for trial before a court of law no matter what their rank may be."

All very disquieting and harmful to Britannia's coveted image of fair play.

May we not conclude, therefore, that, even if some twelve thousand Mau Mau terrorists were killed during the years 1953 to 1956, they were not glory-killings or unnecessary, or doubtful or even wanton. No sane British policeman or soldier enjoys taking life and I am adamant that even if ordered to kill he is still guided by the maxim, "Is the evil I commit not disproportionate to the evil I seek to avert?" The young 'squaddie' would probably have couched it less pontifically—"If I don't stop this son-of-a-bitch breathing now, he will hack some poor bastard to pieces tonight." It all amounted to the same thing really.

As this book is, after all, more of a potpourri, there should be little protest if I go off at a quick tangent and narrate a short story of a personal experience that should do much to dovetail this particular chapter. Once again I would like to stress that the story could be equally true of the hundreds of other 'Kenya Cowboys' who were my contemporaries.

It relates to the capture of my first live Mau Mau and was a noteworthy experience in restraint.

While at my sub-divisional headquarters one afternoon tendering patrol reports and collecting mail, a strange-looking African Kikuyu was seen to walk into the Charge Office. He was interviewed by the station sergeant. I overheard him say that he had been attacked by a gang of about twenty Mau Mau at a point some five miles down the main road toward Naivasha. The gang, he said, had run off into the *kilileshwa* scrub on Waterloo Ridge, an area well known to me, having tracked stolen stock along it on numerous occasions. My ears pricked up sharp with curiosity.

This odd chap had the vague appearance of being a terrorist to me—his smell, guilty air, tatty clothing, hollow cow-horn drinking receptacle dangling from his waist; admittedly his hair was not Mau Mau-coiffured but then that was the reason he was able to walk along the main road without attracting undue attention. Two things were certain—he was frightened and his story was a fabrication. Why?

Being far from incurious I obtained permission for my Tracker Combat Team (such teams had recently been established and I had the command of one) to interview him and to check out his story.

Together we travelled along the highway to a spot about half a mile short of where he alleged that he'd been beaten and robbed. He said that he knew exactly where the gang had crossed the road to sprint over the open grazing land to the cover of thick *kilileshwa* scrub on a ridge about a quarter of a mile distant. His answers to my questions were inconsistent and I had a strong hunch that he had been consorting with a gang and had escaped. A rather unusual occurrence, but some weak members were wont to relinquish the hard life of forest gangsters.

We proceeded to the point where we were asked to believe the gang had jumped on him; even less feasible when I considered that it was a busy main road. In the dust and sparse grass of the *shamba* at the side of the roadway the tracks of several persons were picked up. My team assessed them as about ten hours old. Our informant said they were those of the gang and we followed them toward Waterloo Ridge. On the way I observed a piece of material; it was just the sort of remnant terrorists carried for repairing their clothes. My enthusiasm waxed greatly.

Once up on the ridge I commenced to sweep in a line along it in the direction that our dubious companion said his assailants had taken. He had by this time half-admitted that he had left the gang in that very area a few hours earlier. I was in the centre of the line which, with six of my askari, was strung out over some twenty-five yards. Then the askari on my right suddenly halted, beckoned to me imperatively, and then pointed eagerly to his right. With my Sterling S.M.G. cocked and at the ready I went down the line to the last man who was crouched and bristling behind a thorn bush. Following the direction of his outstretched arm, I saw, right on the edge of the ridge, huddled against a small, shady clump of bamboo, an African who looked to me unmistakably a terrorist. He was sitting with his head resting on his knees and twiddling with his hair. In front of him on the ground was a home-made rifle—it amounted to a butt roughly fashioned from wood with a length of piping attached, a piece of strong elastic affixed to a door bolt that had been sharpened to a point—that appeared to be quite harmless (except to the user!). He was totally oblivious of our presence so near by, which was a great credit to our patrolling skill, and could not have seen us approaching from the road across the open *shamba*.

Pushing the safety catch of my Sterling forward I levelled it at his head, stood up, and said, softly: "*Simama.*"

He could not have been more startled had a lion yawned right in front of him. Springing up and facing me he snatched for his 'toy', then dropped it and, putting his hands up in front of him, moaned, "*Hapana ua mimi. Hapana Mau Mau, hapana Mau Mau.*" (Don't kill me, I'm not a Mau Mau.)

My askari rushed in on him eagerly and I bade them lower their weapons and apply the safety catches. My own finger was nervously curled around the trigger of my gun and, looking about me disbelievingly, for I felt certain that others were in the vicinity somewhere, I went closer.

The first question to him was, "Where are the remainder of your gang?" He whimpered that they had moved on early that morning and that his *rafiki* (who we already had with us) had made the excuse they were sick and wished to rest up awhile. Just to make certain that what he said was true I ordered my team to make a thorough search of the immediate area. I then sat down about ten yards from this terrified fellow and led him to believe that I was going to kill him. I made him to understand that nobody would question his death and that I would say he was armed and had attempted to flee.

His eyes opened wide as he commenced to plead with me, reiterating again and again that he did not know where his gang was now. He went on to say that the gang had recently arrived from Nyeri and were on their way to join up with the self-styled 'Brigadier' Mwangi Wangai. In order to verify his sincerity and to satisfy myself that we would be wasting our time to comb the area for other members of his gang, I decided to test the scallywag's nerve. My own nerves were taut enough as it was and I was still wondering why it was I hadn't fired a burst when he was first sighted.

Menacingly I informed him that I was going to count up to ten and expected him to tell me the truth before I finished. As I counted I went through an elaborate display of preparing my weapon. I then stood up and levelled the gun at him, squinted along the sights, and closed the distance between us to about four yards. The effect of this studied preparation had a terrifying effect on him and he quaked visibly. He then covered his eyes, threw himself to the ground and started to sob and moan.

His performance convinced me; I was also a little ashamed. Even so, I was tense with anticipation. It was never easy to know the mind of a Mau Mau. They had taken beastly oaths to kill and were not easily disposed to renouncing the vows taken during the ceremony. Why the hell should I have believed him? He'd gotten himself into a tight corner and now the crocodile tears; the cowering wretch.

Slowly I lowered my gun, told him to *nyamaza*, then offered him a cigarette. At least, I thought, he might be suitable material for a 'pseudo-gangster'.

I was to learn later that he and his colleague had decided to desert their gang and had hung back early that morning after having gained Waterloo Ridge. Macharia, the one we had located on the ridge, was far too conspicuously Mau Mau to make the journey along the main road without getting himself lynched by Masai or some other unsympathetic tribesmen, so his friend, Gachau, had made the perilous trip alone and concocted the story of the robbery in order to have Macharia captured. I must say it was extremely provident for Macharia that my askari had behaved in such a disciplined manner—or were they overawed?—otherwise he might have been shot up something awful.

The moral of this story is, of course, that restraint was exercised and I like to think it was not just an isolated instance. For me, it was not to be the last time I spared terrorists caught with their trousers down. And, if the reader will accept the official figure of seventy-five thousand Mau Mau held in the emergency detention camps of Kenya, they must believe that the lives of countless numbers contacted in forests and remote places were humanely spared by security forces.

Chapter 11

The penalty for being a Kikuyu and the folly of employing one

In the Tetu location of the Kikuyu Land Unit not far from Nyeri in February of 1931, the same year that Jomo Kenyatta went to London as an ambassador of the Kikuyu Central Association—a visit that was to last for fifteen years—Mwangi was born in the round, grass-roofed, mud and wattle hut of his village headman father, Gichakau. He was Gichakau's seventh child delivered by his third and last wife. Mwangi's father, who had been a driver during the First World War with the King's African Rifles, spent most of his time in another hut with his second wife and her children. His mother was expected to tend Gichakau's maize gardens and to brew his beer. Life was singularly uneventful for him until the night his father was stabbed to death during a wild beer party in the village by a lover of his first wife. Mwangi was fifteen at the time of this incident and had been witness to it. He thoroughly enjoyed his visits to the Supreme Court in Nairobi to give evidence and never really felt much remorse for his father's inglorious end.

The elderly Kikuyu charcoal-burner accused of the murder, and who hailed from a neighbouring village, was convicted of manslaughter and sentenced to a long term of imprisonment. For many months after the trial Mwangi had basked the sunshine of the sudden fame and sophistication that his trips to the city had bestowed upon him. He had stood up to the lengthy examinations and cross-examinations of the *wazungus*, and had received money for his efforts. The youth of his village plied him with questions and admired his quiet confidence. Mwangi grew in social stature as his affection for shallow village life diminished.

However, some months later, odd occurrences began to upset

the even tenor of the family's kraal. Sheep and goats disappeared, their grass hut burst mysteriously into flames one night, then an elder sister fell ill and died, unaccountably, shortly after a visit by a peculiar withered old Kikuyu, who said he was from Mount Kenya and was enquiring into the presence of any angry spirits in the Gichakau kraal.

It became dreadfully apparent that the relatives of the incarcerated slayer of Mwangi's father were engaged in powerful witchcraft. And, as the mother was too poor to employ the services of a professional witchdoctor to counter the disastrous spells and evil curses cast upon her and the kraal, there was nothing else for it but to destroy her property and quit the village with her family. Amid a throng of curious and silent onlookers, the ancestral kraal was destroyed by fire, the few goats and sheep were tethered together and led away by the eldest child and Mwangi carried a cage of noisy chickens. Thus, the third wife of the late Gichakau plus all her progeny straggled out of the village they knew so well just as the sun rose over the lower slopes of Mount Kenya. Mwangi was filled with hate and fear for the intangible forces that had conspired to depose them from their inherited patch of Kenya. The family trekked many miles and, late in the afternoon, deposited itself just inside the forest on the outskirts of Githunguri. Wanjiru, the mother, wasted no time at all in offering her favours to the first eligible bidder who had a house in which the Gichakau brood could continue to grow.

The new location appealed strongly to Mwangi for Githunguri was the place where the Kikuyu Central Association had established a teachers' training college. There were continual arrivals and departures of leading political luminaries for conferences; the college was well known as the retreat of nationalistic agitators and the well-oiled hub of subversion. In the evenings these distinguished politico-educationalists would perambulate in the nearby villages to be wined and dined, and ungrudgingly supplied with coy Kikuyu maidens. They spoke casually, though graphically, of their travels and experiences in other parts of the colony and abroad. And, when such eminent Kikuyus as Fred Kubai, Peter

Koinange, even the great 'Messiah', Jomo Kenyatta, who had returned from his self-imposed fifteen years' exile and was now an accomplished mob-orator, strode majestically about the college grounds, there was always an awed audience of villagers.

Yet, Mwangi's mother drank more and more heavily, potent brews too, like distilled honey and wheat. His life became steadily more intolerable as the stories of his celebrated appearance before a *wazungu* court in Nairobi filtered through into his new environment. The stories were no longer kind; they had become distorted and the version that percolated out of the original circumstances was that Mwangi's father had been killed in self-defence; that the knife had been wrested from his hand and used against him. Mwangi was hearing the word 'stooge' used in a less stagey context to that he had hitherto known it, and the ridicule that accompanied it made his life miserable.

Most of his days he spent high up in the silent, still forests of the Aberdares, searching for honey and the furry tree squirrel. Occasionally he would snare a gazelle, and, one bright, breathless afternoon, he even succeeded in placing an arrow in the hide of a young rhino. It had charged off into the bush and he'd been afraid to hunt it down. Mwangi had heard of the many fatal encounters with rhino and his arrows and spear were inadequate weapons to pit against a wounded animal of the ferocity of a rhino.

His mother, Wanjiru, like all Kikuyu women, was contentment itself clearing and planting the virgin forest land. She would, inevitably, reap rich harvests twice a year for several years and then, when the earth was exhausted, she would leave the plot for nature to rejuvenate in the course of time, and move on to another virgin plot. The forests were vast; she had no time for the horrid counsel of Forestry officials who wanted to preserve the forests to ensure a perennial supply of water on the plains. The *wazungu* was on the plains and if he had insufficient water that was his worry. It was subsistence farming with no care for the future or of land husbandry. Her abiding preoccupation was to provide enough food for today. All her fellow tribeswomen applied themselves in similar fashion so why shouldn't she perpetuate the tribal practice? What was to *serikali* a matter of agricide was to her survival.

The school that Mwangi had attended for some five erratic years at Ihururu in the Tetu location, run by missionaries, had suddenly closed down in 1944. He remembered seeing the quiet, dignified, white-robed fathers climbing into several trucks after a final, brief service in the small church. He had assisted in carrying the few trunks of the Reverend McAlister (Bwana Bleshew, as Mwangi knew him) from his white-washed *rondavel* quarters to the waiting truck. The Reverend McAlister had patted his head and said, in a sad voice: "Bless you, my boy, watch for the serpent in the long grass nearby."

He had not understood the full reasons for the departure of the missionaries but had known for some time that his parents and other elders in the villages were displeased with them. This he knew to be because of their insistence that the tribe discontinue its age-old custom of *kurua*, or circumcision, insofar as females were concerned. The church had repeatedly declared, solemnly, that it was anti-Christian and *shenzi* to circumcise females. Mwangi could never quite make up his mind whether the missionaries were just plain stupid or were deliberately trying to insult his tribe by making such wild assertions. Female circumcision was, as far as he was concerned, as essential to the tribe's social and cultural status as was male circumcision, and the missionaries, for some irrationality, countenanced the practice on males. The mission had also angered his people by preaching that polygamy was an evil thing and that all who practised it would be banned from its churches. What possible connection the wholly dignified domestic circumstance of a man having more than one wife had with God and Christianity, Mwangi was, like his fellows, unable to deduce.

Mwangi had enjoyed the indefinite holiday that followed the closure of the school at Ihururu. Then, towards the end of 1946, there was a colossal gathering one day at the foot of a hill not far from Githunguri. He joined his mother and brothers and sisters, all equipped with an extra foot of sugar cane, and was quite thrilled by the stupendous assembly. He remembered sitting on a rock chewing his cane and listening to a Kikuyu who was called the

Reverend Daidi Maina. This berobed, bespectacled, deep-voiced cleric had exhorted them all to support their African churches and continued to explain that a new church, the African Independent Pentecostal Church, had been established. There had been a lot of loud singing after which the Reverend Daidi Maina had blessed the multitude in the name of *Ngai.*

He enrolled at the school and church that opened shortly after in some old missionary buildings, but he was now sixteen years old and not over much interested in schooling; worse, he didn't care for the stagnant life of the village. Seeing so many well-dressed and ambitious people arriving at Githunguri encouraged him to make up his mind to join those thousands of his compatriots who had already travelled up into the Highlands of the white man and sought work. As far as Mwangi was concerned, whether it was the missionaries or the revolutionary Kikuyu Independent Schools Association, he just was not interested. They were patently politico-religious in construction and the set-up served only to confuse him. In the spring of 1947, Mwangi walked out of his mother's hut with a small bundle and journeyed to Nairobi.

The city he had explored to some extent during those weeks he had attended the Supreme Court as a witness, but he still found himself dissatisfied with it. He revolted against the urban maelstrom, the hot tarmacadam, the rushing motor cars and the nattily dressed businessmen. He could find no decent accommodation, neither could he find work. There were robbers and criminals everywhere. He toured the European residential areas of Kabeti, South-hill and Parklands but all the gardens were well tended and he became sorely tried resisting the temptation to kick away the many fierce dogs that chased him from one street to the next.

Furthermore, he had the not entirely inexplicable feeling that there was an unhealthy political movement spawning in the muck of Nairobi back-streets. That movement, called the Kenya African Union (successor of the banned Kikuyu Central Association) held out a demanding hand, bullying, and gave one no peace. By the summer of that same year Mwangi found himself just outside Naivasha, having obtained a lift in a lorry of the Kenya Farmers'

211

Association. It had cost him a shirt and the old jacket he was left with had to suffice his sartorial needs.

He met a co-villager who was employed by the East African Railways as a linesman and spent the night with him in a railway *lhandi* between Naivasha and Gilgil. The following morning he shared a ganger's trolley with him as far as Ol Kalou. On the way, having looked right down into many abysmal gorges and clung to their steep slopes, he observed, a few miles beyond Ole Olondo station, a large, red-roofed farmhouse about a mile from the line. All around it the fields were neatly tilled and planted, cattle grazed peacefully in slowly moving herds, the water of a dam shone enticingly by the side of a solid thicket of cedar. He could see at least three tractors crawling across the *shambas* pulling shares or fertilizer sprinklers, there were miles of *boma* fencing criss-crossing the wide acres. He spotted a small bevy of *bibbies* with bundles of *kuni* on their heads emerging from a wooded gully close to the line and thought they looked happy and healthy. Mwangi made up his mind to work on that farm and the next day applied. He became a squatter on the *shamba* of *Bwana* Dalton and eventually graduated to be a tractor boy.

He liked the work and never regretted his decision to forsake the reserve. The unpromising political issues that soon began to rage disturbingly throughout the colony concerned him but little. He'd been provided with a hut and a plot of land by his European *bwana*, he drank his can of *tembo* whenever the opportunity occurred on weekends, and found that he could lie with the occasional *bibby* with less fear or difficulty than would have been the case in his reserve. It may be said that he probably felt a vague sort of hero-worship for Jomo Kenyatta, who was hailed as the 'great saviour' of the Africans, but what that stormy person stood for ultimately was way beyond Mwangi's ken. For the next six years he applied himself earnestly on Dalton's two-thousand-acre farm.

Though well aware that many of his tribe held the opinion that all the white man's land should be seized and shared among themselves, he neither disputed nor did he endorse such opinion. He didn't really care what the views or intentions of his compatriots were, just so long as they did not upset his satisfactory life. He now possessed a bicycle, a small radio and had some good clothes, all of which he had no wish to lose. It became inescapably plain, however, that more sinister events were afoot and Mwangi's anxiety gradually increased. There were frequent meetings, secret ones at night, then oathing ceremonies at which his kith and kin made dreadful vows that, if necessary, they would kill the white man to win back their land. Money was collected, or rather extorted, with an increasingly irritating regularity. There was beating-up and even killing of those foolhardy enough to condemn the activities of the money collectors and oath administrators. Mwangi himself had been approached once and instructed to watch closely his *bwana's* habits, where he kept his firearms and his money. In Nairobi there were assassinations and strikes; then, toward the end of 1952, he heard that a European had been murdered by Mau Mau on the Kinangop plateau. This perturbed him greatly— the Kinangop was not very far away. And, more fearful still, he began to hear terrible stories of a plot by Mau Mau to massacre all the Europeans.

Then the first oaths were administered to him, beastly and nauseating ceremonies they were. He'd been ashamed but awed; he felt that, as they had been administered against his will, they were not binding. Such naivety! He soon found that what the ceremony had lacked in authenticity was duly compensated for through subsequent intimidation. This he was made to acknowledge after a very brief interval when, having been asked by a Meru *dhoby-boy* from the neighbouring farm to steal a jerry-can of petrol, he failed to oblige; he found a gang of thugs waiting for him in his hut that night and they beat him up badly. The next day he supplied the petrol they wanted—two days later his own *bwana's* maize store went up in smoke and flames, though not until after most of the maize had been carried off by a gang of strange, wild Kikuyus who had emerged from the Wonjoi forests. Mwangi was unfeignedly concerned by these untoward events and became very reserved; he even went so far as to entreat Mr Dalton to allow him to sleep in the workshop, without, of course, explaining his reasons too fully.

His *bwana*, unfortunately, thought his plea was to enable him to pilfer tools and spares. Mwangi's heart and soul resisted the insidious poison of Mau Mau desperately, almost without knowing why.

But the emulsion of Kikuyu subversion slowly coated his imperviousness to revolt and softened it. Police had made a number of raids on the farm since the maize store incident and several of his fellow 'squatters' were arrested and repatriated to their reserves. This softened his hard shell still more and his sympathies were at last being touched. One dark, star-studded night, the local leader of the Mau Mau 'Royal Family' section put in a personal appearance carrying a Sten gun. Mwangi had listened enthralled to his stories of a meeting with a notorious Kikuyu, called General China, high up on the moorlands of the Aberdares, and of the bloody skirmishes with the *serikali* over in Fort Hall and Nyeri. He was just a trifle unbelieving yet prepared to join the murmurs of acclamation when he heard that so many white settlers were leaving their farms and returning to their own countries. "Very soon," he heard Dishon Kibe hiss, in the light of a flickering fire in the middle of the smoke-filled hut, "all these prosperous farms will be ours, the equipment, herds of cattle, motor cars and—of untold importance—the land, the fertile land that has been stolen from us, will all be ours."

He, Mwangi, had his name inscribed in the 'big book' as serving the great Field Marshal 'Mbaria Kanui', who was shortly to inherit over half the fabulous Delamare estates. It was during this exciting visitation by such a prominent Mau Mau leader that Mwangi learned of a most significant matter, and it served to further undermine his imperviousness to the aims and ideals of the anti-European terrorist organization. This brash, but disarmingly confident local leader, Dishon Kibe, spoke of a co-villager of Mwangi's, a lively, intelligent and rascally Kikuyu who was born in the Tetu location some eleven years before him—one Dedan Kimathi. Colourful accounts were rendered between cups of *tembo* of how Dedan was organizing and training the Land Freedom Armies on the slopes of Mount Kenya and in the heart of the Aberdare forests.

This swashbuckling character had been seen by Mwangi but a few times only while still a child in the Tetu location (though he had known the family as Wachiuru), and he had not been left undernourished of tales of that man's subversive exploits, of his ruthlessness and his cunning. Mwangi could not resist informing the smoky hut's crowded circle that he had grown up not far from the Wachiuru (Kimathi) kraal; the group of squatters and terrorists looked at him warmly; he again enjoyed a measure of pride.

During the ensuing days his thoughts were confused and excited. Was it really going to come true? Were the white *bwanas* being pushed out of Kenya? Would all these wonderful farms belong to the Kikuyus? Yet, still he doubted the rumours he heard. The *serikali* had powerful weapons and many askari; they would all suffer much if those *kali sana* askari came to *shambas* and labour lines. Mwangi was now sitting on the fence and he kept his irksome dilemma at bay only by working hard during the day and keeping to his hut at night. He found that he was suddenly avoiding his *bwana*, too. It had somehow become difficult to look him in the eyes.

Tension grew everywhere as the reports of disturbances and of assassinations multiplied. Then, in next to no time at all, everyone was talking about an 'emergency' having been declared, and of a great purge going on in Nairobi. The following week he was subjected to a humiliating screening in a tent near Ol Kalou police station along with hundreds of other Kikuyu, Meru and Embu tribesmen. He had to be photographed and was later given a *kipande* which he had to carry at all times (or be arrested and handled roughly at the police station). There were curfews imposed and numerous searches throughout the squatter lines on all farms. Soldiers flooded into the area and ambushed tracks and bridges; there were hundreds of arrests and repatriations of his tribesmen and women. He came to hear that the 'Messiah', Jomo Kenyatta, was in custody at Kapenguria awaiting trial for something or other. There were orders that no Africans could enter the forests any more unless they wanted to risk being shot. Mwangi detected a seriousness in the faces of the white *bwanas* that wasn't there before and they were seen to carry their firearms with an aggressive air. The paradise that he'd enjoyed for the last six years was shattered, his innocence was disregarded—he was a Kuke and all he could do was wait until his turn came. It did, some four months later.

Since the huge round-ups and arrests in Nairobi and the sporadic murders on the Kinangop and at Mwiega, a lull had set in. For over a month there had been no raids or assassinations. Mwangi allowed himself to believe that Mau Mau had been crushed by the enormous heel of *serikali*, but he was scoring magpies only; Mau Mau was still only in its suckling stages.

One day in March, 1953, while he sat bouncing up and down on the seat of his tractor that was pulling a rake across the *shamba*, and thinking of his promised night with Njeri, his girlfriend, he was approached by several dirty and unkempt persons. Among them he identified members of a Mau Mau gang he knew to be in hiding in a cave on a rocky hill on Potgeiter's *shamba*. They were raiding that *bwana's* wheat stores almost nightly and demanding clothing and money from the squatter labour of all the farms round about. Two nights ago they had crowded rudely into the labour lines of his own *bwana's* farm insisting on having women—they were quickly provided.

After setting fire to his tractor, they ordered him to follow and off they all sprinted into the nearby gully. It was nightfall before the group, together with the wide-eyed Mwangi, entered the murky cave on Potgeiter's *shamba*. The first thing that the new recruit had to do was turn out all his pockets. The few shillings he had were scooped up and that was the last he saw of them. Likewise with his tobacco and matches. A number of tatty photographs were forthwith destroyed. A shirt he was wearing—he'd only bought it recently too—was taken off his back and put on by a small, ugly gangster called Kariuki, who was the leader.

Within a month Mwangi's hair was proudly coiffed in genuine Mau Mau fashion, he having spent many idle hours combating both boredom and lice by twirling strands and plaiting them. He carried a *panga* and honed it religiously, he had produced a pretty good imitation pistol from wood and gas piping—no ammo though. He also carried a small bag made from a goat's bladder in which were kept pieces of biltong for emergencies. In no time at all he acquired the hard-core terrorist's silent, almost gliding, swift way of walking, his head rotating ceaselessly from side to side, always ready in a trice to charge off at lightning speed and not to pause until absolutely certain that he could not be tracked down.

He learnt to treasure such articles as matches as he would a piece of gold—and to keep them dry; he developed the soles of his feet so that he could disdain footwear in any type of terrain, he became adept at the ham-stringing and noiseless killing of cattle, at sectioning the carcasses and drying the meat. He became accustomed to living on a diet of meat and blood, roast maize and boiled wheat; no more the daily monotony of *posho* and beans. He taught himself to sit for hours in one position without heeding cramp or stiffness, to sleep as lightly as a wild animal and eat as ravenously as one. Mwangi discovered in himself, if not exactly a predilection for the terrorist's forest life, then the capacity for making the most of a destiny he was powerless to reject. He began to indulge in something that hitherto had never been either possible or necessary—to commune with himself. He did what the majority of forest gangsters found themselves unwittingly doing, identifying themselves with nature and her fauna and flora. Their weaknesses were magnified, their vulnerability exposed, their superiority tested. They could not conquer the forces of nature or her elements—they could only hope to come to terms. Their survival depended upon how highly perceptive they could develop their senses, to exist on edible roots and berries, to avoid the bigger game and sense danger, to harden themselves to the biting cold at night and laugh off the viciousness of the mosquito and the horse fly. They were unutterably stripped of every vestige of sophistication or refinement; life was steadily boiled down to its basic ingredient, self-survival. And yet, the raids had to be planned and the *wazungus* had to be harried. The loyal labour had to be scared either off the farms and back to their reserves, or recruited into the gangs, or killed. There were military and police patrols to ambush and cattle to steal. There were firearms in unguarded farmhouses to locate, too. The battle was on and the effort had to be unrelenting. He who shied from the unpleasant or arduous would find scant mercy from the gang's leader; a strangling rope would be dropped over his head with grim aplomb and pulled tight.

Mwangi took the terrible *Batuni* (killer) oath during his first dazed month of gang life and he'd never forgotten the long safari he'd made with several other initiates to a palatial hideout far up on the Aberdare moorlands.

After lying torpidly about on improvised litters for two days and weathering two minor alarms—one when an aircraft flew low over the area several times, and the other when a patrol of askari threaded its way along a game track on the far side of a valley—everyone was shepherded to a grassy clearing just at dusk. In the centre of it was the most elaborate ceremonial archway and oathing paraphernalia ever seen by the initiates. The oath administrator, Mwangi was informed, was none other than the famous witchdoctor, Kingori, whose prophetic dreams and visions were legend throughout Kikuyu-land. The array was frightful and noisome. There was a splendidly constructed tunnel leading from the archway of banana leaves and ferns, at the end of which blazed a large fire. A few yards from the fire, sat on a platform fashioned from bamboo poles, with regal unconcern and roving eye, was a person he'd heard so much about—General China. He was flanked by half a dozen large, well-dressed and scowling guards, all carrying rifles.

What an honour! General China was among the most noteworthy characters in the Mau Mau hierarchy, one of the top three in fact, and had made a safari from his own domain on the slopes of Mount Kenya to preside over this massive *Batuni* oathing ceremony. Not only were there going to be oaths administered to novices but the general was going to appoint official administrators, promote members to higher rank, execute traitors, read out the orders of the day, and have himself a wonderful time in general.

Until the early hours the oathing went on, with due observation for intervals of drinking. Mwangi was, in his turn, subjected to untold degradation. The phantasmagoria of that hideous night would remain with him for the rest of his life. Nothing could ever erase the repugnant impressions, nothing could ever degrade him more, not even the killing of Europeans; and that, of course, was the whole stupendous significance behind the sordid exercise— when the time came his poor conscience would be less likely to trouble him.

Some time the following day, after having rejoined his own section of initiates from Ol Kalou, he was notified of his transfer at the request of one 'Field Marshal' Mbaria Kanui. This self-styled commander had been present at the mighty gathering and had asked that Mwangi be assigned to him as a personal valet. He straightaway took his leave of Section 11 of the 3rd Mburu Ngebo Army and joined his new master, the supreme commander of all Mau Mau fighters operating on Kipipiri and the upper Rift Valley, renowned for his moderate outlook, his leniency and his harem of pretty girls. He was, nevertheless, a strict leader and one who insisted on punctuality, orderliness and discipline in his camps. Tough, he was ruthless when required, but thought to be quietly intelligent. Of paramount merit, he had, like many other Mau Mau leaders, a strange faculty for dreaming dreams in which he was forewarned of danger. This faculty endeared him to his men, and to Mwangi, who became his 'batman'.

What with the wide gap between his two upper front teeth, and being a seventh child (a lucky omen with Kikuyus), Mwangi considered himself fortunate indeed. He'd obviously been selected for such a position because of his clean habits and propensity for the milder forms of terrorism; his preference being for scene-shifting and welfare as opposed to the fighting, raiding and killing. So, for the next eighteen months or so our ex-tractor boy fetched and carried for the 'Field Marshal'. He lived intimately at all times with him in their various hideouts and saw to it that the harem was kept in order.

The two developed a happy relationship; there was mutual trust and the twenty-two-year-old terrorist valet respected his master's pertinacity for fussing and grooming; Mwangi did not let him down or disappoint him—yet.

As the months passed he learned discreetly to guard Mbaria and to accomplish the many secret and often difficult forest calls. By degrees he almost came to believe that Mau Mau was in the ascendancy and that he really would one day work for Mbaria on the rich Delamare estates around the shores of Lake Elementita.

Between his ministerings to the 'Field Marshal' and V.I.P. visitors, 'Private' Mwangi managed to enjoy occasional romps with the women in the camp—though he had to be quite certain that they were only those that the 'boss' had cast aside. None of this, however, was ever really able to atone for his dislike of the rough life and never knowing when the next decent meal would appear before him. At times, when the gang was stretched thin, he would have to take a turn with the cattle-rustling parties and he hated it. He cringed and trembled every time aircraft droned overhead; when they dropped bombs he was palsied and, like most other terrorists, could do nothing but lie close to the ground and pray hard to *Ngai.* The tense atmosphere of the camp whenever a security force patrol was in the vicinity was intolerable, neither could he tolerate the wet or cold nights, or the lean days when he had to suck old bones or chew a piece of maggoty meat or the roots of plants. In short, Mwangi was a poor specimen of Mau Mau for its militant wing. He was convinced that the white settler had too much land for his own needs but was privately unshakeable in his belief that trying to reverse the situation with terrorism was unworkable and wrong.

During May of 1955, the *serikali* continually sent aeroplanes to fly low over the forests. These planes 'shouted' to them in their hideouts below and the voice heard was that of a European who spoke excellent Kikuyu:

"... Many of your comrades have surrendered ... they have realized that it is wiser to work with the government and to destroy Mau Mau ... you have suffered from the bombs and machine-gunning by the planes ... they will return again and again. For the next three days you may surrender without fear of being shot … no patrols will enter the forest … carry with you a green branch and walk into the nearest police or army camp … you have three days … if you do not surrender then you will die …"

Always it was the same—"surrender or die". The planes had shouted it so many times that he felt they must know he and his gang were there, knew their exact location in fact. It was all very unnerving. Mwangi had been told that the person who did the 'sky-shouting' was a police officer and they called him *Kinanjui* (this was Ian Henderson of the Special Branch, to whom credit is attributed for the pseudo-gangster operations that brought the emergency to a much earlier close). Throughout previous months this person, *Kinanjui*, had made repeated excursions into the Aberdare forests to discuss surrender terms. He had been accompanied, too, by a traitor, 'General' China, of all people, who much to the chagrin of all terrorists, had surrendered very early on in the fight. Like his fellows, Mwangi had an uneasy respect for *Kiranjui* but still found it impossible to believe that the *serikali* would sincerely permit them all to pluck off green branches and walk out of the forests carrying them. The askari would sure to be waiting with their weapons trained on them.

Mbaria Kanui and his deputies compelled all those in the hideout to lie down and press their hands over their ears whenever the aircraft flew overhead sky-shouting. During that month the guards were ever more alert; gang members who were away from camp for an inordinate period of time were executed as soon as they set foot inside it. It was impossible to take any form of leave of absence or to visit other gangs. Mbaria himself ceased to exchange visits with other leaders and if any strange terrorists were sighted in the forests, regardless of how genuine they looked, they were avoided; the gang became for many weeks isolated and disconnected from the glorious Land Freedom Army it was once such a proud part of. There was an ever-diminishing trust and if gang members were detailed for a raid in the settled areas and were not back in camp by the time allotted them, then the whole gang would decamp and move on to another hideout many miles away. More and more attention was paid to the trapping of wild game and fishing in the forest streams. They were on the defensive, yet they still constituted a serious threat to the security of European settlers and were capable of fight.

Then, early one morning near the end of June 1955, one member of a food party of five returned alone to the hideout, he had a bullet wound in his shoulder and recounted, not at all uniquely in those days, an encounter the party had had with a patrol on the *shamba* they went to raid. As far as he was aware the remainder of the party had been killed. That night Mwangi sidled across to this unhappy and discouraged companion and they spoke in low voices of their satiation of forest life and of Mau Mau as hunted animals. Chege, the wounded survivor, knew that he'd be unable to stop the infection that had already inflamed his wound and was throbbing with pain. Mwangi knew that the gang would become more hunted, hungrier, more fanatical and steadily less offensive. They made a dramatic compact to desert the gang.

On the morning of the last day of June they both slipped out of the forests of Kipipiri carrying green branches and surrendered themselves to the nearest police post. Before breakfast they were at Gilgil police station chatting and smoking cigarettes with the Tracker Combat Team based there, who were eagerly de-briefing such a rare couple; and from 'Mister' Kanui's outfit too. Well! Well!

I would like for the moment, in order to complete the picture being presented of the antecedents of an average Mau Mau terrorist, to return to Mwangi's ex-employer, Mr Dalton, and his farm. We will therefore leave our disillusioned surenderee with the T.C.T. for a while. He will join us again later after his defection has been fully exploited.

Mr Dalton's nature was an easy-going one, and, having been

farming in the highlands of Kenya since his retirement from the army in 1936, he liked to think that he had the patience necessary for the employment of African labour. His dealings with them were seldom haughty; he administered in a most equable manner. But, that afternoon in March 1953, when he stood staring blankly at his blackened and smoking tractor he felt an all-consuming rage. His bitterness would have been assuaged somewhat had he seen Mwangi lying by the side of it with his head split open; he'd at least have been assured, more or less, that his tractor driver had been loyal. It was just the contrary though—Mwangi had disappeared and, when by next morning he still hadn't turned up, Dalton was forced reluctantly to concede that the Mau Mau had recruited another spirited and youthful member.

"Such a pity, too," he groaned to the police officer who arrived later to investigate the occurrence. "He was quite a cheerful and energetic worker."

The police were provided with a description of Mwangi. Under the heading 'Unusual Features', was written 'large gap between upper front teeth'—and Dalton had added, conversationally, "One day I told the scoundrel that the English considered such a feature to be lucky. His only comment was that everything was *shauri ya mungu,* and I suppose he was right in a way."

As was proved, in the fullness of time, Mwangi was a lucky fellow, very lucky indeed.

The dejected Mr Dalton, though a fearless hunter of game and proficient marksman, tireless and dedicated farmer and known to be unflinching in adversity, was also negligent. His various firearms were to him as the prized rods and reels were to an angler. They adorned the walls of his house and were propped in corners.

With twelve months of the emergency passed, the exceedingly stringent legislation apropos the care and custody of firearms notwithstanding, there were still a disconcertingly large number of seasoned settlers who preferred to remain the best judges of their African labour's loyalty to *Bwana*, Queen and Country, and weapons continued to disappear. The penalty for loss through negligence had rocketed to £200 and should, by the reckoning of many, have been £2,000.

Dalton's Kuke ex-tractor boy was, quite naturally, intimately acquainted with his habits, the geography of the farmhouse, the alarm system and action taken consequent to an alert. The security set-up on the farm amounted to a Kipsigis Special Constable who sat in a tower that was situated between the labour lines, *boma* and farmhouse. He was issued with a whistle and a spear and in the tower was a powerful torch that he could use. If the whistle was blown with long blasts at night, Dalton would tug a lanyard attached to the base of a distress rocket supported in a bracket just outside his bedroom window. Having sent the rocket soaring into the night sky to burst into three red stars, he would, together with his wife and fifteen-year-old son, plus the house guard—a loyal Somali—take up position at the window.

Just a year almost after his introduction to Mau Mau terrorism, Mwangi was detailed by the leader, Mbaria Kanui, to accompany a section of the gang that were briefed to attack the Dalton *shamba*. He was very distressed about this but had felt for some time that sooner or later it had to happen. The gang had not forgotten the information that Mwangi had poured out in a nervous torrent during his first few confused hours with them. The 'positive action' element of the gang assumed that Dalton still kept his firearms festooned about the house, and, although Mwangi had successfully evaded participation in the many raids executed by his lively gang and had clung slavishly to the skirts of his master, this was one action that he had to involve himself in—as guide and adviser.

One dark, wet and blowy night, in April 1954, the police inspector from Spinner's Post raced to the Dalton farm with his askari after a distress rocket had burst luridly above it. He found the owner and his family crouched on the balcony with an assortment of weapons poking over the top. There was no attack and all was quiet except for the mournful lowing of cattle from over at the *boma*, which was the reason for Dalton firing off the rocket. Together with Dalton the police inspector hurried across the two hundred yards to the watchtower. At the foot of it they stumbled upon the lifeless body of the old Kipsigis sentry, a deep gash extended from the front of his head to the nape of his neck, his whistle hung uselessly from its grubby piece of string, now enlivened with spots of blood. Bounding on to the *boma* they were appalled at the next hideous clue of Mau Mau presence on the farm—hamstrung cattle!

Their dark shapes could be discerned here and there in half-sitting postures. Some were shuffling on the raw ends of their slashed haunches and lowing piteously. Many bore yawning *panga* slashes across their flanks, tails were severed and udders were hanging by a thread of skin in the mud of the *boma*.

Shot after shot echoed away across the silent wheat fields and rumbled up and down the valleys of the Aberdares as Dalton and the sympathetic inspector moved from beast to beast.

"Good God!" snarled the inspector. "If only these *ngombes* were Mau Mau instead." He laid down his torch and reloaded his revolver for the third time.

Out of a *boma* of thirty-six fine Ayrshires only nine were separated as being likely to respond to veterinary treatment. The other twenty-seven lay twitching, each bearing its terrible wounds and displaying a neat, small bole in the centre of its forehead. After another circuit of the *boma* to ensure that all were quite dead, Dalton stood back and rested against the *boma* fence. His fury was pent up within him and the choking desire for vengeance was impotent.

He almost sobbed. "Ten years' labour wasted; how can I carry on? It's impossible, the *shenzi* swine. They haven't even bothered to take any; it's sheer bloody-mindedness ..." and so forth did he intone through clenched teeth.

The shooting had attracted other police and army personnel to the farm and very soon all were huddled in eager conference amid the carnage now illuminated by the twin shafts of light from a tractor that had been brought up.

Where were the ambushes and stops to be laid?

Why had no cattle been driven off?

Were the bastards on their way to another farm?

Was this a diversionary ruse?

At this juncture Mrs Dalton strode calmly out of the darkness cradling a heavy Mauser repeater; her face was taut and drawn, her eyes looked tired.

She addressed her husband: "Eric, dear, Musa has just reported that the gang have broken into several of the squatter huts and, according to him, there's a big *shauri*." She completed her report by saying that Richard, their son, had gone over with some farm guards to check.

Mwangi Gichakau and his fellow bandits, meanwhile, had arrived on the far side of the farmhouse and were creeping up to it, hugging the shadows. Ten sinister figures glided from the milking shed, past the water tank, to the back door of the house. Mwangi's guilt flooded his tortured conscience as he stepped inside the familiar kitchen—how often he had shared a cup of *chai* therein with the Kikuyu cook in bygone days—then to the parlour where he used to wait, cap in hand, to receive instructions from Dalton or to explain some technical fault on his tractor. He passed to the balcony and looked wildly across towards the cattle *boma*; he could see the lights of torches and hear the drone of excited conversation. He felt sick with tension.

The audacious gang threw itself upon the Somali house guard they found cowering in the pantry and left him pouring out his life and brains. They ransacked and looted every room, smashed open drawers and lockers until they found what they were after in a locked wardrobe in the bedroom—an old, but still very serviceable, Martin-Express 375 double-action rifle. An additional item of priceless booty was a pair of Zeiss binoculars snatched off the mantle-shelf, complete with case. 'Captain' Moses, the leader of this intrepid and successful expedition, took gleeful possession of these two prizes; he then ordered the final touch of vandalism. A pressure lamp was smashed down on a settee which blazed up hungrily, putting the finishing polish on the scene of havoc and terror. The glistening, black rebels evaporated into the night again, delightedly slashing and chopping at everything they passed.

The valiant posse of security forces, headed by the distraught Mr

Dalton, was soon tearing back from the *boma* and labour lines to the blazing farmhouse, pistols in hand and firing illuminating Very pistol cartridges into the air. Cursing their gullibility, they rapidly cordoned the inferno—it was already too late to enter as choking clouds of smoke billowed forth and kept them at a distance. Then, to conclude the villainous scene of unforgettable drama, several rounds of ammunition, obviously left lying carelessly about the house, started exploding; this totally unexpected peril tended to add to the general confusion and sent the cordon scurrying for cover.

Just after midnight, Mwangi was ensconced, weary and subdued by comparison with his jubilant confederates, in the gang's comfortable and secure quarters on the slope of a dense, bamboo-forested valley on Kipipiri, high above Dawling's farm. The anxious 'Field Marshal' praised them without stint and fondled the Martin-Express rifle reverently. He gave an unusual command—"Prepare *tembo* for everyone."

Mwangi had served his purpose admirably, his knowledge of Bwana Dalton's farm had been exploited fully; another *mzungu* had paid a penalty for employing Kukes. Yet Mwangi felt not at all unlike many other terrorists—he did not mind *shambas* being raided but somehow it was unfair, certainly compromising, to expect them to be the instrument of success for raids on a *shamba* that had employed them for so long—unless, possibly, they had been unjustly dismissed or had some festering grievance. Regrettably for Mwangi he'd been happily employed and the duty he'd performed so well clouted his conscience a hefty blow.

The two ends of our battered circle meet and suffice it to say that the unfortunate Mr Dalton struggled on and overcame his severe setback. As for the rascal, Mwangi, we have not finished with him yet. His activities outside the forest in collaboration with security forces shall be found to be every bit as worthy of comment as those within the forest have been.

Chapter 12
Exploitation of traitors to hasten the turning of the tide

Early in 1955 the authorities experimented with what was called a Stock Theft Investigation Team in the Lower Rift districts. Although police were primarily concerned with this experiment, the administration was more than a casual observer. This was not because of any lack of follow-up action by police when stock thefts occurred as much as a lack of action at the scenes of them. Provincial administration wanted to know whether or not farmers were taking all the precautions expected of them in order to deny cattle to Mau Mau. It usually happened that a farmer would present a claim for compensation whenever he had been the victim of a successful raid on his cattle *boma*; substantial claims at that. Therefore the administration wanted to be quite satisfied that an applicant had not been guilty of negligence before honouring a claim.

There were two parts to this team: a tracker-combat element, that disregarded the actual scene of the incident and got straight on with the job of following up the perpetrators; and an investigation group that carried out a thorough-going enquiry at the scene— recording statements, interrogating stock guards, checking the *boma's* wiring and the farm's security arrangements, etc.

My status hithertofore as a police post commander having been relinquished, I was teamed up with another inspector, one celebrated for his quiet and dedicated approach to 'pukka' policing and who we shall call Cliff. I was made responsible for the tracker-combat half of this team. There is little I shall say about this team except to record that it did not function for more than a couple of months. Two things were responsible for its early demise. Firstly, the information gathered and collated by Cliff and his sleuths after the team had attended some twenty-five stock thefts was sufficient to exculpate the farmers and confirm they were taking all possible precautions to deny their livestock to terrorists. Secondly, Tracker Combat Teams came into being and entered the operational field throughout the settled highlands. These T.C.T.s were expected, inter alia, to follow up stock-theft incidents.

With the fine tracker-combat group developed during the short-lived existence of the Stock Theft Investigation Team, plus two additional good riflemen, I was conveniently appointed as Tracker Combat Team No. 9 and continued to perform much the same except that Cliff and his men bowed out.

Between follow-ups and routine patrols around the forest edge my team always made a diligent practice of thoroughly interrogating all terrorists either captured or surrendered that we could lay hands on. Immediately they put in an appearance at the station a request was lodged to use them. Sometimes they were whisked straight off to the inner sanctums of Special Branch and would not be seen again for days, often to re-appear as pseudo-gangsters and inducted into a Field Intelligence Officer's group. At other times they would be sent direct to those security forces responsible for the area in which they had been sallying to and fro as active forest gangsters.

Many of these surrenderees or capturees became available only after having been squeezed dry of their operational value by Special Branch officers or the F.I.O.s, but, whatever the position may have been I always importuned the services of them as soon as ever possible in order to elicit that final bit of information, to check a hideout or *posta*, etc. My eager and well-tempered contention was that my merry men and me, in the congenial and non-competitive atmosphere of the team's unprepossessing quarters over a bowl of rice, could reduce these enigmatic characters to a compromising frame of mind.

No matter what the time or where the place of operational interest, I was more than willing to mount a patrol and follow an informant to the hideout he'd recently occupied, or to a maize *shamba* he knew his or other gangs to be plundering. More often than not the team drew an unqualified blank; even so, there was infinitely more satisfaction when patrolling with a terrorist who was fresh from a militant forest gang. He was able to show us so much of importance. It was positive activity and we always tingled with anticipation. The very manner in which an ex-gangster threaded his wary way through the bush, avoided soft earth, examined the slightest disturbance of grass or stone, his hyper-sensitive sense of smell, nostrils forever lifted and testing the air, one could almost see the antennae waving in front of his forehead probing and interpreting—it was all so fascinating to witness and we seldom concealed our admiration of his bush-craft, so superb was it. Neither did we restrain our own efforts to emulate his extraordinary bush-craft because, the more proficient we became at aping Mau Mau terrorists when in the forest, the more likely we were to achieve our object of contact and kill.

So it was then that, once having acquired the brief services of a freshly de-fanged Mau Mau, I would systematically and hopefully take him over all the ground covered by him and his gang during the immediately preceding weeks. No inducements were held out, neither rewards nor promises. Rough handling of him was never countenanced and in any case a hostile renegade would only have hampered our efforts. Probably I was guilty of a certain amount of cajolery and always endeavoured to make the fellow as comfortable as my own men were. At every stage of his singular association with the team I displayed a keen interest in the way he had lived and in the raids he had participated in. The one topic that was strictly forbidden, however, was politics, which included the causes of Mau Mau; all such talk was deemed to be unnecessary clap-trap. The capturee or surrenderee was, I might add, left in no doubt as to his fate should he have made any attempt to escape while in the team's company, also as to his ultimate destination—a detention camp. I made it a rule never to prevaricate or compromise. Being in no position to offer any amnesty, I could only have it placed on record that ex-terrorist Kimani had not been unwilling to assist security forces in their forest operations, certain in the belief that it would augur well for him at some later date.

It was, of course, something of a phenomenon that no terrorist, whether captured or surrendered, ever made a run for it; certainly not in my area anyway. They would invariably feel, despite the rapport established, an abiding and almost pathologically morbid fear that once deep inside the silent forests we would seek to requite our earlier defeats by disposing of them. Especially was this fear great should the fellow have already led the team up and down fatiguing valleys only to find the hideout vacated, then to witness the expressions of deep disappointment on our weary faces. Unfailingly, however, I would contrive to effect an air of indifference should such have been the case and my askari were encouraged to display a like attitude; the convert Mau Mau was permitted to believe that "it was an enjoyable ride anyway".

I ought to make it quite clear that, during this phase of my service with a Tracker Combat Team and while exploiting the usefulness of ex-'micks', I had not relinquished my detestation of Mau Mau. I may confess to having paid tribute to their excellent bush-craft and elusiveness but no more so than one would enthuse over the suppleness, cunning and grace of a lion stalking its kill. My private feelings in respect of the beastliness of the monster created by Jomo Kenyatta and his kind were appropriately repressed in the interests of the job; that is all.

These then were the circumstances of my life as a T.C.T. commander in the Kenya police when I laid hands on our old friend, Mwangi, the son of Gichakau. My diary entry for the 30 June 1955 reads:

... last night that wretched phone rang imperatively again with the apologetic voice of Doug (K.P.R. duty officer) on the other end ... cattle, many head, missing from Marula. Out to investigate but nothing could be done until first light. All were recovered after a short patrol—they had strayed! Thence to the Badlands with team for a random observation/tracking patrol. N.T.R. [nothing to report]. Two terrs surrendered this morning, one with a round in his shoulder, the other, a most cheerful and unassuming fellow who is convinced of the whereabouts of one 'Field Marshal' Mbaria Kanui. Certainly a *mkubwa*—a big fish well worth netting. Checked one possible hideout with him on Kipi before dusk but it had just been vacated—tough! Shall try another tomorrow.

Mwangi was bursting with operational usefulness and totally bereft of any conscience as regards the fate of his erstwhile forest companions in arms. He beamed agreeably, displaying the wide gap between his two strong, white front teeth. He spoke affectionately of Mbaria Kanui and told us what a mild-natured person he was. "By what standards?" I wondered. He rendered eloquent descriptions of the hardships being endured by his gang and of its increasingly hazardous efforts to obtain food from the white man's *shambas*. I gleaned enough from him to keep my team busy for months—that is, had the more pressing and mundane tasks of tracking stolen stock permitted.

Deep into the night we carefully chatted to Mwangi, charting his gang's latest movements, pin-pointing the whereabouts of other gangs and learning of the current modus operandi employed by them to avoid contact with security forces.

"Why do they not heed the words of the sky-shouting aircraft and surrender as advised to?" was one of the eager questions put to him.

With an ingenuous air he replied, "It's impossible to leave the forest now. Sentries are posted everywhere at the forest edge and anyone seen leaving without good cause is detained and taken back to the leader who frequently executes them."

And, equally a deterrent to would-be surrenderees was the grave mistrust they had of the gracious amnesty offer. Most firmly believed that it was a hoax and that they would be shot by the askari or the 'Johnnies'. If anything, they preferred to be captured.

It was from Mwangi that we were able to clarify an issue we had often debated among ourselves. Did the bombs showered onto the forests by the Lancasters and Lincolns cause the gangs either casualties or concern? And it was learned, not to our very great surprise, that they were bothered but little and seldom were there any victims of the blasts. They were unhappy about the deafening explosions and fires that were often started but if they lay down close to the ground they stood about as much chance of being hit as a dinghy in the Atlantic by a meteorite. What they were terrified of, said Mwangi, was the wildlife injured during bombing sorties. Animals maddened by the pain of great wounds cavorted dangerously through the forest and would charge out on terrorists quite unprovoked. It was the bigger game, usually so inoffensive, that kept them petrified in their hideouts after a heavy bombing raid on the moorlands, valleys and bamboo thickets.

Having made a rapid, though extremely circumspect, visit to the last lair that Mwangi had occupied, without success, I placed abundant faith in his conviction that the 'Field Marshal' and his die-hard followers had moved two valleys to the left to reoccupy an emergency lie-up site. This they would have undoubtedly done as soon as Mwangi's absence had been noted. They would nevertheless, hardly have been expecting any intrusion quite so soon and would feel reasonably safe, if anxious, for a night in the stand-by camp. Not a moment was to be lost and final instructions were given to my Somali sergeant who visibly bristled with enthusiasm.

"*Sisisote tatoka hapa kesho asabui mapema sana pamoja na huyu magaidi,*" I briefed him. And, despite the lateness of the hour that they all bedded down that night, I had no doubt that he and the team would be up and ready to leave together with our obliging orphan, Mwangi, an hour before dawn as ordered.

As it had seemed to me to be highly probable that substantial numbers would be encountered if my dawn patrol made positive contact, I considered it advisable to reinforce the team with a few military personnel; thus, I took myself along to the Intelligence Officer of the nearby army camp. The Glosters were our resident armed forces and I'd found them always exceedingly helpful and keen to join in any operational jaunt that required some additional sting in it. I was allocated an N.C.O. and four of their best; the I.O. I prevailed upon to ensure that his troops did not turn up encumbered with masses of equipment, "Just their rifles, ammo and a water bottle," I urged. "And no Bren guns, please!"

By 0600 hours the following morning I was breathing heavily, though comfortably, a yard or so in rear of Mwangi. Behind me, with a Sterling gun slung over his right shoulder, right hand gripping its pistol butt, stepped Garry, agile and faintly anxious, a beret set at a rakish angle on his head. Inspector Garry Staff had insisted upon ignoring his duties as Station Officer for a few hours to see how I earned my living. He smiled confidently as he looked up from the narrow track being followed and saw me nod affirmatively.

"This is it, Garry, mate. I feel it. This hide is going to be a hot one," I said softly.

His smile broadened and he panted in reply: "Tuskers on me if there are any 'micks' in it. Don't forget to let me know when we are in the vicinity."

The sun does not find its welcome passage into the towering forests on this side of Kipipiri until late morning and they remain dripping and chill long after dawn. Legs were soon soaked to the thighs and feet squelched in canvas jungle boots. Only the last two or three in the file found they were comparatively dry, most of the dew having been soaked up by the leading members. The game track we inched along was muddy in parts and it was necessary to tread carefully as the incline was steep.

The patrol pressed on, noiseless and watchful. A halt was made to examine a heavy tree lying across the track. It had not been hewn down; its trunk was splintered and pitted. In the vicinity were others looking as if they had been attacked by an army of inexpert and indiscriminate drunken woodsmen, or, better, as if some Colossus had stood in the middle of the devastation swinging an ocean-going liner's anchor and chain round and around. It was, we concluded, the site of a heavy bomb explosion and the ugly scar was a sight that had become all too common during my patrols; pathetic evidence, moreover, of the costly inefficacy of the

R.A.F. blitz on these congested slopes and ridges.

Signalling the patrol to halt I sank down behind Mwangi. He looked as comfortable as if he were strolling through an African location on a Sunday afternoon with a few cans of *tembo* inside him. He took out the hard army biscuits I'd given him and bit warily on one. "*Eee! Ngumu sana, lakini chakula tu,*" he mumbled with a cheerful grin.

I accepted one he waved before me and clamped my teeth on it. "*Ndio, kama mawe* [Yes, like stone]," I rejoined.

"Are we near their *campa*?" I enquired, while poking with a twig at the earth that had somehow become caked inside the muzzle of my Sterling.

"*Ndio, bwana*, not far now. But we are not on the right ridge yet," he replied with conviction.

Although we had entered the forest just before first light I knew that Mwangi wanted to be absolutely certain that our approach to the camp site was not detected by sentries. The route we had taken was a necessarily circuitous one and, in consequence, an arduous one.

"The *mchungas* and guards of Mbaria are everywhere these days," advised Mwangi in low tones, and proceeded to enlighten me as to just how we were going to enter the gang's hideout. There was no conversation between any others of the patrol and, while my own askari sat impassively and stared, enviously I suppose, at the superior jungle clothing of the soldiers, the latter merely sat and enjoyed the magnificent view from our lofty perch on the mossy slope.

The time was 0745 hours and about two hours had elapsed since the patrol had hastened across the wheat fields and thistle-covered foothills. How many times had I done it since my arrival in the district? I was still far from able to distinguish every feature of the mountain but was well accustomed to the terrain and capable of orientating myself with most of its salient ridges and spurs. I was as fondly familiar with the fragrant forests of pine as I was with the abysmal, dark and cool luxuriant valleys that serrated the massive flanks of 'His Majesty', Kipipiri. I knew where not to venture in quest of Mau Mau and was fairly confident of locating water. I knew I'd hear elephants galore and espy abundant evidence of their presence but would seldom encounter them except out in the open or, more likely, in the foothills. Higher than nine thousand feet one would have been lucky to spot buffalo, but at that height of the bracken-carpeted summit a skulking leopard would be no surprise, nor would a chattering Sykes monkey. Mindful also was I of the cruel punishment that this appendix of the Aberdare range could inflict on the body if its slopes were tackled in an over-zealous manner. The principle adopted was *pole pole* (slowly).

Squatting just off the track in the damp foliage I gazed below and whiled away the few minutes' pause while the patrol recovered its wind by trying to identify the various farms dotted among the vast tapestries of rich gold, green and brown.

I felt Mwangi touch me lightly on the shoulder and then speak softly in my ear. "We must go on, they may move away from this *campa* before noon today."

I nodded my assent. Without a word I rose and motioned to the patrol to follow, placing a forefinger over my compressed lips to indicate that silence was still vital. We pushed on again into the all-encompassing and boundless preserves of nature, more slowly now, and pausing at frequent intervals to listen. Every twig that snapped underfoot sounded like a pistol shot and every swish of a branch on clothing like the noisy rending of canvas. Rifle slings would slap against their butts like thunder claps and a water bottle would teasingly find its way round to a belt buckle and clash like an enormous cymbal. Mwangi was forever turning around to stare admonishingly at us and I, in turn, would fix a hostile glare on poor Garry who would then himself turn and carry on the silent rebuke until, I imagined, the last fellow in the file had to shoulder the blame for every bit of noise made by the patrol. Needless to say superhuman efforts were made by all to reduce noise to the absolute minimum. It was plain that the strain of such meticulous patrolling was having an effect on all of us. Weapons were being jabbed expectantly in this and that direction; the bush became more hampering and ever more likely to conceal a few artful Mau

Mau. The tension rose to a nerve-twanging, super-charged agony of suspense.

Every second that passed I expected to hear the ill-fated report of an accidental discharge—a nervous finger curled around a trigger with the safety catch off; it happened so often at the crucial moment.

Garry shadowed me in a state of split-second readiness and once or twice I caught his eye and grimaced in mock exhaustion at him. His features were strained and, like all of us, he found that to walk without stumbling on ground angled at sixty degrees was difficult enough under normal conditions. To keep one's eyes wide and scanning the solid mass of undergrowth on all sides without losing one's footing required tremendous concentration and sure-footedness. A glance occasionally at our military companions assured me of their plucky intentions not to let the patrol down by creating any unnecessary noise. In fact, so religiously were they attempting a silent passage through the matted bush that I felt uncomfortably certain, as their intense expressions tended to confirm, that they had long since forgotten what could happen any second; what little time they would have to do anything about it.

It was now about 0850 hours and we had been pushing and panting through the forest for nearly three hours when, while following up a rushing stream, our valuable surrenderee bade us halt and beckoned me to his side. We conversed earnestly and I learned that the hideout was within striking distance on the opposite slope about twenty feet up and possibly a hundred yards away. It was to be entered parallel to the contour of the slope and we'd chance that our surprise was complete. There was no hope of surrounding the site or of situating stops on escape routes; it was simply a matter of getting straight in and, *'Jambo wagaidi!'*

My final instructions were for every foot of every man to be placed with the utmost care. One human sound would have destroyed completely all the perfect patrolling so far. Indeed, I was so sensitive to the possibility of the mission aborting that I was in two minds about proceeding independent of the patrol in order to reconnoitre the area first.

Tearing a trail down through spiteful nettle and across a babbling stream, then up the other side for about twenty feet, Mwangi picked his way with infinite caution. He was a Mau Mau terrorist again with the alert senses of a wild animal. He selected a semblance of a track that led off to the left and entered. I followed, looking quickly over my shoulder to ensure that all were behind and not too strung out. Another fifty yards of painfully slow progress. Mwangi again paused; I dropped down beside him.

"This is the back way into the *campa*," he barely whispered. "It is very close now and they are definitely here."

He satisfied me that on this approach the gang had no sentries posted. We both agreed, too, that with luck the rush of water, still audible from the stream below, would negate any unavoidable noise that we made.

The reason Mwangi was unquestionably sure that the site was occupied was that he could smell smoke. Such prodigious perception astonished me but I knew better than to doubt it. The only thoughts that stampeded through my head, and which I am able to recollect, were in respect of Mwangi and the fact that he was about to witness the shooting up, and possibly the killing, of those Freedom Army fighters with whom he had lived so intimately for the past two years or so. He appeared to be strangely unmoved. Was he just a callous Kikuyu or was he genuinely antipathetic towards the fanatical anti-European organization? I preferred not to find the answer.

Sensing that the bamboo was thinning out ahead and that we were descending slightly, I closed the distance between Mwangi and me to mere inches. It was one step at a time, then wait a moment or two. I avoided looking down anymore and instead felt carefully with each foot before placing my full weight on it. The folding butt of my 9mm S.M.G. was pulled hard into my right shoulder, its barrel gripped tightly with my left hand.

Mwangi had stopped dead! His position was just on a bend of the narrow game track around which I was unable to see. Frozen, he simply stared ahead as I inched my way up behind him until able to peep round the thick wall of bamboo. There, ten yards distant, standing outside a crude shelter constructed of bamboo and grass, I gazed with stupefaction upon two ragamuffin, tousle-haired wide-eyed characters who were perplexedly staring back at Mwangi.

For an instant the dramatic scene crystallized and assumed sublime proportions, every detail sharply defined. It was a 'still' of the cinematograph film we were acting in. The patrol had arrived at its goal and was on the point of impact with the destinies of a band of fugitive insurgents. The instant passed and the projector of Time whirred at a normal sixteen frames per second again.

Of the following few minutes a coherent account is barely possible; I'd give much for the descriptive pen of Hemingway or London to complete this chapter. It requires detached and objective thought to compound those sentences necessary to convey the thrill and drama of those next rip-roaring moments.

Wordlessly I shoved past Mwangi, firing bursts at the two figures now bounding swiftly past a cluster of rough bamboo lean-to shelters, down to the stream to splash frenziedly across. One stumbled and fell moaning, blood spurting from his bare back. A few yards farther up on the opposite slope a panicking group of five or more struggled to make headway through the virgin bush. Yet another impatient, fleshless form, who emerged from one of the shelters like a startled rabbit, fled with fantastic speed to the far end of the clearing. In a trice they were all out of sight and I triggered short bursts into the green draperies that closed behind them.

No sound came from them as they vanished; only the snapping of branches and splintering of bamboo. I had raced right through the clearing to take up a position some twenty yards from the spot I had fired my first shots. Furious firing and shattering bursts of automatic announced the arrival and excited anticipation of the remainder of the patrol. The featureless ocean of greenery opposite was swept with unrestrained fire and the noise was like a deafening artillery barrage after the celestial quiet of the past couple of hours. But it was all over except for the 'ifs' and 'buts'. Two of my askari leapt across the stream and commenced to hurl themselves up the other side in hot pursuit but, being morbidly afraid of accidents, I commanded their immediate return. Surveying the scene of contact I hardly dared to believe it had not all been hallucination.

There were two bodies lying in the water, one was dead and the other was looking blankly at the soldiers who stood over him awkwardly, and apparently in some doubt as to what should be done next.

My tall Somali sergeant in a startled voice said: "*Iko moja ingine huko,*" (There's another over there) and sprinted off upstream. I hurried to join him but there was no need for the rush; the fellow was about to expire. The sergeant, however, loath to leave anything to chance, levelled his rifle and discharged a single shot. It entered between the dull and unseeing eyes; the lids slowly closed.

The remaining wounded, half-naked, scraggy wretch died a few moments later, coughing blood and still staring vacantly at the strange faces above him. It was a last glimpse of security forces that he'd probably been instinctively awaiting for months past and was now glad that it was all over and done with.

Mwangi, rather sheepishly, made his way up to me.

He looked frightened and peered stonily at the bodies lying lifeless in the stream. Without any trace of emotion he informed us that one of the two was the gang's doctor and the other was a 'captain'. The third fast-cooling member upstream was the cook. The doctor, Kimani Ndindi, according to Mwangi's information, had been a gentle person, never one for fighting, and devoted a lot of time to the study of medical books whenever he had been able to acquire them. In one of the small simple shelters, that were nothing more really than inclined roofs, a first-aid kit in a haversack was found. (This odd item of Mau Mau bric-a-brac had been removed from a Harvard spotter plane that had crashed some months previously.) Useful documents were recovered that included one or two surrender leaflets that had been showered onto the forests from the air.

Mwangi was surprised to see them; he believed that Mbaria destroyed such leaflets when they were found. Souvenirs were rapidly gathered up and the half-dozen shelters destroyed. I was worried to an irritating degree settling the various claims of the soldiers for the vigorously contested ownership of souvenirs— *pangas*, cow-horn drinking receptacles, fly whisks fashioned from the tails of cattle, a couple of ludicrous home-made rifles, and so on—all five of the young and excited Glosters wanted some evidence of the patrol's successful foray. Someone then produced a camera and in the shafts of sunlight streaming through the mists of early morning, spent and elated, we all gathered around the dead 'micks', now laid out in a shallow depression, and posed with hard-set expressions. The possibility of a concerted and angry counter-attack by the large gang that had melted before us was blithely ignored. The patrol was triumphant and satisfied that the remainder of the gang were still running as fast as their skinny legs could carry them.

Three dead and most certainly some wounded, perhaps to die unseen in the jungle; their ignoble graves a hyena's stomach. As the day was still in its infancy I decided to leave half the patrol in positions near the hideout area in the remote possibility that any gang members absent during the skirmish should return blissfully unaware. A fresh army patrol would be mustered and sent up during the afternoon with one of my askari as guide to attempt the tracking down of the fugitive Mbaria and his cohorts.

By mid-morning, legs still soaked to the thighs and twitching with the effort of a swift descent, we were speeding back to base in the team's Land Rover with half the patrol hugging its cherished souvenirs.

Garry gave himself up unreservedly to the glory of the occasion and chuckled repeatedly with disbelief at the lightning success of the encounter. "Bloody hell! When I heard your first burst I thought it was an accidental triggering of my own gun. It was impossible to push through that damned narrow track any faster and even then I almost tripped over Mwangi who had gone to earth ..." he cited enthusiastically.

"I think the contact was an object lesson for our Gloster friends, don't you?" I queried.

"Christ, yes! As you told them before we started, there are only a few seconds in which to loose off a burst and record hits. I honestly think that those in rear saw nothing at all of the flushing."

And that was just so; once contact had been made action had to be at top speed ... plus! It is impudent of me to refer to the gratifying session as being an object lesson in combat logistics for the military alone, for it is well that I remind myself it was my first ever killing contact too. Though, strangely at the time it was as if the experience had been mine many times before. Natural enough I suppose when reconciling the incident to the numberless patrols of an equally gruelling and exacting nature carried out to tactically logical, though unavailing, conclusions.

At the station there were congratulatory comments for Garry and me. The askari were praised and thanked and promptly dismissed with an extra ration of meat. Mwangi was feted and drawn more closely to the bosom of Tracker Combat Team No. 9.

I could never make up my mind whether the cheerful and co-operative surrenderee was just stoically facing up to it all or whether he was downright, unashamedly disgusted with his ex-comrades. Quite honestly I came to believe that he simply never gave the matter much thought. Life or death was not his by choice, any more so that he was entitled to cling assiduously to either the hope for longevity or for a merciful end. It was all simply *shauri ya mungu*.

Indeed, Dame Fortune had at last delivered to me a live 'mick' whose services as an active hard-core terrorist now terminated, could have his immeasurable usefulness placed at the disposal of his former enemies. He was white-hot with operational value; his gang were agitated and on the move; it would take them several days to reorganize, to establish new hideouts, *postos* and food stores. The food-foraging parties would have to be called in and all game traps gathered up. Mbaria Kanui would be taking a long and sobering look at his reduced and disrupted ranks.

Mwangi was no less voluble or cheerful after our fruitful exploitation of his timely desertion to our lines. It was just over twenty-four hours since he had thrown in his lot with us and the torrent of information continued to pour forth—the farms on which small independent terrorist cells, in some cases renegades, were living off the growing crops; the heavy elephant gun that Mbaria proudly possessed without, alas, any ammunition; the increasing tendency of gangs to hold pseudo-religious ceremonies presided over by witchdoctors. He rambled on about the re-oathing among forest gangs in an effort to reinforce morale. There was a note of terror in his voice as he described their fervid attempts to avoid contact with the *serikali's* pseudo-gangster teams and went on to narrate a dramatic story of his own gang's discovery of twelve dead terrorists, all strangled, high up on Kipipiri above Sattima Point.

To all this and much more besides my faithful band and I gave a cocked ear. We learnt an unprecedented amount of vital intelligence from our pet surrenderee and it was all noted accordingly for future reference. Special Branch was anxious to recruit him as a 'pseudo' but I importuned stubbornly for permission to complete my series of expeditions with him. Realizing that there was a strong possibility of further successes, my superintendent interceded on my behalf and Special Branch yielded.

During our talks well into the night of the same day as the team's successful contact on 'Kipi', Mwangi spoke speculatively of a food-foraging party that had been detailed to trap game and catch fish in the Kasariga gorge on the North Kinangop. The party was expected to remain in the area and would be relieved periodically of its catch by other gang members who would carry it back to the larder. Here then, was another odds-on chance, should they not have become aware of Mwangi's traitorous *volte-face*.

There was much speculation on whether Mbaria Kanui had been present in the hideout on Kipipiri when we barged in to interrupt the meditations of its occupants. Mwangi seemed to think that Mbaria had ventured elsewhere with two of his favourite *houris*. Could they have gone to visit the party operating in the Kasariga? The possibility heightened the incentive to have a 'look-see'.

On the morning of 4 July, before the cocks started crowing I drove out of a slumbering Gilgil with my team. On this occasion the army were not in tow but I again had Garry who had enjoyed himself to such an extent the previous day that he had decided to make himself an honorary member of the team. I also invited along a fellow 'bush-basher', a red-headed, broad-accented Scot named Derick Rush, an ex-matelot and as tough as tarred oakum. Having recently acquired a high-velocity .22 Hornet rifle, he was anxious to try it out on 'micks' instead of the usual bush buck and python. The three of us sat engrossed in our own thoughts in the cab of the team's Land Rover; Derick nursing his Hornet and smoking numberless cigarettes, and Garry poring over a map to check whether or not we would have to bulldoze into the area of Geiter Mill Post.

"We should be alright if it's the Kasariga and not the upper Mkungi that this native chappy's taking us to," said Garry. "Even so, it's bloody doubtful that old Tug Wilson [Geiter Mill's inspector in charge] will be found crashing around in a gorge at this insane time of day."

We bounced along the rough farm roads towards the bottom end of the Kasariga and cleared the last squatter lines without any inquisitive Africans observing our bright and early appearance in that area.

Derick's guttural voice was lifted above the whine of the vehicle as he addressed me: "You haven't forgotten that you are leaving for Mombasa today, have you? It is today, isn't it, that your leave starts?"

"Depends on this little *shauri*," I replied. "Anyway there's no tearing hurry. I want something to celebrate while at the coast and, to tell the truth, I'm beginning to have fun with this fellow. Perhaps I should postpone my leave for a week or two. What d'yer think?"

"Don't be such a daft bastard," Garry exploded. "Who the hell do you think is going to recommend you for an O.B.E., eh? While you flog your guts out chasing 'micks', someone in Nairobi will be collecting the laurels. Take your leave, mate, and get pissed from dawn till dusk."

Chuckling, I replied, "Agreed, wings! It would be too bad if the A.C.P. decided to toss me a commendation; it might just inspire me to accept a permanent appointment. What a horrible thought, a second tour with this mob!"

Having rammed the vehicle into the middle of tall elephant grass at the edge of the Kasariga gorge we all alighted and slipped into the dark, leafy, chilly depths to grope a passage down to the river, two hundred feet below, where we waited silently until a watery dawn trickled over the top of the Aberdares sufficient for us to proceed without slipping and sliding too much.

Mwangi was soon off the mark and pointed out a distinct muddy footprint on a rock at the side of the swift-flowing waters. "*Jana* (yesterday)," he announced without hesitation. "This is a place where they fish."

During the next hour we stalked, ever sharp-eyed, in a zig-zag course along the suspect side of the gorge. Climbing to within a few feet of the top, then slowly descending again to the river, checking and rechecking every sign in the most thorough-going manner.

Shortly before 0900 hours, with the sun just beginning to coax the little rock rabbits out of their warrens and encouraging the strutting secretary birds to bid each other good morning, Mwangi bent down and turned over some earth near a young silver oak tree. He exposed some anaemic-looking human excrement. He looked up and about him, expectant and bristling, sniffed the air, then whispered in the lowest of tones, "They are around here somewhere."

I took over then and signalled the patrol to fan out.

The bush was much less congested and the slope less steep. It was possible to proceed in extended line. Mwangi remained close by my side and evinced an expression of such imminency that I found it almost impossible to stop myself shaking with anticipation.

In two or three furious minutes it was all over and the stuttering automatic fire in glorious disharmony with the cracks of rifle shots was still echoing up and down the gorge, broadcasting that a few more rebel pests had been purged from Kenya's beautiful forests and fertile valleys. The high-pitched hum and whizz of ricochet filled the ears, muffling the excited shouts of askari and groans of the wounded.

There had been three that I saw as I eased through the foliage into a small, grassy glade. All, I felt certain, had received some disabling attention from my smoking Sterling gun. One was lying still on his face, a *panga* grasped in his right hand.

Another was whimpering, "Don't kill me", and the third had careered off between two large boulders, dripping blood and hard-pressed by Derick and an askari. Somewhere below could be heard the crashing of other askari in frantic pursuit of our cunning prey.

I can remember screaming, *"Simama! Hapana kimbia,"* as I released my first bursts of lead but everything happened so quickly it was impossible to know who stood still and who didn't.

From the corner of my eye I'd seen a brown-jacketed, heavily built, ugly brute slide off a rock upon which he'd been basking in the warm sun, and simply dive out of sight straight down the side of the gorge. Running over to the breach in the densely woven foliage where he'd disappeared, I saw another swathe cut through the undergrowth. There were smears of blood on the leaves and grass, obviously from the fellow that Derick went after and who, judging from the chorus of wild firing and shouting below, had succeeded in bringing down.

Turning my attentions to the 'mick' lying in the glade, still alive and moaning with fright and pain, I yelled: "How many were you?"

"Five," he croaked, in Swahili, eyes rolling.

He was sat up, a youngish Kikuyu with the embryo stubble of a beard. He looked to be tolerably well dressed in a patchwork quilt jacket fastened at the waist with a leather strap. He was supporting a limp and shattered left arm and before him, spread on a piece of dirty linen, were some old bones and a handful of boiled wheat, also a *simi* and several strips of cycle inner-tubing. The whole while that I glowered down at him he moaned piteously, *"Kamata mimi, bwana, kamata mimi* [arrest me]". For moments I stood in an agony of indecision, compassion wrestling with insensitivity.

As I was about to examine his wounds, compassion in the ascendancy, Derick reappeared, sweating and red-faced, through the tall curtains of grass. His voice was full of grim eagerness.

"Christ! Not still alive surely? What do you plan on doing with him? You're not going to carry him out of this bloody jungle, I hope. Here, let me finish him off before he draws that *simi* across your throat."

"Easy, mate! Curb your bloodthirsty spirit. I'm not decided yet," I hedged, as I drew closer to the cowering specimen of half-human, half-animal. "You know how useful the bastards are if interrogated—you've only to look at Mwangi for your proof. If he's able to walk we'll toddle him back with us."

As it happened my cursory examination of him revealed multiple chest wounds and bloody spume was already frothing from his mouth. He started to cough and it sounded like a release of air under water, the scarlet spume turning to a steady flow to drip upon the pathetic pauper's meal before him. I assented abruptly that it would be better to get it over with. The futility and the savagery of this dirty quasi-war suddenly overwhelmed me. With mounting anger I yelled: "Well! Now, what are you waiting for? Do you want me to blindfold him for you?"

Derick stared querulously.

Long seconds ticked by as we stood regarding one another with an odd suspicion, our weapons held tightly at combat readiness. The croaking and gasping of the crumpled terrorist became more laboured and my hatred of him reached a visceral intensity. I wanted him to do the decent and proper thing and die—NOW!

Then Garry appeared on the scene, face glistening and looking haggard. He walked a few yards into the clearing, gazing about him wildly and growling, "Where the flaming hell do they *toroka* to? There must be more of them but ... WHERE? WHERE?" Warily he trod a circuit of the rocky knoll poking his Sterling into the bush until he almost tripped over the dying wretch who very slowly swivelled his head to peer up at him. The glazing eyes had no time to register his last emotions—if he had any, for he suddenly twitched violently and rolled over, quite dead.

Could his timely demise have been accelerated by the merciless look on Garry's face? Several enormous rooks took wing nearby to caw questionable approbation from above.

Turning to Derick I questioned, "What about the others, how many did you stop below?"

"As far as I know we've only accounted for a third and he's lying in a small gully below. The askari intercepted him as he dropped like a stone through the bush. He looked pretty bad when I saw him."

We followed the tunnel that had been torn and clawed through the undergrowth until we came across two askari who sat staring at the ill-clothed and under-nourished form of the third terrorist lying head down, sprawled and limp. His eyes were open but unseeing and his chest heaved in long inspirations. It was but a matter of minutes before he would join his comrades in Hades.

Nothing was said, faces were impassive; there seemed to be a tacit understanding between us all. The .22 soft-nosed bullet had entered the moribund gangster's forehead high up and the smallest of holes appeared, though instantly his left eye popped out and hung as an indeterminate blob of white and red upon his shiny, black cheek. His chest sagged in a final expiration and another Mau Mau brute was in our bag, a leader too, according to Mwangi a 'colonel'!

Having gathered up all the usual minutiae of hard-core forest terrorists, the patrol sat and smoked and yarned over the gratifying engagement, particularizing and spawning the substance from which would undoubtedly emerge countless colourful, if somewhat exaggerated, accounts of this well-deserved encounter in the Kasariga gorge. Mwangi was quite noticeably less smitten on this occasion. The mentality of these Kikuyus really was baffling. Once they had made up their minds to transfer their allegiance it was with incredible finality.

Subsequent identification of those three Mau Mau despatched so uncompromisingly in this, the team's second fruitful contact in two days, showed they were not the small fry we thought we were after but three of a party of five *mkubwas*. They had made a most unpropitious visit to ascertain the food position and were, in fact, waiting to rendezvous with the small party of trappers that we ourselves had entered the gorge to locate.

By the side of the rock which I had glimpsed the brown-jacketed individual slide off to make good his streaking escape, I had picked up a monkey-skin peak cap—an excellent piece of sartorial ingenuity that was to become one of my rare souvenirs of Kenya's emergency. It is significant to relate that about six months after its owner's lucky escape, on New Year's Day to be exact, high up on the wind-swept and desolate moorlands of the Aberdares, the quartermaster of the 3rd Mburu Ngebo Army, attired in monkey-skin trousers and jacket, surrendered himself to the intrepid Special Branch officer, Ian 'Kinyanjui' Henderson and his equally gallant team. It was the headgear of his natty durable suit that I had picked up and had identified as that of Maina Gati. This arch Mau Mau personage, who had so narrowly avoided perishing in the encounter with my patrol, was to become one of the sharpest, if not the sharpest, instrument in Henderson's hands, and rapidly underwent the remarkable metamorphosis that made him the fulcrum of the most successful group of pseudo-gangsters ever developed by Ian and his colleague, Inspector Richard 'Mac' Maclachlan, during the emergency.

In which case, despite my deep chagrin, when excitedly informed by Mwangi that the cap I stood studying in that grassy glade in the Kasariga had belonged to none other than the quartermaster, Maina Gati, I like to feel that his escape was pre-ordained in the longer-term interests of anti-terrorist activity.

That same night, weary but satisfied, I was jolting across the arid Athi plains in a train dropping rapidly from the White Highlands, and Mau Mau, to the coast, where I reclined torpidly for fourteen days' leave and recreated mind and body. After so much ceaseless and enervating operational enterprise over so many months it was to take several days before my tracker-combat machinery ran down sufficiently for me to relax properly. Malindi, Shelly Beach, the old Dhow harbour and the exotic, bustling Arab bazaars remain imperishable memories.

Chapter 13

'Kenya Cowboys' vs Mau Mau rustlers

The administration soon came to require mandatorily that all cattle *bomas* be adequately fenced, that they should not be widely dispersed, that a stock guard suitably armed and trained should be employed, that a high watchtower be erected nearby, that grazing cattle be tended by a reliable herdsman, and so forth. Claims for compensation for livestock lost to Mau Mau through negligence would not be honoured; moreover, the claimant would be liable to prosecution. Mau Mau had to be starved into submission or at least exposed to greater risks when raiding *bomas* for the provender their hollow tummies were so desperate to receive.

It was yet another turn on the economic screw and the farmer settlers fumed and stamped. Wasn't it further erosion of their paradise by rules and horrid regulations? They reflected moodily upon bygone days when hundreds of head of cattle could wander and graze to the far distant corners of their properties with virtually no supervision. It was of little consequence if the occasional steer or heifer strayed into the forest or some scallywag of a Masai helped himself to a nice boran that he fancied. The great herds were as free and unfettered as their owners. Now they had to be watched closely day and night, every single beast had to be accounted for. Miles and miles of multi-strand wire fencing had to be erected which also meant hundreds of fence posts, soaked in creosote, too.

The paradise was crumbling rapidly; the farmer settlers wondered with derision and frustration just how it was that one tribe of 'coons and kaffirs' could jeopardize the privileged freedom from bureaucracy they had enjoyed for so long. Those nice rose-tinted spectacles worn by the whites of Kenya—their perquisite for being white, in fact—and why they probably went to Kenya in the first place, were being replaced by the clearer lenses of reality. The view was, of course, so much less enchanting!

And yet, despite all their conscientious efforts, livestock continued to be rustled. However, our hardy, fanatical insurgents would now sneak into a *boma* far more surreptitiously and silently to slash the throats of one or two beasts only. These would be sectioned and rammed into sacks to be carried off to the hideout. The practice was disliked by them, being both arduous and insufficient for the gang's needs. Whereas when they were able to drive off anything from fifteen to twenty on the hoof, it would require but a few of their number. The beasts could be driven, their tails twisted cruelly, deep into the forest onto the rustic tables of their ravenous comrades, almost.

In time, experienced tracking teams found they were confronted with either one of two quite different situations when there was no more spoor to follow assuming, that is, the spoor had not been obliterated by rain or lost through some other circumstance, such as passing through rocky terrain—and in neither of these situations would the beasts be discovered whole.

With the most common of the two situations a determined team would catch in its nostrils the unmistakable odour of livestock offal. Then, in a clearing or near a stream, it would espy the nauseating remains of the cattle it had been following. The evidence would be abundant; heads lying around in pools of congealed blood, all minus their tongues—a delicacy thoroughly enjoyed by gangsters; intestines would be scattered like huge mounds of some elephantine worm's droppings; the masticated contents of stomachs would be strewn about like wet straw and smelling like a stable; dung and a few legs and udders would be mixed in with the sanguinary scene. The stomach, bladder, tail and, quite often, the horns, would not have been seen for all such items were priceless to outlaws who were not able to obtain their bags, drinking receptacles and fly-whisks in the normal way at the local *duka*.

Such grisly work would have been deftly executed, *pangas* having made the incisions, severed the limbs and extracted that which was inedible, with the skill of a surgeon and the thoroughness of a primitive and starving people. Each beast would have been sectioned into four quarters, one quarter being about all that a wiry terrorist could manage.

After examining such a scene, and if it were possible for the team to continue tracking the Mau Mau rustlers, the pursuit would be easier due to the deeper impressions made by them in consequence to shouldering their heavy loads. Apart from this there was little else that could be achieved.

With the second of the situations that equally often presented itself, the team, or patrol, had to be extremely observant and cautious. It was a situation created by terrorists few in number who had driven off a large herd but were unable to proceed as far as they would have wished (insufficient time, orders not to attract security forces too near the hideout, difficult terrain), and had chosen to halt and to butcher their bovine contraband at the first convenient and reasonably inconspicuous spot en route.

The chopped-up portions would have been hidden in the immediate vicinity—under bushes, behind rocks, in holes in the ground and even up trees. These hiding places would never have been far from the killing arena and all the offal and other evidence of slaughter would have been left where it was, it being well nigh impossible to clean up the blood and gore to an extent that no clue was left. However, their efforts at concealing the flesh were, if hasty, most cunning and painstaking. They would then, with equal thoroughness, have gone to great pains to eliminate every sign between the place of slaughter and the places they had hidden the meat. Their exit would have been made on the far side where they contrived to leave an abundance of heavy spoor, even throwing down a hunk of meat here and there for a hundred yards or so in the direction they hoped to lure any tenacious trackers. One of the rustlers would then have doubled back to conceal himself in a position where he could observe the area while the remainder returned to the hideout to report on their nefarious activities and to solicit the assistance necessary to return and carry in the fleshy spoil.

Only this type of situation allowed security forces recourse to some form of counter-activity. One method often practised was the ambushing of the area in which the meat was hidden. The method was far from being easy to accomplish and its success depended largely on the size of the patrol and the lateness of the hour. Taking full cognizance of the fact that somewhere in the vicinity was one of the enemy, squatting watchfully in some vantage point and aware of the patrol's discovery, success would also, therefore, have to take into account that observer's shrewdness. Had he counted the number in the patrol? If the patrol or team leader wished to chance an ambush and shooting up the bold perpetrators he had to answer, no!, then to proceed with his plan. So, with the patrol making a convincing show of casting around to pick up the tracks of the gang leading out of the area two or three askari would go to ground suitably concealed where they could command a view of the places in which the meat was hidden. The rest of the patrol would form up, perhaps carrying some of the discovered meat, and make its conspicuous exit the way it had come and keep on going.

There were obvious risks run because if the gang was a large one, or worse, armed, then the ambushing party could itself be stalked and set upon. The major weakness was that the European team leader would have had to depart and could not possibly partake in these counter tactics. He being the only white skin present and easily recognizable, what hope had he of outwitting the silent watcher? At least the white skin had to remove himself. Therefore the African askari, courageous and artful as they frequently were, had to be left to spring the ambush and take what offensive measures they thought best. It is regretted that in most instances they were found to be over-eager and trigger-happy and exposed themselves long before the appropriate moment, or their shooting was wild. It wanted but the slightest rustle of a leaf or even heavy breathing and the hyper-sensitive terrorists, crawling back to collect the ill-gotten flesh, would vanish as effectively as the little dik-dik out on the hot plains when a lion was sensed in the vicinity.

A wicked seed that was sown in the mind of many an anguished and thwarted member of the security forces, and which was not, I can safely say, allowed to take root, was poisoning of the meat—sprinkling it with strychnine. It was indeed an evil seed and had such a practice been resorted to it would doubtless have resulted in the destruction of much wildlife, not to mention the lives of innocent and loyal Africans who sometimes availed themselves of Mau Mau's uncollected spoils. Frankly I heard of no instance where security forces yielded to the strong temptation to poison slaughtered livestock they were unable to deny the enemy, though talk of such was common.

I shall never forget being handed a bottle of strychnine by a rural colleague who'd not had the temerity to use it himself but who thought that as my work took me deep into the forests after stolen stock I might like to sample its efficacy in known terrorists' lairs. The stuff gave me nightmares for days and I was everlastingly scrubbing my hands lest some of the deadly substance had leaked from the bottle. In the end I disposed of it in a deep latrine pit; probably it arrested the process of putrefaction of the faeces by destroying the active bacteria but how relieved I was!

I remember, too, when I first hit on the idea of denying terrorists the meat they had gone to so much trouble to thieve by destroying it, I reasoned that this would give the team as much satisfaction, if not more, as would carrying it all away, generally an impossible task anyway. Actually I have no reason to doubt that most trackers conceived of various schemes whereby the meat was destroyed. But, to destroy the flesh of several large cows, either sectioned or whole carcasses—sounds easy enough, but give it some more thought.

Burning it was the only practical proposition, or so it seemed to me. On but one occasion only did I attempt to do so. It sufficed to convince me of the futility of such a method of denial. What made it worse, humiliating in fact, was that the bloody terrorists, and only they, were the beneficiaries of the folly. When we gave up at dusk in disgust our attempt to reduce the mound of meat to cinder it was just nicely roasted. It was easy to visualize the watering mouths of insidious Mau Mau watching from their perches our every move.

In the early stages of the incinerating we cut tender slices from the roasting carcasses and ate our fill, laughing and joking the while, mockingly, at the ruthless manner in which we were depriving our tormentors of their plundered beef. Ah! Their expressions of anger when they see a pyre of charred flesh instead of succulent joints, sides and quarters. Wood was sought and stacked around the meat; the leaping flames soon engulfed the mound until it sizzled and crackled. The outside quickly turned black and became rock hard. After three hours stoking the fire and feeding ourselves the top ashes were cleared away to view the expensive venture (expensive indeed, for one good heifer could fetch as much as fifty pounds). Someone slashed at the nearest haunch with a *simi* and cut cleanly into beautifully roasted beef, a little underdone if anything. Pulling away the uppermost portions to expose those in the centre of the pyre we saw with mingled amazement and pique that the meat was raw—as raw as my mood at that moment. Instinctively I looked over my shoulder fully expecting to see a couple of emaciated Mau Mau with slavering mouths peering at us in general and at the pyre in particular. I could hear the words they might well have gleefully uttered: "*Asante sana, bwana. Wewe nasaidia sisi sana.*" (Thank you very much, *bwana*. You have helped us a lot.)

My team and I were inconsolable after this abortive effort to destroy the purloined victuals of terrorists. They were, I'm sure, fully aware of the immensity of such an enterprise and it was one of the reasons why they would lure trackers as far away into the bush as possible before killing the stolen stock. Few and far between were the occasions when Mau Mau were completely denied their spoils. I might add, too, that the horrid felons were never so charitable as to abandon cattle unharmed. If they were not slaughtered then they were always hamstrung, or sadistically slashed. All that tracking teams could ever hope to achieve really was to discover where the gangsters were in hiding, or to narrow down the area and then arrange for the army to saturate it with patrols, sifting and chivvying. Sometimes if our intelligence was reliable an F.I.O. would move in with a pseudo group.

From the Kikuyu escarpment, north up the Lower Rift Valley through Naivasha, Gilgil, Nakuru and on, was splendid ranching country. Mau Mau had a wide choice of *shambas* and it was not difficult for them on most nights to find one or two cattle *bomas* indifferently guarded. Reference to my operational diary shows one particularly interesting incident that occurred on 8 June 1955. The routine, though exacting, nature of a Tracker Combat Team's work is illustrated rather well.

At 1100 hours on that Wednesday a report was received that sixteen head of cattle were missing from Marula Estate, about six miles south of Gilgil. We were bid to stand by as personnel from Marula police post together with some local Masai were following good spoor along the Waterloo Ridge, north.

That same afternoon, having heard nothing further from the Marula party, and my own team becoming restless, we mustered and drove out to a water reservoir situated on the Cole Estate, from where we proceeded on foot up the highest knoll in the area— an almost vertical climb up its 250-feet side and we were able to look across the Badlands and over the wide, shimmering grazing country toward Marula. No sign of any tracking forces and, apart from a huddle of shy bush buck at the foot of the knoll, everywhere was tranquil and lethargic in the heavy heat of the afternoon.

We sat for a further ten minutes watching, me through binoculars and my askari through the sights of their rifles taking make-believe pot-shots at the buck. From our position it was possible to paint a delightfully variegated and captivating picture. To our right some two miles distant stood the strong, white brick bungalow of Lady Eleanor Cole, suggestively Moorish in character, set in attractively landscaped grounds and surrounded by tidy farm buildings and labour lines. Most of the rich grazing pastures within a three-mile radius belonged to her. The estate had been capably run by her since the death of her husband, though she employed a manager, a charming Dane with a beautiful, willowy, golden wife. Farther to the right the mirror of Lake Elementita with its splash of pink flamingos harmonizing delightfully with the pale green-blue of the calm water was as pretty a postcard as one could wish for. Away to the left stretched the green scrub and rugged patterns of rocky outcrops of Waterloo Ridge, and beyond still, the glint of Lake Naivasha. In front and to the westward the sombre bulk of Eburru and the Mau heights soared to nine thousand feet, the topmost peaks just puncturing the soft ivory cushions hovering above them. Between them and the pinnacle we occupied were the Badlands, an expanse of volcanic lava rock; mysterious, barren, uncharted and forbidding. Like its impenetrable cousin, ten miles to the south on the edge of Lake Naivasha, the inhospitable papyrus swamp, it was an area eschewed by security forces, eliminated with bigoted finality, as being totally unsuitable for any kind of human habitation, even subhuman which meant Mau Mau. Occasionally the tracks of a gang had been followed to its perimeter and lost; the conclusions had been that gangs entered only sufficiently far to shake pursuers off their scent. Recently, however the feelings in anti-terrorist circles had hardened considerably and a few days previously some exhaustive operations had been carried out in the area. For the moment I'd like to reserve the comment I wish to make on those operations.

The Badlands cover some twelve square miles and is, or was, atrocious stuff in which to patrol. Comprised of endless undulations of lava rock, like large sand dunes only less rolling, the surface being like glass-paper magnified hundreds of times to give it an unholy and altogether frightening appearance rather like one imagines the silent, lifeless surface of a distant planet to be. It is a vast jigsaw puzzle of pin-cushions—with the pins left in—or gargantuan porcupines laid end to end and side by side. The only tracks to be found being those made by buck; but for all practical purposes the Badlands are trackless featureless and waterless.

From atop the hill they looked deceptively flat and devoid of any forbidding features. This is due to the incredibly hardy tough perennial bush that flourishes to a height of six feet and more; coarse grass, holly tree and thorn bush also manage miraculously to exist. But, no matter what the vegetation, it all looks tired brittle and dry—nay, parched. Once one penetrates this wide area of vicious lava-rock 'sea anemones', it is hopeless to obtain orientation. It is frightfully easy to lose oneself in the bewildering moonscape up and down, round and round, along scarcely discernible animal tracks that all disappear after a few yards. Patrols had either to take along a good compass or be prepared to wander aimlessly for hours, sometimes days, in a bone-dry, unearthly and sinisterly quiet wilderness in which the rasp-like surface of the rock could destroy a heavy pair of boots in a day.

The Badlands could rightly be described as the 'hairy mole' on the fresh and attractive face of Kenya's highlands just as that damp, squelchy, leech-infested papyrus swamp close by Naivasha could be adequately called its 'Sargasso Sea'.

"God! What a swine of a place," I thought, while sat scanning the weird formations of rock. Just twelve days earlier six hundred soldiers, police and home-guardsmen had surrounded the vile area and invested it for a week or more until aircraft were made available to blitz it. It was my own T.C.T. that had initiated the operation after having successfully tracked a large gang into its eerie depths. Two starving, mad-with-thirst beggars had surrendered themselves to the stop-lines, the Glosters had shot a self-styled 'brigadier' and another had been captured by Masai herdsmen after having broken through the tight cordon.

In the main, however, security force commanders had groped in the dark and had only 'seized the nettle' to show that they were unafraid to chance their luck. It had been a nightmarish, confusing and unco-ordinated performance, the major object of which had been to contain the area until the R.A.F. could blast it with H.E. (high-explosive bombs). Everyone had been confident that the 'micks' would scuttle helter-skelter into the arms of the cordon. But no such spectacular end-product was witnessed. In theory it had all been okay, but in practice horribly out of tune with reality and fact—namely, that nobody was certain just where in the twelve-square-mile area they were skulking or whether, in fact they were still within the cordon, or if they had a source of water somewhere. (As it happens, they did. They used Cole Estate's abundant supply!) It was all guesses, hope, obey orders and bash on, regardless!

A vulture appeared from nowhere and commenced to circle over us. It served to pull me out of my reverie and I decided we should take a walk. Taking a last look around from atop the knoll we slithered down the other side with the intention of making a desultory circuit back round to our vehicle; being antipathetically disposed to the Badlands I had no desire to cast about too diligently for spoor only to become embroiled in anything like what we had recently set in motion. Any enthusiasm I may have had for siege campaigns had been stifled and I felt bilious just to think of it—an interminable thrash through an operation based on conjecture and boosted with hope.

Really! How bolshie and delightfully cantankerous of me to think thus. What about the plethora of cattle-hoof impressions that were picked up almost immediately on a thread of track that skirted the foot of the hill we descended? And of our ever-mounting excitement as they were followed deep into the hellish underworld of the Badlands? Professional pride if you like.

With an obstinacy that negated altogether my aversion for the infernal region of lava rock we thrust slowly on. The tracking was painfully tedious. Sploshes of fresh dung here and there confirmed that my two Wanderobo trackers were hot on the trail. I cursed the fact that it was now late afternoon. We were not equipped for a night in such a God-forsaken place and, in any case, though we may well have stumbled upon the slaughtered beasts or the remains of them, what of the gang? What hope had we of locating them? We had, just a few days earlier, discovered how exasperatingly easy it was for Mau Mau to slip from our clutches in the Badlands. As it happens, even while deliberating abandonment, it was a most bizarre contingency that influenced my decision to discontinue the tracking.

It had already occurred to me that our route was taking us

through territory that military forces had scoured during the recent operation. Then, when I heard the ominous high pitched buzzing sound, I knew instantly what it was and halted the patrol. The angry hum grew louder and filled the hollow we had halted in. It seemed to assail us from all sides and we apprehensively stood and swivelled our heads to see where it came from. 'It' was a swarm of bees and it was plain that the bees were in ill-humour.

Several of the wooden cylindrical hives lodged in trees had been passed en route and it was obvious that some local Masai or Kikuyu squatter labour, or even Mau Mau themselves, had established the hives and removed the honey from time to time. Cautiously we edged across the hollow, through a narrow pass in the clinker rough lava rock into another depression. There before us hanging askew in the fork of a thorn tree was a shattered hive. To the side of it was a dark, amorphous mass that was fraying at the edges as bees sped hither and thither. Already we were swatting at bees that buzzed hostilely around us.

Then I remembered and froze with fear. "*Toroka! Toroka!*" I shouted to the team, and we made our hasty withdrawal.

What I had remembered was that during the recent operations a patrol of the Glosters had suffered a fatality, though not by Mau Mau. One young and foolish member of the patrol had decided to amuse his buddies by directing a burst from his automatic into a hive. Perhaps the young, sweat-soaked, plodding soldier sought only to enliven a dull patrol. The infuriated insects swarmed outside their violated hive, conferred briefly as to who among these inconsiderate humans had been the perpetrator, then descended on him in their hundreds, each to inject its painful, poisonous little sting, until the poor fellow writhed in terror and agony before his horrified comrades. Before he lost consciousness and his agonized screams changed to laboured, stertorous breathing his head and face swelled with enormous bumps until he was grotesque and unrecognizable. His alarmed and aghast companions rushed him back for medical attention but he never recovered from the massive stinging.

This must have been the scene of the tragedy that had so shocked police and army personnel during the big Badlands operation several days previously. What had flabbergasted most of us was the singling out by the bees with such uncanny instinct of the one soldier responsible. Needless to say, I wasted no time in making my exit from that place and allowing the bees to continue making the best of their sundered hive.

Before moving on from the subject of stock thefts it would be as well to record the noteworthy fact that it was not only Mau Mau that stole cattle. Our colourful and picturesque friends, the Masai, were occasionally found to be the culprits. Though, in fairness to them, I must add, that they would never treat the beasts in the cruel manner that Kikuyu terrorists were wont to, such as twisting their tails, severing udders or hamstringing. To a Masai cattle are second only to his love of freedom, and even his wife takes third place.

Significantly, it was by courtesy of some Masai employed on the Cole Estate that we were presented with yet another bizarre spectacle before our 'routine patrol' was over that day. It was rather more impressive than the bees and quite as unnerving.

Having emerged, with no little relief I may say, from the Badlands we were returning at a brisk pace to the team's Land Rover. Rounding the hill we had earlier scaled it was not long before the vehicle and water tanks came into view, as also what appeared to be a group of Whirling Dervishes!

Quickening our pace we covered half the distance before identifying this agitated group as Masai, about a dozen of them, all naked and each carrying a spear and *simi*. They were in a wide circle and each in turn was leaping high into the air as if in competition with each other. This was not at all an unusual game-cum-exercise with young Masai warriors who were famous for their ability to spring up and down on the spot three feet and more in the air. This they did without noticeably bending their knees. However, these Masai were not doing it for either exercise or entertainment—they were preparing to engage the enemy! This leaping in the air was known also to be a preliminary limbering up. They were oblivious of our approach and we stopped at a discreet distance to observe.

What a fantastic sight it was; several of them had erect penises, so worked up and excited were they. I had heard that this erotic manifestation was not unusual with them prior to combat. The expressions on their faces were trance-like and some looked quite mad. Every muscle was taut and the whole body rigid, their spears held high and menacing while they grunted in a sort of sing-song chant. On and on they went while we apprehensively gazed on.

Why were they behaving like this so near our vehicle? I was anxious to find out. Surely they couldn't be angry with us for some reason? We had never had any quarrel with this proud and dignified tribe and greatly admired their stubborn refusal to change their traditional tribal habits.

Well, there we were, and it would have been rather embarrassing to back away. I said to my Somali N.C.O., who regarded the group with a disdainful eye, "*Piga bunduki yako upande kitchwa yao.*" (Fire your rifle over their heads.) This he did and it had the desired effect.

The cavorting circle of tall, black, glistening nudes stood absolutely still and turned towards us with not much friendliness on their faces; their chests heaved, their erections drooped and spears were slowly lowered. Without hesitation I led my team straight into the centre of them, looked quickly around at their still taut faces and selected the oldest of them. He I addressed with the Masai salutation, "*Soba!*", then gripped his upper left arm and squeezed it—an accepted gesture of peace. For fully half a minute he stood unmoving and his steady eyes bored into mine. Tightening my grip around his bicep I could feel the pulsating of a big vein that stood out like a tube inserted under the skin. My lips felt dry and the smile I managed to form on them was tight and awkward. The heavy breathing around me gradually subsided.

"*Soba!*" he replied in a sonorous voice and, jabbing his spear into the ground, reached forward to grip my left upper arm. The spell was broken. Suddenly everyone was jabbering away in Swahili. Several Masai women appeared carrying ochre-stained blankets and one or two gourds. With the blankets our lithe, clean-limbed warriors covered their nudity to some extent. The gourds were offered around and only my two Wanderobo askari, who are somewhat akin to Masai, slaked their thirst with the contents. The remainder of us were not partial to a beverage of milk and blood!

We soon discovered the reason for their gala performance. They had seen us head into the Badlands and believed it highly probable we would flush out the Mau Mau known to be hiding there. Throughout the emergency these Masai on the Cole Estate had had to tolerate the sporadic rustling of their employer's livestock. They were always on the lookout for their detested traditional enemies, the Kikuyu, and if they happened to be Mau Mau as well then nothing could stop them from venting that hatred.

During the recent operation they had rendered valuable assistance to security forces and one of them had been set upon and castrated by a group of terrorists he stumbled across lurking just inside the cordon. This had, naturally, served to intensify their hate. Had our patrol sent any terrorists scurrying in their direction that afternoon they would have been accorded the same savage treatment as General Ngome had been, several months before not so far from this very place, too.

So yet another 'routine' stock-theft patrol was concluded. Once again the devils had out-manoeuvred us.

Chapter 14

Operation Bullrush: the waning moon of Mau Mau over a papyrus swamp

30/12/55. Govt. Vet. Stn. HZP.7320. R.V.P. T.C.T. 9 found hide with 30/40 terrs. Patrol opened fire but no known cas. Cooking pots, pangas and clothing found in hide and destroyed. Terrs scattered into papyrus and two parties of 10 and 2 were later seen by K.P.R. spotter aircraft but no contact by ground forces. R.H. mortared area. Area surrounded during the night by 2. coys Glosters, 4 pltns G.S.U., police from 3 posts, 45 H.G. and 3 R.V.P. T.C.T.s. 2300 hrs 30/12/55, 10 terrs tried to break out at HZP.710267, were driven back by Glosters, no cas. 1 bag of maize recovered. At HZP.302395, 40 terrs tried to get away, time 2359 hrs. 5 got through, no cas. Others left 6 bags maize when driven back ...

The above is a factual extract from a consolidated sitrep in respect of an operation initiated in a papyrus swamp on the shore of Lake Naivasha and which became officially referred to as Operation *Bullrush*.

Before presenting the full details I should explain that the government veterinary station referred to at the beginning of the sitrep happened to be situated at the edge of the papyrus swamp about four miles from Naivasha township. It was not the spot at which the Mau Mau gang was contacted but for convenience of identification on the map this salient feature was used. The various figures preceded by letters are map references and the reader is kindly requested to refer to the glossary of terms at the back of the book if he should wish to decipher the jargon and abbreviations employed throughout this chapter.

What had happened was this: On 30 December 1955 as the early morning mists were still swirling around the lush, green impenetrable and leech-infested swamp on the northeastern shore of Lake Naivasha my T.C.T. and I, aided by a recent Mau Mau capture, located a gang estimated to be between forty and fifty strong. Fire was opened but the contact aborted and there were no known casualties. A most bitterly disappointing (for the team) start to one of the most spectacular and expensive operations launched during the three years that Kenya's emergency had raged—three years of relentless and untiring effort to rid the colony of the scourge of Mau Mau. Memories of this particular enterprise by the armed forces have remained with me, vivid and exciting, and, no doubt, the full facts of it will one day be set down by a qualified military historian who has the facilities and the ability to obtain and marshal the plethora of facts and figures. I shall be content to record as faithfully as possible some of the highlights and wider issues, especially with regard to the inception of the mammoth operation that blossomed. The technicalities I prefer to leave to the experts whose task will be, if more laborious, certainly more competently dealt with.

A word or two on the swamp itself is necessary first. It covers some ten square miles; hippopotamus abound in it as also shoals of leeches. It had never really been charted and there were only a couple of jeepable tracks that traversed the watery wastes. To explore the swamp more thoroughly one had to use the channels made and used by hippos! Not recommended but often adopted nevertheless. The reed grows to a height of ten feet or more, as dense as a tropical rain storm and quite as damp. To struggle through it is how a mouse must feel threading its way across an unmown lawn. Include the stinking water, the disgusting leeches, the hazards of hippo and the fact that wide tracts are completely impenetrable unless cut through and you have a general idea. It is, even so, almost impossible to describe accurately the full horrors and discomforts of working in papyrus as profuse and luxuriant as it grows around Lake Naivasha.

There had at odd intervals been a number of minor operations, more in the nature of sorties, in various sectors of the swamp. Terrorist gangs had been known to seek refuge in the silent labyrinth of reed and the occasional 'mick' had been sighted. Reports of a high grading were from time to time received by R.V.P. Special Branch officers that gangs were using the abominable expanse and had constructed substantial hideouts in the drier parts. Patrols, however, had all returned with the same verdict—as a place for regular habitation, even by hardy survival-conditioned Mau Mau, it was absurd to imply that there were 'bed & breakfast' facilities in a Little Venice!

It was the fabled Badlands all over again, but the desultory patrols had never discovered anything of operational significance—no large hides, no frequently used tracks, no food stores, game traps, *postas*. What! With all those vicious leeches and those enormous hippos splashing along narrow waterways! Security forces hated the swamp and regarded any excursion through it as downright punitive. But, for all that, they were as naïve as the Honourable Mr Gladstone was when he concluded that the Mahdi in the 1880s was just a religious mystic with no 'savvy'.

Late in December 1955 a certain terrorist was captured by some Masai herdsmen between Gilgil and Naivasha. Special Branch authorities instantly whipped him in and within a few hours the usual astonishing metamorphosis had taken place. From being a fugitive, hunted, predatory animal moving from one lair to another, living on the corn he could pick from the standing wheat and sucking bones long since cleaned of flesh, he became the co-operative agent of security forces. He had been handed over to the F.I.O. in whose area of responsibility he had last roamed and terrorized with his gang. The F.I.O. lodged him with his pseudo team to visit his last used hideouts, to check *postas*, learn of the tracks and watering places used and so on, but the programme with him showed little promise and his usefulness was soon exhausted. It was time to off-load him to C.I.D. for their action—

possibly they had some evidence with which to prosecute the fellow for a criminal offence (apart from the offence of being a member of an unlawful society!). Criminal procedure always seemed to be somewhat cock-eyed during the emergency.

I was able to solicit successfully for this knave and he was then quizzed most patiently by my team, as had been the practice so often before. The scruffy individual went by the name of Henry and during our talks he made mention of having left a very large gang in the Naivasha papyrus swamp some two months previous. He'd never been back to the *campa* since but as the gang was comfortably ensconced when he left it he had no reason to suppose that it was not still there—and neither had I nor my team. The fact that we had made over past months countless safaris into forests and gorges with similar de-terrorized Mau Mau on similar information and with similar glimmering hopes in no way deterred us. The same strange thrill and satisfaction was always derived from stalking through gloomy forests into recently occupied hideouts behind freshly captured or surrendered terrorists.

So it was then that with six members of my T.C.T. together with the 'Kenya Cowboy' whose bailiwick included the swamp we followed Henry to the edge of it. The Land Rover I left with its driver and a guard and we got down to business. There is a river that skirts the periphery of the swamp in the sector we had entered and was utilized for irrigation purposes by an Italian who owned a few hundred acres of fine maize adjacent to the papyrus on reclaimed swamp land. It was possible to inform this Italian several days later, with no little ire, that his sumptuous maize *shamba* had been the major source of food for scores of terrorists for many months past; it had been a veritable larder right on the gang's doorstep.

The banks of this river, or stream, were shallow and muddy and, after following it round the edge of the papyrus for a while, a single footprint was spotted. The owner of it had jumped across the water and had left the one deep impression. It was not long before we were following with great ease a beautifully clear set of naked footprints through the enveloping curtains of papyrus.

Silent progress soon became practically impossible due to the deep, water-filled, muddy channels that were followed, but at this stage it was not considered necessary to exercise perfect combat-tracker drill. Very shortly Henry assured me that the spoor was that of a *mutu ya misitoni* (forest gangster) and that it led in the general direction of the hideout he had told us of. He was able to remember where it was situated and, as the spoor of the terrorist being followed was headed towards it, we were entitled to assume it was hot.

From then on the spoor was disregarded; it was almost impossible to detect anyway due to the ever-increasing tracts of water. With waxing excitement and weapons poised and cocked we splashed our way on as close to Henry as we could. I was immediately behind him and ready to rush past as soon as he ducked down, this being a pre-arranged signal that he had sighted either the hideout or Mau Mau. Ex-terrorists that led security forces back to their hides were always, understandably, morbidly nervous of the fire that would be directed over and around them, therefore it was imperative they were given complete assurance that if they lay down then no harm would befall them.

The Marula Post inspector and I toted our issue Sterling sub-machine guns and my six askari had their .303 rifles, now of the No. 5 pattern (shorter and not so heavy as the S.M.L.E.). I felt sure that their rifles would be quite useless in this location and regretted not having issued some of them with Greener shotguns instead. I had my inspector colleague, Dave, brought up behind me and we continued to inch along. I began to tingle with expectation. I'd made safaris behind enough ex-terrorists to sense that Henry knew fairly confidently just what lay ahead of us. He would certainly not have been practising such expertise in his movements or have mentally detached himself from the patrol, were he not so confident.

The waterway being followed was about a yard wide and the tall papyrus crowded in stiflingly on all sides. My imagination refused to remain in check and I could feel the eyes upon us. During every few yards of our tedious progress I had seen the flitting shapes of a score of terrorists and had heard a provoking repertoire of sounds purporting to be a gang put to flight. Noise of splashing was unavoidable and we were all giving each other angry and reproving looks.

Henry stopped, bent low, turned round and stared at me beseechingly. He said nothing, his mouth opened then closed. He started to shake and then made jerky gestures with his right arm in a direction ahead and to the right. I dropped down beside him with racing thoughts; my dilemma was huge—should I give a signal for the team to rush ahead? If there was anyone there and they were not revealed within the next few seconds they'd never be spotted at all.

"*Mlinzi yao! Mlinzi yao!*" stammered the quivering Henry. He was referring to a gang sentry. That was enough incentive for me.

Despite being able to see nothing beyond the green lattice of the formidable reed, I lunged forward. The water that was now ankle-deep prevented any semblance of speed and, having gained several yards, an opening appeared on my left. It was like a tunnel and the earth was firm and dry. It was just large enough to permit passage in single file. Not knowing what to expect and utterly heedless I raced on for another twenty yards when a sort of rustic gate was arrived at. Incongruous as it struck me, I threw myself against it, noticing as I pressed past that there was a little platform by its side, probably for a sentry. Plenty of time to examine it later, I thought.

I then found myself in the middle of a dry, well-trampled clearing, a fire still burning, clothing spread out to dry, piles of maize and firewood, chattels and personal effects but, no dwellers! I could smell them alright and they surely could not have fled far. I gave them full marks for having a very alert sentry system. What consternation I experienced as I beheld some six or seven tunnels in the wall of papyrus around the clearing that the fleeing terrorists could have used. I selected one that looked a bit wider and more well-worn than the rest and plunged into it. Dave and my askari followed closely. The thin strand of a path twisted and turned, was sometimes swamp but more often an almost solid screen of reed, the staves of which, as thick as one's forearm, had to be forced apart. There was no lack of evidence to suggest that it was the route they had taken but how far would it penetrate? Was it wise to chase them too deep into such a morass?

There was a bend to the right and while contemplating the merit of determined pursuit I glimpsed movement ahead. Barely discernible figures had pushed onto the track and then vanished just as suddenly. Were we being ambushed? Was it another exit route from the hideout that joined this one? God! How exasperating that the damned papyrus should forbid a clear view ahead.

Checking my spurt forward I raised my Sterling, flicked the safety off and, in a glorious spasm of pent-up elation, released an entire magazine in short bursts. I fairly raked the whole of my right front hoping that the 9mm rounds would drill through the staves of papyrus to find more fleshy targets. As the grateful applause of the stuttering detonations died away I pressed the magazine catch, removed the spent magazine and smacked on a spare full one, then charged on, half-expecting to see a dead 'mick' or two sprawled on the track, or at least some red stuff to follow. There was nothing! Nothing at all, and ahead it was as quiet as a mausoleum. We all stood and stared dumfounded into the verdant gloaming, feeling a trifle foolish. There was, however, scant opportunity to analyze the situation, the gang had been routed and there was nothing to gain from castigating ourselves for failing to have come to closer grips with whomever it was we had flushed. I permitted the team to press on for a further hundred yards or so and to punctuate its progress with prophylactic fire just in case there was a bold group who had decided to make a stand.

It was safe to assume, anyway, that some of them would have diverged from the escape route and launched themselves into the forest of reed hoping, quite soundly, that we would hare off along the main track. During the follow-up many an interesting article dropped by the rapidly dispersing gangsters was picked up. Tatty notebooks (always of value to Special Branch), sacks of food, chattels, home-made firearms, a carved walking stick, an old boot, a string of colourful beads. It was all collected up before the team retraced its squelching footsteps and re-entered the palatial hideout.

In a moment I would like to describe in more detail this unusual hideout of militant Mau Mau gangsters. For the present, now that contact had been made, abortive or otherwise, the real problems materialized. It was now that decisions and appropriate action were necessary. Here in the swamp was a gang estimated to be some fifty strong, and something had to be done quick smart.

After spending a few minutes ascertaining the full extent of the hideout and collecting up all the abandoned junk, which was dumped into a large heap in the centre of the clearing, I made my way back to the team's vehicle with two askari. We were, in fact, not more than twenty minutes' walk from it.

Among the pile of *taka taka* (rubbish), so called, Henry had drawn my attention to a leopard-skin valise and had informed us with conviction that it was the property of none other than the 'Field Marshal' himself, Mbaria Kanui. (How young Mwangi would have opened his eyes had he been with the team. He had long since been on the payroll of the Glosters as a tracker.) But the staggering thing was that Mbaria should ever have emerged from the high forests and security of Kipipiri where he had eluded us so successfully for so long. It had been his avowed practice never to expose himself out in the settled areas. Why, of all the atrocious places, should he deposit himself in the papyrus? Answers to such questions and many more were readily forthcoming from Henry. According to his knowledgeable account all the gangs of the Rift and of Kipipiri had been instructed to attend a *baraza* in the hideout of another famous gang leader, 'General' Mekanika—his was the 'spread' we'd just located—in order to listen to the visionary sermons of the celebrated witchdoctor Kingori and to receive his sacraments! This charlatanic Mau Mau's prevalent sentiments were known to be non-aggressive and he was counselling a back-pedalling policy to enable leaders to negotiate for a general amnesty. The wily old witchdoctor had had dreams in which he'd had divine insight into what was in store for all hard-core terrorists. What was in store, apparently, was misery and hardship, and with the rider that they'd all be *impuissant* to alleviate it.

There it was then: with a stupendous stroke of luck, plus a hunch and the determined use of a capture, the team had achieved something that had been denied the armed forces for months. Never since 1954, in fact, when a large and well-armed gang had been surrounded at Dundori on the outskirts of Nairobi and progressively blasted to smithereens, had the discovery of such an interesting concourse contained within one well-defined area been made. (During that heavy engagement on 14 October 1954, eight terrorists were killed, three were captured and seven precision weapons were recovered.) But, what an area! How slender still the chances of eliminating any of them.

As I called up Control on the Land Rover's V.H.F. radio I guessed what frenetic activity was to ensue. I knew that what I was about to set in motion, which must involve an immense assembly of security forces, would have to be answered for in unequivocal terms. I knew, too, that they, the brass, would not be at once convinced of the authenticity of such a report—imagination! exaggeration! hallucination! glory-hunting! However, I had the inspector from Marula Post to corroborate the report. I diluted my sitrep as much as possible without detracting from its urgency.

"... Control to Tracker Nine, reading you loud and clear. Come in, over."

"Tracker Nine to Control. Priority, Betty. Have just discovered large hide in papyrus at approx. HZR.724190. Team opened fire but so far as is known there are no casualties. Gang strength estimated at forty to fifty. They were followed to a point due west where the papyrus opens on cleared land below the vet station. Am now returning to the hide to destroy all food, clothing and equipment recovered. Will destroy by burning and the fire will guide any spotter plane available so that a more accurate reference can be obtained ..."

Half an hour later, while busy back at the hideout destroying everything that could be found, the spotter plane arrived and circled overhead. It then buzzed off and was seen diving and making aerial enquiries over different parts of the swamp. It was yet again an occasion when the team had omitted to take along a portable V.H.F. pack-set and I cursed our inability to communicate with the K.P.R. Airwing pilot above.

Before going on to narrate those significant events that followed hard on the heels of this momentous discovery I will pause for a moment to describe more closely this incredible home of Man Mau, so radically unlike anything the team had ever come across before. It was doubly fascinating by virtue of the fact that everyone's conviction had been that no terrorists would, or could, live for long in the wicked swamp without succumbing to some ghastly fever or being sucked bloodless by leeches.

Around the central clearing radiated exits that were really half tunnels, and the lofty reed closed over above so that it was necessary to either part them or to bend double to gain entry. Once inside the all-concealing labyrinth of sturdy reed there was a maze of minor passageways each leading to and inter-joining small rectangular recesses in which were crudely fashioned sleeping litters. Some of these were elaborate affairs and comprised a strong structure of papyrus, each stem of which was secured to another stem with strips of dried papyrus skin and interlaced with the foliage, a spray of which crowns each reed. What a durable and versatile plant it is. Although there was less water in this particular part of the swamp, there were numerous patches where one had to wade ankle-deep; it was the dry season too, and it occurred to me that with any rise in the level of the lake these elevated platforms, or litters, would be essential if the occupants were to keep dry. The overall layout was a classic of improvisation and of a coming-to-terms with nature. Survival from exposure played a role of paramount importance among militant Mau Mau and hereabouts they certainly had brought it to a very fine art indeed. There were reed-lined pits with cleverly disguised lids for the storage of food, drainage channels hoed around the sleeping recesses, perfectly adequate drinking receptacles fashioned from cow horns, serviceable kit-bags from animals' stomachs, combs carved from bamboo, needles from bone and small pouches for matches and tobacco ingeniously prepared from hides; even instruments for grinding maize were found and which, too, were fine examples of primitive craftsmanship. It was an intriguing reconstruction of Stone-Age mankind.

Every path other than the main entrance and the tortuous exit trail came to a dead end in the eerie, loathsome depths of the papyrus. From above nothing could be identified to indicate inhabitation by Mau Mau because the fuzzy foliage atop the reed overlapped so densely that to a spotter plane it was just an ocean of green, very similar to bamboo thickets. An astonishing feature of the hideout was the complete absence of excrement, or even the smell of it. It goes without saying that terrorists obeyed calls of nature much the same as everyone else, but they did so well away from their lodgings and covered it over as would cats. They were alert to the torment of huge horsefly and mosquito through the presence of refuse and offal so it was in their interests to be as sanitary as possible. Notwithstanding which there were myriad insects buzzing around all sectors of the swamp; this I remember only too well for it was my misfortune to stew in the pot that I'd put on the fire during succeeding days.

Before that eventful day at the end of December was over a military-police operation of major proportions began to take shape. The lean, slightly stooping and indefatigable Chief Inspector Jimmy Jamieson, who was assigned as El Supremo of the proceedings, latched on to his fearsome responsibilities with an enthusiasm that quite belied his already onerous position as the officer in charge of a busy town station. He duly joined me for discussions at the team's location on the edge of the swamp. I will admit to having found it rather difficult to conceal my amusement to see him dressed in an athlete's track-suit, but then Jimmy was known to be a little eccentric at times.

There had in the meantime been several reports from K.P.R. Vultures of small pockets of terrorists at various places in the swamp and, having debriefed me, Jimmy was fully sold on the idea that here indeed was a target worth going all-out for. And he really did pull out the stops; the planning was spontaneous and ambitious, all with the concurrence of the superintendent at Naivasha, of course. Units of the Glosters and the Rifle Brigade, Police General Service Units, the Kenya Regiment, Kikuyu Homeguard, T.C.T.s, and lots more besides; all were poured with a mighty splash into the operational area and that first night the swamp was contained by a cordon the circumference of which, excluding the lakeshore, was something like thirteen miles.

The reader may well wonder how it was possible to contain such a huge area. It was precisely this enormous problem that the various commanders had to grapple with from the beginning to end of the operation. It was achieved in the main by the employment of saturating rifle and machine-gun fire. Security forces in the cordon were spaced approximately every twenty or thirty yards; if the terrain was open, then this distance was increased. Each man was instructed to fire off a certain number of rounds at irregular intervals throughout the night and to be ever-watchful during the day. Upward of seven hundred men were required for the cordon alone! This, plus para-illuminating flares fired from two-inch mortars at intervals, during the night, was sufficient to deter any major breakout—or was believed to be, anyway!

As the days wore on the forces increased and the cordon thickened until soon there were over two and a half thousand armed forces pitted against the wily foe. The combat débâcle was enjoined in earnest.

Every night the barrage rose to a deafening crescendo; seldom had so many soldiers enjoyed such a one-way shooting match. It was like an annual militia camp with the accent on realism. In all Kenya's, indeed East Africa's, colonial history it was an unparalleled military extravaganza. Thousands upon thousands of rounds of ammunition were expended, the tracer was spectacular and together with the flares dropping slowly beneath their small silk parachutes it was comparable to a gala Brock's fireworks display.

Each morning as the sun rose patrols moved off from so many points on the perimeter while all fire was strictly withheld. They would check most thoroughly every possible sign that might have indicated a breakout and strove their utmost to allay the oppressive fear that the sector commanders entertained as weary day succeeded weary day—"Are we wasting our time? Have they broken out? How can we be sure that the bastards are not now somewhere else, scoffing at us?"

Doubts about the justification for continuing the investment ever increased and all patrols were tediously debriefed. Three days passed and there was no sign of a terrorist body dead or alive. I can assure the reader that I made myself scarce, I had no wish to be accused of having allowed my imagination to run riot. As it was, events were largely out of my hands and, apart from being consulted now and then on the topography of the area or being requested to check and categorically report on some suspicious circumstance, I just endured the awful suspense waiting for something to happen.

I heard many an authoritative critic describe the *Bullrush* operation as farcical and an unmitigated waste of money, materials and effort, not to mention the drubbing to British prestige! A letter to the *East African Standard* decried it as a "costly and foolhardy venture, the epitome of military bungling and in the same category as Mons".

Actually I have no intention of expressing an opinion one way or the other; humble police inspectors who commanded T.C.T.s were expected to retire deferentially into the operational background once having played their part in locating the elusive foe. Those who decreed that the onslaught should proceed apace had access to far more intelligence than I and, quite possibly, the Special Branch and military intelligence officers were already in possession of reliable information to support my own findings. I prefer, however, to remain rather sceptical on this point for, and subsequent events tended to confirm this, there was at the start of the 'battle' a wide-scale operation being conducted on the slopes of the Aberdares designed to net those very gang leaders and their followers who were at that time contained in the great cordon around the papyrus swamp. I do not even consider it necessary to sympathize with those security-force commanders who failed to satisfy the bystanders who, and often vociferously, awaited glorious and justifiable results after so much controversy. Not always would they have been as correct in their decisions or wise in the planning as the critical audience thought they should have been. But what I feel constrained to comment is that it took courage and experience, honesty and inflexibility to continue the bombardment and maintain the tight cordon night after night on the sole assumption that, in the absence of any real evidence to the contrary, the rebels must still be trapped in the encirclement of security forces and that, logically, they must therefore be smoked out, starved out or bombed out.

An exceedingly frustrating assumption, no less so because it was, in the circumstances, unavoidable. But, when senior military officers have once committed themselves in a major operation it is seldom they will admit to being in error. Somehow they always find a tactically logical excuse for dedicating all their forces and energies to the bitter end.

As it was, there was nothing they needed to fret over because, sceptical as they may have become, even to the extent of morbid anxiety, those they sought to annihilate were still splashing, fatigued, petrified and hopeless, among the leeches and the hippos of the accursed swamp. They were there, so bombard and decrease the cordon, bombard and sweep, bombard and hope, bombard and enjoy it!

And so the 'Battle of the bullrushes', as one sardonic correspondent described it, leapt sensationally and vigorously through thirty days to herald a new year that was to damage irreparably the malleable backbone of Mau Mau's subversive anti-European organization.

As mentioned already, my T.C.T. was edged into the wings somewhat after the initial contact. We were relegated to those unpretentious and menial tasks of all other police units around the swamp and, of course, rightfully so. Not long was it before the mediocre police enterprise became an almost exclusively military display. The mercurial Chief Inspector Jamieson, who had elected to continue his appearances incognito in the track-suit, was relieved of the overall command by the C.O. Glosters and subsequently concerned himself with administering the assorted police units, of which there were ample to satisfy his relatively lowly status among the *Bullrush* hierarchy. It was Jimmy who demanded, and was granted, the right to concentrate all police units in one clearly demarcated sector of the cordon instead of their being dispersed throughout the army contingents and subordinated to their whims and capricious requirements. We police had always considered that the army tended to bog down with rationing arrangements, white-washing stones and conforming ritualistically with Company Orders—if a soldier did not wait until the N.C.O. in charge of his patrol told him that the scruffily dressed, spiky-haired individual carrying a bag of maize and a *panga*, wading along a hippo trait was a terrorist before opening fire he'd find himself on defaulters' parade before his adjutant—to a most irritating extent. So it was, therefore, that the police G.S.U.s, T.C.T.s and forest post personnel took over a two-mile-long sector; it was now that the rivalry commenced in earnest!

It was the sector nearest a number of lakeshore estates and our H.Q. was sited just below a settler called Hopcraft. This venerable Kenyan had been yelling at the authorities for months past to clear the gangs out of the swamp. We all firmly believed that it was the sector most likely to yield results. Our own shrewd tracking and local knowledge told us so. There was one unabashed fear we had and that was of the hail of rifle and machine-gun fire of the Rifle Brigade who were situated diametrically opposite and who laid down a terrifying barrage throughout the night. At times the elevation of their artillery happened to be inordinately high and stray rounds frequently hummed over our lines. It was never considered to be beyond the realms of deliberate provocation! However, this unfair suggestion was never openly expressed; we relied far too heavily upon their charitable offerings of compo rations and flameless fuel heaters for us to be rude to them.

Six days after the cordon was hastily thrown around the swamp and patrols without number had criss-crossed the watery hell, locating the occasional hideout and caches of foodstuffs, an incident of stupendous moment occurred—in the Hopcraft sector too! The notorious 'General' Mekanika and remnants of his battered gang were contacted and shot up just inside the stop-lines in chest-high water.

What happened actually was that during the night there had been an attempted breakout, one of many, and the usual heavy bombardment was set up to drive them back. Several terrorists were reliably reported to have been hit and the following morning T.C.T. No. 10 followed up. Within minutes they recovered the body of one shockingly emaciated rogue and found the tracks of several others. The team shortly found itself in knee-deep, cold, stagnant water, but pressed on undaunted. (We were, in fact, by now convinced that while security force patrols were wending their way around the swamp's periphery, the terrorists backed away into the more inaccessible reaches, where in many places they would have been up to their necks in water, and there would remain until the patrols had passed on.) It was with the aid of a K.P.R. spotter plane liaising brilliantly overhead, which had sighted a group of heads and shoulders through a gap in the papyrus and then dived low over them, that the team had caught sight of its quarry. As a result of some first-class shooting by the team's commander one of the group was shot dead and soon identified as 'General' Mekanika himself. The jubilant members of that T.C.T. spent many gruesome minutes after emerging from the swamp removing leeches from their limbs with lighted cigarette ends.

It was exactly what everyone had been waiting for to quell the increasing doubts. Despair had sunk to its nadir and both the army and police alike were in urgent need of some sort of strong stimulus. This success provided it, plenty of it at that. Efforts were renewed with great purposefulness—if Mekanika and his brethren were still roaming the fetid swamp then so must many others. What exuberance was displayed over the success; yet most were disinclined to vaunt the chance encounter because their sighs of relief were every bit as real as their cheers.

But that was only the start; it was but a confirmatory incident, and as the days passed so the trapped gangsters were steadily accounted for. There were no super battles or fire fights or even substantial contacts. The animal-like, obdurate Mau Mau were tediously, almost unnoticeably, eliminated one by one. A patrol would report finding one that had been killed by mortar fire, a K.P.R. spotter plane would radio that a group had been sighted near the lakeshore and that he was bombing it—lobbing 20 pounders over the side of the cockpit!

There were a few token surrenders also. These surrenders were a pitiful experience and scarcely worth rejoicing over. Their dishevelled and skeletal appearance invoked feelings of the most stinging humility and compassion. Some broke out at weak points in the cordon, many died within that would never be known of, a few were captured and still others were tracked down after they had successfully made their escape.

It was the vexing inability to satisfy the question "How many are left inside?" that rendered the task so difficult. So significantly did the entire fate of the operation depend upon the answer. Upon it hinged the imponderable 'Was it worth carrying on for the remainder?' Especially was this so when, under the direction of District Officers, hundreds of Kikuyu homeguardsmen were assembled for a gigantic sweep.

It had been decided, after several 'O' groups attended by worried 'Acorns' and respectfully assertive 'Sunray Minors' to progressively reduce the area of operations to more workable proportions. To send in patrols over ten square miles and hope to contact a few terrorists was ludicrous. The conference of the various sector commanders agreed that so long as the cordon was maintained intact and tight it was tactically proper that its circumference be reduced until there was but a square mile or so to work in. The order of the day was, therefore, 'whittle the scheme down to manageable proportions'.

With the army behind them, the home-guardsmen, equipped

with sharp *pangas* and *simis*, extended over a front of four hundred yards and commenced cutting the formidable papyrus. Such a development in the *Bullrush* saga was of unprecedented interest. The sight was spectacular to say the least; acres of ten-foot-high reed falling before an army of glinting, slashing, weaving *pangas*, like an impossibly enormous human scythe. And so they went on all through the hours of daylight, clearing, advancing and tightening the cordon.

The odd dead 'mick' and decomposing carcasses of bullet-riddled hippos were revealed; illusory live 'micks' and a few home-guardsmen too far ahead of the line were sportingly potted at! The bobbing, flailing line of Kikuyu loyalists, each wearing a white band around his head to identify him as 'friend', was maintained as straight as possible with the assistance of K.P.R. Vultures that dropped coloured smoke markers on the flanks. It was really quite fascinating as they inched forward and laid flat vast areas but ... it was not to be. The vile and hindering fastness of papyrus defied even this desperate attempt to conquer it. The effort was too great and it was rapidly realized that it would take weeks and weeks to shorten the circumference appreciably. Brave though the decision may have been, it simply couldn't be done within the narrow time limits imposed.

There was one particularly significant setback in consequence to this futile venture to raze Naivasha's fabled papyrus, a heartbreaking setback that led to anguished criticism and angry recrimination. One evening after the home-guardsmen had finished their labour and retired for the night, the army omitted to knit together the essential cordon in the sector just cut away. There happened to be a wide gap left unstopped. It was not discovered until the following morning and the bother it created had many frightful ramifications for young subalterns and N.C.O.s. It was impossible to say conclusively whether any lucky Mau Mau had exploited the grave oversight and, after a T.C.T. had huffily done its best to find evidence of a breakout without success, the lamentable *faux pas* was hurriedly forgotten with everyone hoping that the (by now) extremely desperate terrorists had not seized their heaven-sent opportunity. But they had!

The wily and aggressive Kibe Kimani, notoriously familiar in the Naivasha and Kinangop districts, and several of his gang had crawled to freedom and made a dash to their old haunt near Longonot. Being driven by fear and hunger, 'General' Kibe Kimani was lax in the exercise of his usual bush-craft; a pseudo-gang entered his hideout within hours of the fugitive group's reoccupation of it and shot them up. The affair, it is regretted, was not all of the success that it could have been and, courageous as the action of the pseudo-group was, always was in fact, it failed to account for Kibe himself. Several of his gang, however, terminated their short-lived liberty and it was very interesting to listen to their stories of the misery and distress of the many still trapped in the swamp.

The following morning yet another batch breached the cordon, this time they were members of Mbaria Kanui's clan. They were tracked to the Badlands where they sought refuge in an old hideout (the very one that my team and I had stormed some months earlier) but were not permitted to relax for more than a couple of hours before another pseudo-gangster team pounced on them. It was again a rather lame sort of engagement and during the ensuing chase over the disagreeable lava rock two terrorists were bowled over and another was captured.

My T.C.T. managed to accompany the pseudo-group, under the energetic and able direction of a settler-cum-F.I.O. from Ol Kalou, and was in a position to impart its intimate knowledge of the Badlands. I am, moreover, able to assure the reader after chatting with the captured terrorist that the experiences of all those Mau Mau incarcerated in the swamp were by far and away the most hazardous and frightful they'd had to endure since becoming forest fighters of Jomo Kenyatta's Land Freedom Armies. And even those few who escaped with their lives from the swamp's lethal investment to enjoy a few fleeting hours of deliverance knew that somewhere, sometime, a bullet would find them.

❖❖❖

I doubt I shall ever forget those first couple of weeks under canvas at the edge of the swamp. My astonishment as TAC H.Q. mushroomed and spread until it resembled Benger's Circus, including the clowns! The dust along the road that led to the site that became deeper and deeper until it was quite impossible to travel closer than two hundred yards behind any other vehicle along it, or the dust-devils that snaked up to heights of several hundred feet, whirling across to blind and choke us. Every night just before dark a shattering bombardment would initiate a tremendous arc of flashing fire as seven hundred soldiers began to pump lead into the common target area until dawn broke and the light blue haze hovering above the cordon was slowly washed away by the rising mists of the swamp. Two-inch mortars fired para-illuminating flares at irregular intervals and they would hover eerily over the papyrus, burning brightly and shedding light over an area the size of a football field, during which time all forces in that sector would blast away demoniacally with Bren-gun, Vickers, rifle and mortar fire. It was an extremely brave or foolhardy 'mick' that ventured too close to the perimeter seeking a gap through which to sneak to safety.

Among my most vivid recollections is the sight of the Gloucestershire Regiment mortar platoons lined up for a rapid-fire bombardment. Watching such displays it was difficult to appreciate that human beings were possibly on the receiving end of the storm of explosives. In one such demonstration of military might, which lasted for an hour, something like 2,800 bombs were flung into a square-mile target area of the swamp—a casual expenditure of about £20,000! The normally peaceful farming area around the swamp fairly shook with the incessant explosions and it seemed indeed that a real battle was being fought. And, interspersed with all this, during lulls, there was the 'sky-shouting' from aircraft that flew low over the swamp to play amplified recordings exhorting "Come out or die!" Such optimism! Such condescension!

So the thud, thud and the whine and the zipping and humming through the forest of stately papyrus became a commonplace thing in our lives—one even found the faculty eventually to sleep soundly through it all.

One tragic aspect of the proceedings was the havoc caused to the hippopotamus and just how many were shot in mistake for terrorists by jittery soldiers will never be known. The morning patrols invariably came across a dead or dying cow or bull hippo at a point where the stop lines had reported an attempted breakout.

The fine weather broke and rapidly deteriorated with rain that fell steadily, soaking the young 'Johnnies' lying in their pup-tents with just the snouts of their rifles poking out. Morale became more and more difficult to maintain as the inclement days were ticked off; the fruits now soured.

Then the exalted 'Field Marshal' himself was at long last netted. Mbaria Kanui, while attempting to break out with a number of his devoted followers, was fired upon and driven back into the swamp. He was located and captured the following morning. What a prize! And what another fillip to sagging morale. Dressed in a tartan shirt, khaki shorts, fraying woollen pullover and an old, wide-brimmed felt hat, with brass ornaments through both ears and a scruffy growth on his chin, he was still the immediate personification of a Mau Mau leader. And yet, unbelievably so, he was every bit as susceptible and apostatic as his idolatrous subordinates. Some hours after his identification as the celebrity he was, bedecked in army jungle-green shirt and trousers, he was handed to my T.C.T. for such activity as I deemed appropriate.

For a whole day we roamed the swamp with him checking sundry hideouts to no avail; he was, in any case, weary and confused after the terrifying ordeal he'd only just managed to survive. There was an anxious hour or two while we had penetrated deep into the swamp and had ventured too near a sector that had been designated as 'out of bounds', being a mortar-fire field of fire. The bombs fell within a hundred yards of us with fearful explosions and, while it may have added to the excitement of the patrol, it is to be admitted that I felt extremely uneasy and veered away as soon as the first bombs began to crash in. However, the experience at least proved to us that mortaring was quite futile in the dense growth of papyrus unless an almost direct hit was scored; so dense, in fact, was the stuff that hardly any impression was made on it at all. The illustrious 'Field Marshal' appeared to be perfectly accustomed to the deafening explosions and was well aware that short of a direct hit there was nothing much to worry about. I learned later that the army had withheld fire for some time while deliberating the exact whereabouts of my team and suffered considerable disquiet until we emerged safe with the valuable capture.

Mbaria's capture set in motion a tragicomic series of events largely due to his exceptional affability, straightforwardness and honesty. It was decided to attempt a surrender campaign. Thus, Mbaria was carefully briefed on the broadcast he was to make and was sincerely in favour of encouraging his erstwhile companions to surrender. A recording van was brought up from Nairobi and, together with a team of four police officers, of which I happened to be one, Mbaria was sat atop the cab of the van, microphone in hand, and we drove slowly along the few tracks that penetrated the marshy papyrus. The group always went in completely unarmed and looking as unaggressive as it could. Everyone wore the regulation white band somewhere on his person to distinguish him from the 'foe'. It was a rather disappointing affair and I record that even though the entire swamp was saturated with rifle and mortar fire after each surrender tour the response was a bewildering, incomprehensible blank. They simply would not leave the trap they found themselves in. I hasten to add that the softening-up bombardment was never commenced until after the expiration of a prearranged interval during which the rebels could safely surrender themselves to personnel in the stop lines.

There is one very humane facet to all the drama and sensationalism that I have recounted and it discomforted, or rather, humbled, many of us. It concerns the likeable insurgent boss, Mbaria Kanui, who was reputed to be such a great one for the ladies. The stories were that he spent his days on Kipipiri attended upon by his girls. They used to groom him and titivate him, prepare his meals and vie for his favours; he'd even left his forest haunts, most reluctantly

I might add, in company with several of his fairest maidens for the big *baraza* in the swamp, one of whom he was captured in the company of. She had fled with him quite as agilely, slept as fitfully upon damp reeds, suffered the same torment of leeches, ran the gauntlet of bullets and bombs, until, while attempting their ill-fated breakout, she was hit in the thigh and disabled. Mbaria had remained with her and nursed her until, at first light, a police T.C.U. had found the two of them a few yards from where they had been spotted and fired upon during the night. She was a handsome, sturdy and mild-mannered Kikuyu girl, yet every bit a Mau Mau terrorist and blindly dedicated to the movement's perverse ideals. One could see the venom and evil that lay behind her subdued exterior. We all knew that Mbaria Kanui could have made good his escape had he not elected to remain and comfort this forest mistress of his. Such an example of strange, almost matriarchal devotion defies understanding. The Kikuyu had so many strange customs, of course, many far beyond our comprehension.

The gathering of the terrorist clans in the Naivasha papyrus swamp was impossible to repeat ever again during the emergency. Chastening though it was that so many broke through the cordon to a short-lived freedom the ultimate score was an impressive one. The total number of Mau Mau terrorists in various hideouts at the time my T.C.T. made contact was estimated to have been in the region of fifty to sixty, sometimes quoted as seventy to eighty even, and the final analysis of casualties that the gangs of Mbaria, Mekanika and Kibe suffered directly or indirectly as result of *Operation Bullrush* were:

- 'Major-General' Mekanika—killed by small-arms fire
- 'Field-Marshal' Mbaria Kanui—captured while escaping
- 2 killed by K.P.R. spotter aircraft
- 3 killed by patrols in swamp (army)
- 11 killed in follow-up patrols after escape (pseudo-teams)

- 1 female captured while escaping, wounded
- 2 killed by mortar bombs
- 4 surrendered

The total eliminated was, therefore, twenty-five, with one rifle and masses of equipment recovered. A post-mortem on the efficacy of the operation by any military yardstick revealed that it was most gratifying for us and most damaging for Mau Mau. The more far-reaching effects were even more disastrous for the hard-core gangs which were sent scampering without pause until weeks later when they were utterly disorganized, dejected, desperate and more vulnerable than ever before.

A final word: Such a concerted storming of the swamp against its fifty-odd trapped terrorists would seem at first to be not a little lop-sided. Nevertheless, with a cordon, the circumference of which was seldom less than ten miles, considerable numbers of personnel were required. The conglomeration of fighting forces was unprecedented during Kenya's emergency and at the height of the operation became quite staggering—something like three thousand, in fact, which excluded the battalions of Kikuyu home-guardsmen.

And so it went throughout January of 1956 with the rest of the colony watching with bated breath and with high hopes. But where were the two most important leaders—Dedan Kimathi and Stanley Mathenge? Still squabbling with each other up on Fey's peak no doubt! But their knell, as well as that of the remaining Mau Mau fanatics, was booming loud in the ears of all.

Chapter 15

The dreadful cost in life and money: for what? Land?

The spate of security force successes grew in volume throughout 1955–56 and irrevocably turned the tide of Mau Mau terrorism. This bright new complexion on the emergency was attributable largely to the ruthless exploitation of the Kikuyu, Meru and Embu's apostasy once captured or surrendered. With the absolute minimum of delay or fuss he was turned round and shooed back into the forest, into his old stamping grounds, in front of a patrol. It was the surest path any gangster could tread to mitigate the appalling guilt he must have borne after the months of predatory and repugnant life as a member of some section of the great Land Freedom Armies of Mau Mau.

There have been more than a few purblind detractors of this course of action adopted by Kenya's security forces; they snapped that "it wasn't cricket" and that it was compromising justice with expediency. What they meant, of course, was that such methods prejudiced the poor, misunderstood insurgent's chances of survival, that they had a perfect right to demonstrate their dissatisfaction with oppressive colonial rule by taking to the hills and making themselves a criminal nuisance. It was all supposed to be healthily and fairly conceived opposition. I even recall that some U.K. newspapers took to referring to the murderous fanatics as 'resisters', of all the barmy descriptions. These sneering detractors of Kenya's security forces, in particular the police, and more particularly still, the 'Kenya Cowboys', regarded the blood-thirsty, anti-European Mau Mau terrorist organization much as they did the fox and stag hunts, the so-called blood sports of the landed gentry, that periodically call for a protest march to

Westminster or a tiresome debate therein.

With the lengthening table of anti-terrorist achievements, so the foe grew wilier. They had to be winkled out with ever more subtlety and patience. The era of pseudo-gangsterism was ushered in and, by degrees, the greater portion of security-force activity in the forests and gorges was conceded to the 'Special Effort' teams who, when fully operational, were indistinguishable from genuine Mau Mau terrorists—except that one or two of their number would be found to have white skins if stripped.

T.C.T.s and G.S.U.s, the teeming military units and all other orthodox forces were excluded ever more frequently from the dense forests and confined their endeavours to the settled areas, tying up wheat stores and squatter labour lines, denying the itinerant gangs freedom of movement and patrolling the forest fringes, flushing out gorges and generally harassing gangsters back into the towering Aberdares, Kipipiri or the slopes of Mount Kenya, where the pseudos could account for them. It became, towards the end of 1955, no longer a matter of locating the various gangs in their entirety but of individual personalities—the leader of the 'Royal Family' section known to be skulking around the Sugenol Hill area, or Kibe Kimani eluding his tormentors between Hell's Gate and Longonot. Security forces came to learn of the predilections of prominent Mau Mau individuals, their modus operandi, possession of any precision weapons or who it was wearing the leather police belt and jersey taken from a constable murdered two years before near Kabeti. They were slowly identified and labelled as minor targets or exclusive game. Naivasha would have its own pet gangster to hunt down and Nakuru its. The Kinangop would plan a trap for the wriggling leader of Section 15, still wanted for the part he took in the Ruck murders, and so on.

My T.C.T. continued to do its bit, the restrictions increased and great care had to be exercised with regard to just where we ventured in pursuit of our quarry; the pseudo-Mau Mau teams roamed everywhere. It was an invidious state of affairs but we had to re-orientate and adjust accordingly.

It really was incredible how the crushing efforts of H.M. Forces began to tell during 1955. A typical 'Operational Intelligence

Summary' as issued fortnightly by the District Intelligence Committee evinced a picture that was still far from heartening at the start of that year (*See* Appendix V):

Potatoes were stolen from *shambas* on Knight's and Weaver's. This may be labour stealing for Mau Mau as it usually is, or labour stealing from each other. Caches of potatoes marked with signs have previously been found in the vicinity of these farms.

A gang of food carriers was reported in the forest at HZR.0613. Another gang estimated at about 100 strong was reported at HZR.0100.

A gang of unknown strength attempted to raid the dairy on Gledhill's farm at HZR.0238. The terrorists were driven off by farm guards.

A patrol of the Royal Irish Fusiliers surprised a small gang in a hideout at HZR.081297. The patrol killed one terrorist and recovered some useful documents.

A gang of some ten-plus strong raided the Manera *lhandi* stealing money, clothing and food. The railway *lhandi* like others in the district, though wired in, present easy targets for the terrorists because:

a)   of their isolated position
b)   the wiring is not good enough
c)   the *lhandis* are not guarded
d)   they are well supplied with food and money

A farm guard who was wounded at Hopcraft's farm HZP.6922 and had his shotgun taken from him by a party of terrorists was walking along on his own contrary to the orders for farm guards who are supposed to travel in threes.

In this particular summary the District Intelligence Committee had this to say under the heading 'Mau Mau Aims':

Gangs now realize what strength they have to contend with at *bomas* and come prepared to deal with the two or three guards. They usually make a noise to allow the farm guards to then fire, before the guards can reload—a slow process with their type of gun (Greener shotguns)—they rush them.
The noise made is sometimes deliberate to draw fire while the raiding party are busy at another point of the *boma*.

Later that same year the D.I.C.'s summary had quite a different story to tell, one that reflected the ascendancy of security forces (*See* Appendix VII):

On 26 October at HZP.923565 a lone gangster was killed in his hide. S.F. were led to this contact by a surrenderee.

During the military operation *Excalibur* on 2 November one gangster was killed and another captured. Information from the capturee led to a further military operation resulting in the contact of this gang again.

On 5 November a gangster from Mcharia Kimemia's gang surrendered at HZP.8837. He led S.F. back to his hide, HAR.0931, where Karioki Nduati was killed and four precision weapons were recovered together with a quantity of documents. Among those in the hide were ... and the three sheep which were taken from Nightingale's farm on 4 November by this gang.

At HZP.7745 on 8 November on information a gang of three was contacted and eliminated, two being killed and the third captured. The capturee led S.F. to the capture of a further two of his gang on the 10th at HZP.9150.

And so the annihilation of monstrous Mau Mau gangsters continued and was speeded up by the swift use of capturees and surrenderees. Mau Mau were now well and truly set upon a course of self-destruction. Any *entente cordiale* that had existed between the various gangs was abrogated and relationships became worse than bitter. The outlawry that was once such a pleasant life rapidly deteriorated until it became a trial of wits, a morass of conflicting loyalties among gang leaders, and the poison of treachery spread insidiously throughout the forest. They distrusted each other, squabbled and fought. The executions increased and they voraciously gobbled each other up. Security forces received their greatest impetus from the dissension among the murderous gangs and not from their own superior numbers or materials of war.

Gone were the days when forest-post personnel, army patrols, T.C.T.s and the like could swan off into the wide tracts of prohibited and restricted forest for a quiet *pole-pole* saunter or sweep a gorge on whim or information. It was instilled into all units that with pseudo-gangster teams operating more extensively every day, absolute clearance had to be obtained prior to take-off. Nevertheless these pseudo-teams took tremendous risks and could hardly blame an unsuspecting army or police patrol if they were shot up before being able to retire or identify themselves. They aped Mau Mau to perfection and quite often strayed outside the bounds of an area that had been cleared for their peregrinations. (*See* Appendix VI)

I firmly believe that most police and army units grew to be so jittery and uneasy about the uncertainty as to exactly where a pseudo-team was operating that they gladly and graciously bowed out of the operational arena in deference to the 'Special Effort' sorties.

At the turn of the year the mammoth *Bullrush* operation, splashing and blazing away in the papyrus swamp, was as indicative as any operational yard-stick that the moon of Mau Mau subversion was waning. The gangs were not just on the run, they were scuttling, and throughout 1956 the Commander-in-Chief, Lieutenant-General Sir Gerald Lathbury, and the Commissioner of Police, Mr Richard Catling, had the situation well in hand; a gradual rundown of the armed forces began. By the end of January, I had handed in my Sterling gun, jungle-green clothing, binoculars and maps and had taken to wearing stiffly starched khaki drill and a peak cap. As a duty officer in the Operations Room at Colony Police H.Q. in Nairobi I came to enjoy working regular hours, sitting down, saluting 'brass and scrambled egg', and listening to the exploits and hardships of others over the V.H.F. radio sets it was my duty to operate. I was, moreover, for the first time since my arrival in the colony enabled to view the overall picture of anti-terrorist activity. So highly efficient and smoothly geared was the machinery at Colony Ops—the religiously maintained historical and current incident maps, farm villagization charts, location of every S.F. unit marked with coloured pins—that I came to recognize and applaud the central master-brain behind the vast internal security offensive; a confident, composed faculty that co-ordinated the mighty and disciplined force that was twisting the tail of Mau Mau. And, while witnessing the noose being pulled ever tighter about the neck of the terrorist hordes, I found I was in a position, too, to observe the facts and figures. I feel, therefore, that it would not be inappropriate if I were to wind up this final chapter with a general summary of those more conspicuous statistics. It will be seen as a rather revealing and interesting summary, I am sure.

By the end of 1956 the Mau Mau pestilence was all but purged from Kenya's fair face. The scars were left to disfigure but, from a distance, they were unrecognizable. In terms of character, of determination and of pride, her face still evinced great resilience— and of hope, too. But, of strength and trust? No! The bitter struggle had been a fatiguing one; the economic wounds continued to cause discomfort and not all were quick to heal.

The figure of European civilian casualties had totted up to thirty-two killed and twenty-six wounded. This may not appear to be a very disturbing figure when compared with an appalling total of 2,735 loyal civilian Africans, of whom nearly two thousand were killed, but what one is asked to remember is that those fifty-eight Europeans were killed or wounded in singularly horrific circumstances. People are killed in their thousands on busy streets, or in air disasters, there being little time for reflection, or to do much about it or even, for that matter, to suffer much. Others are killed in battle where there is, to some extent, glory and heroics. Again, the majority of us forsake this world after long illness and have plenty of time to reconcile ourselves to the inevitable. By the time our demise is pronounced we have been able to tidy up the loose ends of our lives and leave as little chaos as possible. But let us examine the passing of those Kenya settlers a bit closer.

In the first place they were not ordinary run-of-the-mill folk; they were pioneering types of rugged potential and practical intellect, resourceful and with spunk. Most had made momentous decisions to establish a future in Kenya and were imbued with hope for a useful and happy relationship with the indigenous population. Proudly they declared Kenya to be their home. Alongside the African they were confident of their ability to elevate the colony to a place among the great farming nations of the world. The majority of them lived intimately with danger and primitive evil, no less on their nerves—uneasy nights, fearful doubts as to the loyalty of the native, every moment expecting the ghastly to occur. Their nights were filled with unrelieved tension, always waiting, taut and sweating, starting at the slightest noise and grabbing for a gun a hundred times, fighting numberless desperate mental battles with villainous Mau Mau. Then it would happen, at the most unexpected moment—black savages, slashing *pangas*, cruel hacking, murderous assault—a pitiless, defenceless, helpless nightmare until they were left dismembered in a pool of blood.

They were no ordinary deaths and each was the equivalent of ten in terms of fortitude, valour and prospects. Each of those mortal encounters with Mau Mau brutes was an excruciating wound in the vitals of Kenya's hopeful future.

In terms of economic value those slaughters of white settler farmers on their isolated farmsteads were immeasurable and constituted as sharp a warning as could possibly have been sounded of the dreadful threat Mau Mau terrorism had become to the lives of all those who occupied alienated land, no matter how sincere, zealous or valuable their contribution to the colony's agrarian development. However, the evidence is that the great exodus of Europeans that began soon after the emergency was over has never been halted. They have quit the land which they toiled to make productive and upon which the whole economic viability of Kenya depends so urgently. It is for others to decide whether or not the, ironically so, victorious, freedom fighters who have taken over so many of those fabulous farms have been successful in perpetuating the accomplishments of the *bwanas* that were so violently ousted.

During the same period of the emergency casualties among European security forces totalled one hundred and sixty-four, of which about two-fifths were killed. The grand total of European casualties by the end of 1955 then was in the region of two hundred and twenty-two, a by no means inconsiderable number. They were, nonetheless for that, but *one-nineteenth* of the total African casualties sustained (excluding terrorists) and we are left in no doubt that it was the loyal African who bore the brunt of the Mau Mau onslaught.

In four years nearly two thousand loyal African civilians, mostly Kikuyu, perished and almost half that number again were wounded. To this must be added African security forces who met their deaths and who totalled over one hundred together with a shocking figure of one thousand five hundred wounded. It will be readily appreciated, therefore, without wishing to pester the reader with a riot of austere figures, that fatalities among the native Kenyans outnumbered those of the European by approximately thirty to one!—a sobering and jarring comparison? Worthy of some comment, too, and this I propose to do in a moment.

A safe estimate of the grand total, European, Asian and African, deaths by the sword of Mau Mau over the four-year period is two thousand and is but one-sixth of the terrorists killed. Few people can have had any real conception of the staggering numbers that have, with reasonable accuracy, been compiled in respect of Mau Mau casualties, and, despite the degree of unreliability, guerrilla warfare being what it is, it is possible to submit that almost twelve thousand were killed during the black years of the emergency.

Upwards of forty-three thousand (excluding 'grey' suspects), and the greater part of whom were Kikuyu, Meru and Embu tribesmen, were accounted for—either killed, captured in action, arrested or surrendered. Of these the most provoking figure happens to be the meagre two and a half thousand captured in action—it is explained in an earlier chapter how unlikely it was to capture a forest gangster and any that survived the firing when contact was made never stopped running until several ridges had been put between they and their pursuers—and this figure is further inflated, enormously too, by those captured by pseudo-gangsters later in the emergency. The bulk of the forty-three thousand-plus were arrested during township sweeps and raids on farm labour lines when, quite often, although it was impossible to classify them as hard-core terrorists they were quite definitely Mau Mau adherents of varying shades of nastiness.

Only during the early months of the Mau Mau uprising did European civilian casualties soar to between twenty-five and thirty. Once the vast machinery of the emergency hummed into action and security forces swamped the settled areas, the terrifying raids on remote farmsteads eased considerably. There can be little doubt that further delay in His Excellency's declaration that a State of Emergency existed in Kenya and the comparatively modest figures of thirty-two killed and twenty-six wounded would have assumed grievous proportions. We only have the gallantry and indomitable spirit of the settler farmers themselves to thank for the obdurate opposition displayed against Mau Mau during the early stages of the holocaust that swept the settled White Highlands.

Yet, even while the Crown was prosecuting its counter-offensive so vigorously, the terrorists still selected their victims and swooped with all the savagery of wounded wild animals. As late as October 1954 they were still able to horrify the world with their wickedness.

On the 13th of that month at Kiberiri, near Nyeri, seventy-year-old Mr Arundell Gray Leakey, his wife and step-daughter, were enjoying dinner in their delightful little farmhouse when a Mau Mau gang battered its way in and wasted no time in strangling Mrs Leakey in the presence of her husband. For him they had other more evil, more maniacal plans and he was abducted. Before leaving the house they chopped up the cook-houseboy—the step-daughter for some inexplicable reason was left unharmed; they probably considered that she would suffer far more if left to live with her ghastly memories. Subsequent intensive police enquiries and dogged searching disclosed the grave of Mr Leakey five weeks later situated in thick forest some five miles from the farm—he had been buried alive. The horrors he must have endured before he died are surely indescribable.

As I have stated earlier the total of thirty-two may not at first appear to be very impressive but they were no ordinary deaths; each was the very essence of callousness and fiendish to the point of insanity.

What now of that shocking total of loyal Africans I mentioned a few paragraphs back? Two thousand butchered and almost another thousand maimed, disfigured and mutilated. Upon them was wreaked the full fury of madmen and it is particularly pitiful because it was Kikuyu decimating Kikuyu in a desperate, ruthless endeavour to intimidate and corrupt every single member of the tribe. Fortunately for Kenya the Kikuyu tribe showed that it still had many thousands of decent God-fearing families who wanted nothing more than to benefit from the white man's skills, medicines and western attributes.

Had it not been for the formation of the Kikuyu Homeguard and the staunch loyalty of the Tribal Police it would have been scarcely possible to check the havoc. It is this category of the senseless slaughter that represents the greatest tragedy of the emergency. Shall I ever forget when, as a Duty Officer in the Police Colony Operations Room at Nairobi H.Q. during 1955–56, almost every sitrep received from Nyeri, Kiambu, Fort Hall, Thika and other Kikuyu locations, included a gruesome total in respect of the bodies of loyal Africans recovered. It is certain that the full toll will never be known for many a family vendetta was successfully concluded under the blood-soaked cloak of Mau Mau.

This figure of two thousand quoted above refers mainly to those loyalists as they were called, murdered by terrorists because of their obstinate refusal to assist Mau Mau in its nefarious exploits, or to hand over the subscriptions demanded. Their deaths fell into two groups—strangulation and decapitation. In most instances they were buried in shallow graves. It was during early 1956 onward when 'confessional *barazas*' (meetings at which those who had taken Mau Mau oaths were called upon to renounce their allegiance to the organization and were thereby purged) began to bear fruit that these graves were discovered and shown to police. No Kikuyu was safe from the depraved monsters who descended on their villages at night, demanding food, money and clothing, raping the women and abducting those maidens they fancied.

So urgent was the necessity to protect themselves from these frightful nocturnal visitations that, with the assistance of the administration, the loyal Kikuyus dug a colossal ditch, ten feet deep and five yards wide, between their reserves and the forest. It was many miles in length and in time was manned by a tribal policeman or homeguardsman at one-hundred- to two-hundred-yard intervals along its entire length. It was, in fact, this very ditch that was so dramatically responsible for the cunning Dedan Kimathi's undoing. On that fateful morning of 21 October 1956, having been hounded relentlessly for weeks by those intrepid pseudo-gangsters of Ian Henderson, he was spotted and shot while trying to climb out of the ditch—by his own tribesmen, too!

It is, therefore, wise to remember when talk of Mau Mau is deemed to be synonymous with Kikuyu that the tribe itself suffered as no other did. It may well be that they now have the most to be thankful for, but, their treachery and schizophrenic behaviour notwithstanding, they should rightly stand in the forefront of Kenya's parade of heroes and brave souls.

❖❖❖

Having provided the facts concerning the cost in death and suffering let us finally examine the facts in hard cash. A fabulous sum was absorbed by the gargantuan blotter of five years of the Mau Mau emergency. The Kenya government was obliged to foot half the enormous bill and its contribution halfway through the final year had reached the impressive figure of £26,500,000, representing a crippling inroad into the colony's revenue. The generous British taxpayer poured into the insatiable coffers another £24,250,000 as a grant plus a further £5,250,000 in the form of loans. There can be no illusions, therefore, that, looking at the astronomical figure of £55,500,000 from any angle and in any light, the emergency that Kenya endured so stoically was a costly solution to subversion and insurgent mayhem. Such vast sums are difficult to comprehend for the man in the street and are, of course, the reason why so many asked, "Was Kenya worth salvaging at such expense?"

Many cynical authorities would, I've no doubt, submit a table of very convincing calculations purporting to show that the marketable value of all European-owned property in Kenya hardly added up to £55.5 million and such a submission obviously does not end there. May I suggest, however, that it was not so much the marketable value of property in Kenya as Kenya's market potential that mattered. Hanging on to the colony in the teeth of such violent and bitter opposition, not to mention serious impugnment of the prestige of the Crown, was not to preserve the existing settler palaces and plots but to protect the agrarian potential together with, in variable measure, the strategic value of the territory politically. The lamentable realization was, nevertheless, that the poor abused and ridiculed settler had been living on borrowed time; many would, I imagine, allege on borrowed land too.

Racialism, be what it may, a much bandied and misconceived word, can be resolved in an atmosphere of trust and compromise but land? Never! It was, and possibly still is, the abiding cancer that afflicted Kenya and all the diplomatic healers and all the political surgeons in the world could not prevent the spread of hatred around it. One might just as well attempt to exorcize the spirits that abound, according to African legend, on Mount Kenya.

On this point I beg to quote from an address by Mr Eliud Mathu, who was an African-nominated member of Kenya's Legislative Council, at a meeting in May 1951, in Nairobi. Mr Mathu, by the way, was a very distinguished African politician with a moderate outlook. He said:

"It is on the land that the African lives and it means everything to him. He cannot depend for his livelihood on profits made through trading, he cannot depend upon wages, he must go back every time to the only social security he has—the piece of land ... without land the future of the African people is doomed. God will hear us because land is the thing he gave us."

The theme of his address was 'Give us back the stolen land', and as far back as seven hundred years the Kikuyu tribe, living in the forested areas around Fort Hall, were seeking to remedy the problem of congestion. They expanded into Nyeri and Kiambu, then pushed out the nomadic Wanderobo who, fortunately for the expansive Kikuyu, were hunters and not agriculturists. And now the same problems, only more urgent in this age of improved health services and lower infant mortality rate, beset the volatile Kikuyu—land congestion!

I've heard a hundred anxious settlers, if I've heard one, declare seriously and soberly that to yield the White Highlands of Kenya would provide but a temporary relief only; that until the African has been completely educated in the arts of land husbandry there will never be enough land for all with the traditional practice of subsistence farming. The only possible salvation was, they said (and can we deny the logic?), to establish other industries. But, where was the money? In the land! And the land you couldn't see for the tumult over it!

Epilogue

In 1938 a book entitled *Facing Mount Kenya: A study of Kikuyu society* was published in London and, while it is doubtful that many will have either read or heard of it, they will almost certainly have knowledge of its author, though not by his real name of Kamau wa Ngengi. How much, one wonders, were the chances of success for that esoteric publication improved by the *nom de plume* adopted by its author or by the exciting illustration of him dressed in leopard skins on the book's jacket.

The author was Jomo Kenyatta. Needless to say the name was thought to have just the right ring of pretentiousness to it and how unquestionably (in)famous it was to become, though not as an author, despite three later publications (*The land of conflict, My people of Kikuyu* and *Harambee.*)

But so it was that, as a promising young graduate of the London School of Economics and with a diploma in anthropology, Kenya's first prime minister and life president, Johnston (a baptismal name) Kamau wa Ngengi, assumed the pseudonym that was to acquire such notoriety in Kenya and Britain. The choice was, despite its fortuity, quite inspirational and provided him, Kenya, and no doubt his publisher also, with a personalization and marketable image his tribal name never could have had at that time. And could he then, fourteen years before the emergency in Kenya was declared, have been even remotely aware that his adoptive name was to become so intimately associated with a sinister and subversive organization that was to spread like a cancer over the then White Highlands of Kenya? An organization of insurgent extremists, the name of which was to strike terror in the minds of people of all races around the world.

For Jomo Kenyatta and Mau Mau became indivisible, of this there can be little doubt. To both were to be ascribed the same condemnatory adjectives—barbaric, savage, heathenish, primitive, vile. Mau Mau was execrable. So also Kenyatta.

What might have been his thoughts and ambitions while, as an agricultural worker in the sleepy Sussex village of Storrington, he whiled away the long war years? Certainly he must have fitted in rather well with the English way of life and even married an English girl, Edna Clark, in 1943. She bore him a son, Peter. Throughout his lengthy sojourn overseas he remained a dedicated and tireless campaigner of African advancement, though never violent. And then, in 1945, he apparently decided he should do something positive about it; he returned home. By all accounts the gestation of Mau Mau then began.

Jomo Kenyatta was Kenya's Ataturk, though with this significant difference. The latter legendary soldier-statesman earned his overwhelming popularity by leading his countrymen physically; he was a fearless and redoubtable soldier, not overly fond of the niceties of parliamentary protocol. Kenyatta, by contrast, preferred to employ his gifted oratory and his remarkable talent for *double entendre*. Later, as was inevitable once committed to lonely exile, he became a national inspiration. His martyrdom was to supply the dominant Wakikuyu (the tribe to which he belonged) with the sort of patriarchal totem they so urgently needed if they were to exploit their success as the tribe with the temerity to challenge the imperial authority of the British. Still later, when the time came to elect a national leader, few will doubt that Kenyans chose wisely, notwithstanding a conspicuous absence of any serious rivals or contenders for the presidency in 1963.

Not by chance is it that Kenya's coat of arms should surmount the word 'Harambee'. At political assemblies Kenyatta's mesmeric oratory was invariably preceded by screeches of "*Harambeee!*" (a Swahili word meaning 'let us pull together'), and the ecstatic crowd would respond with an answering roar "*Harambeee!*" after the oratory. It was to become his rallying slogan and its incorporation in the coat of arms of an independent Kenya is entirely appropriate.

Kenyatta always had an indefinable quality as a political leader, call it psyche if you will, that enabled him to achieve some semblance of *harambee* among Kenya's disparate tribal groups. There have been, and are, many in Nairobi whom one could say were possessed of more professionalism, but what they seemed to lack, apart from Jomo's inimitable patriarchal profile, has been the preternatural gift he had for telling the people what they wanted to hear, irrespective of the facts.

So, like the Turks during the 1930s who felt impelled to affectionately dub their hero Mustafa Kemal Pasha with the name Ataturk—father of Turks—we witnessed the deification of our Kenyan hero's pseudonym. However, the word *mzee*, meaning 'old man', was to replace the familiar 'Jomo' and it is considered to be more respectful to refer to Mzee Kenyatta, which is, after all, probably another way of saying 'Father of Kenya'.

On 8 April 1953, at Kapenguria in Kenya's northern frontier province, there was little of the future sage or dignified statesman about the bearded, corpulent Kenyatta as he sat unquailingly before Mr Ransley Thacker, the presiding judge at his trial for complicity with Mau Mau, yet he deviated not an inch from his chosen course as the saviour of his people.

Deferentially he listened to the ponderous summing-up and judgement. He must surely have realized that the British had no alternative other than to condemn him. The vociferously hostile white settler community had already judged him and he was guilty. Guilty with nothing in mitigation. It was in no mood for legal semantics and required his immediate removal from the political scene, preferably hanged, no matter how insubstantial the evidence might have been against him.

"I am satisfied that you masterminded a plan to drive the Europeans out of Kenya. Your Mau Mau has slaughtered hundreds of men, women and children in circumstances which are revolting ..." intoned Judge Thacker with much feeling.

To which the defendant was eventually to reply in a style so characteristically that of 'Jomo': "None of us [he was arraigned with several others] would condone the mutilation of human beings. We have families of our own. If you think that in working for African rights we have turned Mau Mau you have been misled. We feel that this case has been so arranged as to bring Mau Mau on us as a scapegoat ..."

So much then for judicial condemnation and the unrepentant rebuttal. His plea of innocence of the charge that he had created the monster which went on a rampage of bloody genocide was not believed by the British at that time; would it be now? And, if he had not been the creator, then who was?

Ironically, however, and perhaps unfortunately for Kenya's expatriate white settlers, the British government was champion of not only nineteenth-century colonialism but also of twentieth-century democracy. The two ideologies were, and are, quite incompatible excepting at great cost and intolerable strain. Hence, the exiled 'scapegoat' lived on to enjoy an honour and veneration comparable to that enjoyed by the former Ethiopian emperor, Haile Selassie. The wheel of African fortune was slowly but inexorably turning and it was not long before Kenya's first president could claim to be one of Britain's former colonial empire's foremost national celebrities.

Mzee Kenyatta's suits were made by a famous London tailor. The jackets had special embroidered labels sewn onto the maroon silk lining that read, 'Made expressly for His Excellency President Kenyatta'.

From vilified and pilloried instigator of Mau Mau to His Excellency! *Uhuru*, then, was apparently acknowledged to have been the legitimate aspiration of the people of Kenya. To have been Mau Mau was to become a hero, provided he managed to survive the Kenya Cowboys and the Soldier Johnnies. Few of the militants did.

On the occasion of Kenya's tenth anniversary of independence an article by an erudite African, Peter Enahare, appeared in the magazine *Africa* (28.12.73). The following is an excerpt of some significance:

If multi-racial Kenya failed, [then] the white supremacists

would claim vindication and sympathy abroad for the African liberation movements would diminish. But Kenya has become Africa's showcase that racial integration under black direction can and has worked.

In the same issue it was said that:

Not before or since was the independence of an African state [on 18 December 1963] greeted with more scepticism, fear and derision.

Clearly the prophets of doom have not lived to witness an African rule in Kenya that has led to chaos and disintegration. The first decade of independence was not all roses and honey; and we have to admit that some patches have been decidedly sinister. The deaths, whether by assassination or misadventure, of several outspoken critics of the Kenyan government of whom three—Tom Mboya, Ronald Ngala and Josiah Kariuki—were members of parliament, are consistent with a pattern of ruthless subjugation of rivals. There have, too, been insinuations of nepotism involving high office that cannot be ignored. And yet, ominous as these events may be there has been scarcely any evidence of what one could call destabilization and the country's vigorous growth and viability has continued to amaze the cynics.

Who, for instance, could have believed that after twelve years of uninterrupted rule by a Kikuyu-dominated government there would be over a hundred farms still under the ownership of whites? Or that Britain would provide ten million pounds to facilitate the nationalization of them? This of itself surely indicates that those white settlers who were prepared to reconcile themselves to being governed by those militant extremists (for, dare we refer to them now as Mau Mau?) they once so vehemently denounced were not, after all chased off their *shambas* by vengeful *panga*-wielding savages.

Perhaps we ought to conclude therefore that the 'scepticism, fear and derision' that greeted independence was simply last-ditch racist propaganda. This is what we should all sincerely hope anyway.

But those magnificent highlands of Kenya are no longer white and the Europeans who stayed on could never hope to recapture their erstwhile privileged lives as *bwana mkubwas* in an earthly paradise. Yet, by comparison with so much that has happened and is happening in other parts of Africa they have much to be thankful for and to be proud of. The many thousands of Europeans who have adopted Kenyan citizenship must prove, as conclusively as anything can, the unalterable lure of this beautiful country.

The convulsive rise and fall of Mau Mau was a regrettable episode but will have faded in the memories of many. It is not easy to reconcile the horrible activities of that violent rebellion to Kenya's remarkably moderate record and prosperity since independence and there is much that will probably never be forgiven by some.

However, history will have to decide the right or wrong of the principal contenders and the contenders' principles.

Postscript

In the first edition of this book the blurb inside the front cover commences: "Thirty-five years after its jubilant attainment of *Uhuru* Kenya can claim with some justification to have matured as an independent sovereign republic".

With this later edition of my book, a further ten years have elapsed since the ceremonial handing over by the Duke of Edinburgh of the symbolic instruments of state to Johnstone 'Jomo' Kenyatta. However, while Britain's former colony may have continued to mature as a sovereign republic its progress towards implementing those constitutional reforms so desperately imperative for it to be hailed as a manifestly, multi-party incorrupt parliamentary democracy leaves much to be desired. The regrettable inescapable fact appears to be that, having won its precious *Uhuru* after such a long and bloody struggle against the British Raj, it has done little to stop its unchecked drift towards the rotting pile of other failed African states that have become entangled in webs of nepotism, corruption and destabilizing tribalism.

In Kenya the inexorable downward slide has been less conspicuous or worrying as elsewhere during the past four decades. This is due to it having been masked, to some extent, by the passive acquiescence of the many thousands of former white settlers who elected to remain when it ceased to be one of those nice red patches that splattered maps of Africa. Added to which, has been the generous infusions of Western aid, a thriving and lucrative tourist/safari industry and, by no means least, its strategic geographical location having a long seaboard and sharing a border with five other states. All of which, when reinforced by an electorate in thrall to one powerful ruling party, has allowed the fledgling ship of state to remain, by and large, on such remarkably even keel. Until now.

Kenya's quinquennial general election last December that, allegedly, returned Mwai Kibaki for a second term of office, became the catalyst for widespread unrest and public disorder. All those thousands of erstwhile passive and deferential minority tribes-folk have begun to display a bellicose dissatisfaction with the status quo as perpetuated by the ruling Kikuyu oligarchy. Intelligent, bold and articulate leaders capable of the sort of inspirational oratory—that hypnotic harangue so effectively practised by the inimitable Mzee Kenyatta himself—have begun to emerge from the political shadows. One such is the founding head of the only, grudgingly permitted, opposition party, the Orange Democratic Movement, Raila Odinga. Being vociferously adamant that he was cheated of the presidency he brought his dissenting and angry supporters onto the streets of Nairobi and other main centres in their thousands. Unsurprisingly, of course, they were soon to be dispersed by the republic's highly trained police General Service Units (the Red Berets). Mr Kibaki was in no mood to tolerate such democratic protest and had no qualms about seeing them sent scampering with bloody noses and not a few fatalities.

Not at all a very auspicious start to Mwai Kibaki's second term in Nairobi's imposing State House.

At the time of penning this postscript the death toll has passed one thousand, rising almost daily, and many thousands have been forced to flee their homes. Indeed, so alarming and explosive has the situation deteriorated that the former UN Secretary-General Kofi Annan, was called in to lead mediation talks, though it appears, to no avail and tempers have yet to cool.

A question hovering on the lips of many Kenya observers is: "With the highly volatile tribalism and simmering ethnic rivalries can the country ever enjoy parliamentary, Westminster-style, multi-party democracy as was Kenya's original ambitious intention?"

Perhaps a yet more appropriate question would be: "Is democracy fashioned on Western/European constitutional ideals and human rights really so necessary at all?"

When the doughty 'Mzee' Jomo died in August 1978 he had been president of one of the most prosperous, promising and stable African nations for almost twelve years. (The presidency passed to Daniel Arap Moi, the vice-president, who was confirmed in office at the elections of December 1979.) The government he had presided over with such autocratic, though hugely popular, authority was universally considered to be Western-orientated, foreign-investment-worthy and much favoured by Nairobi's large diplomatic and UN communities. The many thousands of expatriates engaged in Kenya-based commerce, industry and tourism found little cause for concern during his benign presidency.

Even his audacious amendment of Kenya's constitution within a year of taking office to ban all opposition, renounce allegiance to the British monarch and declare a republic within the Commonwealth caused but the slightest tremor of anxiety in the corridors of Westminster or Whitehall—if not overtly acquiescent, exactly then most certainly discreetly tolerant of the ominous shift towards autocratic rule. There appeared to be an inexplicable unanimity among world leaders during the years following this departure from the accepted norms of Western parliamentary democracy. As election followed quinquennial election, in which Kenya's highly tribalized populace was coerced into accepting a one-party state dominated by an all-powerful Kikuyu elite, there were few demurring voices heard.

Few would doubt that Kenyatta metamorphosed from being a painful thorn in the side of Kenya settlers and the erstwhile colonial administration to an avuncular, equable elder statesman; a president in whom they quite happily, or prudently, placed their trust, future security and privileged expatriate lifestyles. The sensible course, it was believed, was to allow the flamboyant rascal to enjoy the trappings and pomp of his high office and the reverence of his people. As long as he eschewed the rapid nationalism that had resulted in his long incarceration by the British in Kenya's remote and arid Northern Frontier District (NFD), what did it matter if a little corruption or artful nepotism had to be ignored? True, no longer was it the carefree "squirearchy on the Equator", as Evelyn Waugh had described it. But for many thousands of white expats it was still an enviable place in which to live and work, so, why rock the boat! They needed no reminding that their presence in an independent Kenya was tolerated only on the understanding that they confine themselves to making money and ensuring a steady inflow of foreign currency and aid. And politics? Well! only as long as it favoured the Kenya African National Union (KANU).

One white Kenyan-born citizen who had the temerity not to toe the party line is the celebrated palaeontologist and conservationist, Richard Leakey. In 1995 he took full advantage of President Moi's sudden and surprising relaxation of the government's much-criticized, unjust proscription of political opposition parties (legislation enacted by Kenyatta thirty-one years earlier) and promptly formed his own party to oppose KANU, which he named the Safina Party. Leakey had no illusions as regards the perilous political journey he embarked upon with the bold formation of a new party crossing ethnic and tribal boundaries, a major goal of which was to force constitutional reform. During the eighties he was President Moi's choice to head Kenya's ailing Wildlife Services but soon forfeited his patronage and support upon swopping conservationism for opposition politics.

His courageously forthright condemnation of government ineptitude and rampant corruption was to create a great deal of unease among the 'white squirearchy' gaily lunching on the terrace of Nairobi's fabled Muthaiga Club—still so nostalgically redolent of those halcyon colonial times when the 'Happy Valley' settler aristos gathered for their wild parties. They, along with many a sycophantic Western leader, may not have approved of either Kenyatta's or Moi's authoritarian administrations but there was quite enough strife and violent instability throughout the African continent without stoking the fires of Kenya's many disaffected tribes.

Nevertheless, while in London during July of 1995 for the making of the BBC TV documentary *African Wildlife Warrior*, Leakey made clear that as a Kenyan-born citizen he was deeply disturbed that his decision to form Safina was being criticized as racist or that he had grandiose political aspirations.

"I want to stop the rot," he told the *Sunday Telegraph*. "Our platform is to try to put back some integrity into government, to put back accountability and service to the public."

Such fine words. Ringing with crusading zeal. So sad that the embryonic Safina found it such a hard and daunting struggle to make any real or lasting impression on a cowed and submissive electorate, black or white. His laudable anti-corruption crusade had even pitted him against his brother Philip who, until being ousted in the 1992 elections, was Moi's foreign minister, and had preferred to display solidarity with KANU's popular, if tarnished credo.

Notwithstanding Moi's placatory gesture to allow multi-party elections in December 1995, doubtless due to the threat by Western nations to withhold their generous infusions of aid, the ruling KANU party remained unassailable.

Moi's successor, Mwai Kibaki commenced his presidential term in December 1997 with the most worthy of intentions, having vigorously campaigned with promises to purge government of corruption and to expose to public scrutiny all the institutionalized sleaze and scandal.

For awhile the fresh green shoots of integrity and trustworthiness sprouted around the higher echelons of government. The sweet scented air of optimism presaging democratic constitutional reform wafted into the twitching nostrils of Kenyans of whatever colour, tribe or political persuasion. But, it was not to be—Mr Kibaki was no paragon of virtue about to lead his people into a bright, noble and righteous twenty-first century. He had already been clothed in the tawdry mantle as worn by his predecessors. Never mind that he made such a determined and convincing attempt during his first year in office to wage war on bribery, corruption and malfeasance. He was soon compelled to cool his reforming ardour by the avaricious elitist hierarchy of his own tribe, the Kikuyu.

With commendable zeal and commitment he commissioned a public enquiry into the disappearance from the Treasury of some

$600 million (the enquiry came to be known as the Goldenberg scam) during the 1990s. The highly trumpeted and diligent investigation was able to report that substantial amounts of the stolen money was traceable to bank accounts in the names of several senior figures in official positions. Once this embarrassing information had leaked out any expectation of punitive or disciplinary measures rapidly receded and the whole sordid affair was discreetly allowed to gather dust in the Attorney General's chambers.

Again, there was the four months' investigation that concluded with a draconian purge of the judiciary. Justice Aaron Ringero, formerly head of Kenya's Anti-corruption Authority, appointed by President Kibaki to conduct the enquiry, was soon able to establish with credible, well-founded evidence that a wide range of serious offences had been revealed including: direct corruption, want of integrity, unethical conduct and judicial misbehaviour. The Ringero Report was duly presented to the Chief Justice, Esau Gicheru, in October 2003 and the list of shame named eighty-two magistrates and twenty-three Appeal and High Court judges. The over-powering stench of rot and decay throughout Kenya's judiciary was impossible to eliminate without the connivance of the higher echelons of government, so unequivocal and damning was the evidence.

So, what then was the outcome? They were suspended!

The tribunal set up so hopefully by Kibaki had been expected to set the stage for further far-reaching purges. Regrettably, as is now known, the much-vaunted crusade foundered abjectly before the year ended.

It was indeed fortunate, however, that this failed attempt by Kibaki denoting a break with Kenya's corrupt past, did not deter the IMF from endorsing his three-year reform programme in November 2003, agreeing to a multi-million-dollar loan which, when added to an extremely generous EU aid programme, did much to salve any troubled consciences.

And what has there been to show for it all? Why, in spite of such international tolerance of his government's shortcomings, is Kibaki and his Kikuyu-dominated administration held in such contempt by the teeming disadvantaged, disenchanted, landless thousands in the stinking slums of Nairobi, Mombasa and many other large urban centres?

The venerated 'Mzee' Jomo Kenyatta bestrode the Kenyan stage just as iconically as did Cecil Rhodes in his own fiercely jingoistic eponymous British colony, with the notable exception, I should add, that the latter's white settler-farmer community, being of a more robustly obdurate Afrikaner disposition, succeeded in prolonging Rhodes' ideological dreams a decade or two longer than did Kenya.

It is, however, fair to say that Kenyatta's was an act impossible to follow. He shaped the mould for the country's political future. Never a consummate political exponent, immensely charismatic with gifted oratorical talent, and his reputation as the messiah of his people, his was a dazzling, inimitable performance. His flamboyance and sage worldliness were such that Kenyans across the entire disparate tribal spectrum, involuntarily almost, coalesced around magnet persona. His powerful demagoguery ensured his electability unopposed.

Unfortunately for both Moi and Kibaki, neither found it possible to emulate the evangelic-like Kenyatta charisma that precluded any serious inter-tribal enmity or strife during his three terms in office. And yet, it has to be said that, revered father of his people as he may well have been, self-aggrandisement was a perk of office that appeared not to trouble his conscience. The corrupt abuse of supreme authority that he so deviously indulged without incurring much public censure or disquiet was to set the pattern for his two successors.

Shameless acquisition of land became the guiding beacon for so many fortunate or corrupt enough to attain influential position in public office; attributes of probity and altruism were simply glib election rhetoric and Kenyatta's example of unabashed self-aggrandisement and nepotism came to be the excepted standard for Kenya's disdainful ruling clique, as the following extraordinary statistical data will indicate all too clearly. The figures quoted have been collated by several independent surveyors and Ministry of Land officials and, as far as is known, have not been disputed by anyone in authority.

Apart from a residual class of white settlers (such as the extensive Delamere Estate around Lake Elementita) and a group of former State House toadies, the biggest land owners are by far Kenya's two former First Families and that of the present-incumbent Mwai Kibaki.

The extended Kenyatta family alone owns an estimated half a million acres—approximately the size of Nyanza Province—spread throughout the former White Highlands. The Moi family land, owned in the names of his sons and daughters and other close family members, totals a more modest, though still impressive, one hundred and thirty thousand acres. The Kibaki family's acquisitions have been rather less at almost forty thousand acres, but is not at all meagre for a president during his first year in office.

Thus, Kenya's descent into the slimy pit of corruption, malfeasance and nepotism continues apace. Could it be otherwise however? It remains to be seen, with the inter-tribal violence and anti-Kikuyu, anti-KANU fury growing more ominous by the day, whether Kenya's emergent combatant minority tribes will be able to persuade their political leaders to espouse some long-overdue constitutional reforms.

The brutal and bloody inter-tribal clashes spreading relentlessly throughout the Rift Valley is all horribly reminiscent of what so shocked the world in neighbouring Burundi between Tutsis and Hutus some years ago. I wonder if the person now so boldly challenging the legitimacy of President Mwai Kibaki's second term in office, Raila Odinga, has ever had the opportunity to read those prescient writings of another Odinga, a Luo, forty years ago.

The following passage is from *Not yet Uhuru* written in 1967 (Odinga Odinga founded the Kenya People's Union (KPU) to oppose the ruling KANU Party, though with little success):

Inside Kenya the struggle before us will be stern and exacting.

We are struggling to prevent Kenyans in black skins with vested interest from ruling as successors to the administrators of colonial days.

What form will the struggle in Kenya take? Is our country to see government and high office riddled with corruption and men in power using force and manoeuvre to block the expression of the popular will?

But in the long run, the wishes of the people must prevail.

Could the current bout of genocidal savagery be sardonically dismissed as *déjà vu?*

P.R. Hewitt
Barnet
February 2008

Glossary of Swahili words

asante sana	thank you very much
askari	native soldiers or police
bibby	unmarried native girl
boma	fence or stockade
bunduki	firearm
bwana	title of respect—something like mister
chakula	food
chunga	look after
duka	shop, store, kiosk
effendi	sir—used for police or military seniors
fatina	intrigue, trouble-making
gari	motor car, vehicle
hapana	no
jambo	greeting
kabisa	absolutely
kal	strict, severe
kamata	arrest
kanzo	long gown worn by house staff
karani	clerk
kiboka	whip
kipande	identity card
kuke	colloquialism for a Kikuyu tribesman
kune	firewood
kwa heri	goodbye

liandi/lhiandi	railway goods yard/store
moshi	smoke
m'kubwa	big person, senior
myingi	many, much
ndio	yes
ngai	sacred spirit (on summit of Mount Kenya)
ngoja kidogo	wait a little
ngombe	cow
nyapara	foreman
nyumba	house
panga	long, broad-bladed knife, machete
piga	hit, strike, shoot
pole pole	slowly
pombe	native beer brewed from maize
posho	ground maize meal (staple diet of natives)
rafiki	friend
rondavel	round hut made of mud and wattle with thatched roof, though nowadays corrugated iron has substituted thatch
sana	very
samaki	fish
serikali	government, the Crown
shamba	farm, cultivated land
shauri	trouble, matter, affair
shauri ya Mungu	God's will
shenzi	uncivilized, wild, savage
simama	stop
squatter	native employed by a settler and living on a plot of land provided for him
sufuria	bowl
sundowner	a drink of two before dinner

taka taka	rubbish
tayari	ready
tembo	intoxicating distilled liquor
toroka	flee, run away
toto	child
villigization	concentration of native labour lines inside one *boma*—in more recent context, a 'protected village'
wapi	where
watu	people
wazungu	European, white person

Glossary of army and police abbreviations

Acorn	Intelligence Officer (Military)
Coys	companies
FIO	Field Intelligence Officer
Glosters	Gloucestershire Regiment
GSU	General Service Unit
HG	Homeguard
Johnnie	European soldier
Kenya Cowboys	sobriquet given to those Kenya police officers recruited during the emergency
KPR	Kenya Police Reserve
nan tare roger	nothing to report (radio speak for NTR)
O Group	operational conference, or 'Orders' Group
RB	Rifle Brigade
RVP	Rift Valley Province
schedule (sched/sked)	routine calls on VHF radio
SF	security forces
sitrep	situation report
Sunray	OC operational forces
Tac HQ	Tactical Headquarters
TCT	Tracker Combat Team
Vulture	KPR Airwing spotter plane

Appendix I

'Your turn may come'

A directive published by the Department of Information, Nakuru, for the Provincial Emergency Committee

Now that the increasing tempo of operations by the Security Forces are denying to the terrorists supplies of all kinds, keeping them on the move, and, in conjunction with heavy bombing, driving them from the forests, gangs are entering the Settled Areas in increasing numbers in search of food supplies, clothing, arms and ammunition. There is no doubt that as they see the tide of battle turning against them, the terrorists are becoming more and more desperate and ruthless. The probability of attacks being made against European lives and property in the coming months is therefore greatly enhanced.

In some parts of the Province there is still room for a great deal of improvement in the Security precautions which some people are taking. In some instances these precautions are even yet woefully lax. It should not be necessary to remind everyone that every successful theft of food and supplies prolongs the Emergency and, where firearms and ammunition are stolen, the lives of the Security Forces and loyal citizens are greatly endangered. Please also remember that every incident which has to be investigated deflects the Security Forces from their task of hunting and fighting the terrorists.

In your own interest and that of the most efficient prosecution of the Emergency, you are therefore asked to attend at once to the following details of your personal and property security.

IN THE HOME

LOCKING-UP
Do this yourself. Don't leave it to servants.

WINDOWS

Have these protected with bars or expanded metal. Ensure that opaque curtains cover the windows properly.

DOORS

Fit doors with bars or barrel bolts on the inside.

KEYS

Keep all keys yourself. Don't give servants a key to the veranda or other outside doors.

SERVANTS

Do not employ Kikuyu servants. If you have an outside kitchen have a covered way to the house wired in with expanded metal. If you cannot do this then lock all servants out of the house before dark. Do not admit servants to the house after dark unless absolutely necessary. If they have to enter the house ensure that their entrance is covered by a gun.

CHAIRS

Do not always have these in the same place. Move them around from time to time. Never place a chair with its back to a door.

ON THE FARM

THE LABOUR LINES

Make all your employees live in the Labour Lines. Do not allow any of them to occupy isolated huts. Have the Lines concentrated as near to your own house as is practicable, certainly within sight and sound. Have the Lines wired in, if possible, or at least within a thorn or bamboo stockade.

ALARM SYSTEM

Ensure that each hut in the Labour Lines has a gong or a whistle. Instruct each hut to sound their alarm as soon as they hear anyone else doing so. Rely on this sound alarm to give you warning of an attack on the Labour Lines, not on a runner who may be killed 'en route'.

FARM GUARDS

Check up on your Farm Guards and Watchmen as often as possible. What about a Watchman's clock, the record of which will show you whether your Guards are on the job at night? Never allow one man with a rifle in the open. He must be accompanied by three or more spearmen.

FOOD PROTECTION

Have you done all you can to get rid of the wheat from your farm? If you still have wheat on the farm get it into a secure store somewhere near the house. Do the same also with maize and other foodstuffs.

CATTLE

Ensure that these are always in a secure boma at night, within sound of the house, and under guard. Stock Guards have proved a great deterrent to terrorists. Get as many cattle as possible fitted with bells. Know how many cattle you have. Count them in the morning and in the evening.

MONEY

Don't keep large sums of money on the farm.

DOGS

Keep a good watchdog which barks and always keep it in the house after dark.

FIREARMS

In the house after dark always have your gun loaded and ready for instant action close to your hand. It is useless in its holster, in a cupboard or a handbag. When a gun is wanted it is wanted instantly. The speed with which you can have your gun in your hand may well mean the difference between life and death.

RATIONS AND SUPPLIES

Have a strong room, accessible from inside the house, for emergency rations, rockets and other supplies.

FIRE EQUIPMENT

If your house is at all inflammable, have buckets, or containers of water and earth always filled and ready.

OUTSIDE LIGHTS

Illuminate the exterior of your house where possible.

FIELD OF VIEW

Have a good field of view all round the house. Cut down all bush and undergrowth for a distance of at least 50 yards.

GUEST HOUSES

Don't use these unless there are sufficient people to be able to protect themselves. Farm Managers or assistants should sleep in the main house.

OUTSIDE LAVATORIES

Never use these at night.

ROUTINE

Don't keep a set routine for eating, sleeping and other activities in and about the house. Do not always lock up in the same routine. Ring the changes.

ABSENCE FROM THE FARM

Don't leave the farm at regular times and don't advertise the fact that you are leaving it. If leaving the farm in the hands of Africans, post a sentry some distance away to run or ride for assistance if your farm is attacked. Never leave firearms in the house.

ALERTNESS

Be suspicious of unusual occurrences, e.g. Kikuyu employees suddenly asking for leave. Always wear your gun and don't be afraid of showing that you are ready for trouble at any time.

RECORDS

Keep a record of your employees so that they can be traced if they abscond. Try to know them all by name and/or sight.

GENERAL

HAVE A PLAN
Have a plan ready against attack on the house or the Labour Lines. Make sure everyone knows what the plan is and get your household and the labour to practise its operation. This is very important. The gangs are looking for 'easy', disorganised farms to attack. In almost every case where attacking terrorists have encountered any resistance they have fled. Have a good rocket alarm system with firing switches in different parts of the house, not only in one room. DON'T rely on the telephone: the wires are invariably cut before an attack.

ROCKETS
Do not dissipate the efforts of the Security Forces by unnecessary firing of rockets. Make sure that you really need help before discharging rockets.

KNOW YOUR K.P.R. LEADER
Know your K.P.R. Section Leader. Invite him to look over your security precautions. He might spot an important snag you hadn't foreseen.

REMEMBER THAT PRACTICALLY ALL THE EUROPEANS WHO HAVE BEEN MURDERED BY TERRORISTS WERE THOSE WHO WERE TAKING INSUFFICIENT OR NO PRECAUTIONS AND HAD NO PLAN READY WHEN THEY WERE ATTACKED.

Appendix II

Inspector P.R. Hewitt
Police Station, Gilgil
Ref: POF/PRH/32/55

I append below copy of a letter received from Ascompol, Nakuru, the original of which has been placed on your Personal File.

ASPOL – NAIVASHA

Ref. S.53/275

Letter of appreciation: the Carnelly Raid

The following is a copy of a letter which I have received from Mr. C.T. Hutson of Box 306, Nairobi. The letter is self-explanatory but I too would like to add my praise for the good work done by Inspector Hewitt and the pilot, Mr. R. Pakenham-Walshe. I would be glad if you would inform Inspector Hewitt that his good work is appreciated, and that a copy of this letter is being placed on his personal file.

My wife and I were staying on our fishing plot on the Turasha River at the time of the Carnelly incident and were fairly close observers of the efforts that were made to catch the Mau Mau gang. We would like to pay tribute to the work of Mr. Hewitt of the Police Post at Ol Magogo and above all to the person who piloted the spotter aircraft. It was a brilliant and breath-taking effort to lead the ground forces to the gang. We are very grateful and sincerely hope you will succeed in catching the gang.

(Signed)
L. Griffiths
Ascompol
Nakuru
10.1.55

Appendix III

G.H.Q. East Africa

Nairobi

Kenya

30th November, 1953

Message to all officers of the Army, Police and the Security Forces

I must remind all Members of the Security Forces of the Instructions I gave them on the 23rd June. It is absolutely imperative to the success of the operations and to the honour of the Forces operating under my command that every single member of these forces—Army and Police—should carry out their duties strictly in accordance with the letter and spirit of my instructions.

I will repeat the most important part of that instruction: "I will not tolerate breaches of discipline leading to unfair treatment of anybody. We have a very difficult task and I have no intention of tying the hands of the Security Forces by orders and rules which make it impossible for them to carry out their duty—I am practical soldier enough to know that mistakes can be made and nobody need fear my lack of support if the mistake is committed in good faith.

But I most strongly disapprove of 'beating up' the inhabitants of this country just because they are the inhabitants. I hope this has not happened in the past and will not happen in the future. Any indiscipline of this kind would do great damage to the reputation of the Security Forces and make our task of settling MAU MAU much more difficult.

I therefore order that every officer in the Police and the Army should stamp on at once any conduct which he would be ashamed to see used against his own people. I want to stand up for the Honour of the Security Forces with a clear conscience—I can only do that if I have absolutely loyal support and I rely on you to provide it.

Since I issued this instruction there has been a satisfactory General Standard of Conduct. There have however been some complaints which lead me to think there are still a few individuals who are taking the law into their own hands and acting outside my orders—I am out to catch and punish such people—there must be no ground for complaint—even one act of indiscipline can tarnish our reputation.

The responsibility for enforcing this instruction will lie particularly on the Senior Officers in the Police and Army who must be most vigilant on my behalf.

(Signature)
General
Commander-in-Chief

Appendix IV

Headquarters, The Kenya Police
P.O. Box 83
Nairobi
17th October, 1955
Ref. No. sEC.373/1/81

All Provincial Police Officers
All Officers in Charge of Districts
All Officers in Charge of Divisions
All Officers in Charge of Sub-Divisions
Assistant Commissioner, C.I.D. Nairobi
Assistant Commissioner, Special Branch, Nairobi

Ill-treatment of persons in Police custody

1. On 3rd December, 1953 the then Commissioner of Police felt it necessary to draw the attention of all superior officers in the Regular Police and Kenya Police Reserve to breaches of discipline resulting in the ill-treatment of persons in police custody. A copy of this instruction is attached. It still stands.

2. We have recently seen yet another shocking case of the brutal handling of two Africans in custody proved in open court against three Police Inspectors of South Nyeri Division.

3. I wish to make it quite clear that I am determined to eradicate such despicable behaviour within the Force by every means available to me. I emphasized this determination publicly on 30th December last when assuming command and have constantly reiterated it to all ranks since when visiting police formations throughout the Colony. I repeat again that the Kenya Police cannot do its job unless it has the respect and co-operation of the public of all races and nothing is more calculated to destroy respect and prevent co-operation than disregard of the law by police officers of the kind disclosed at the South Nyeri trial.

4. I would remind you all that where evidence of brutality by police officers comes to light I shall continue to have no hesitation in submitting their cases to the Attorney General for trial before a court of law no matter what their rank or ranks may be. Where indiscipline does not amount to criminal liability the case will be dealt with under the Police Ordinance in the most severe manner, if necessary to the extent of dismissal where it is within my power or recommending dismissal to Government where it is not.

5. Every man in the Force, of whatever rank, will constantly bear in mind that his responsibility as a police officer is above all to give protection and service to the law-abiding community and that his behaviour and discipline must be impeccable. The maintenance of the rule of law in Kenya demands first of all respect for the law by the Kenya Police whose profession it is to uphold it, and this will be so.

6. Finally I would remind you of the vital need to ensure that persons in police custody are properly held and that in every case legal authority to do so exists. A summary of the powers of detention of police officers, both under the permanent law and under the Emergency Regulations, is attached. These powers cannot be exceeded. This is a simple guide which will be adhered to rigorously. Officers in charge of formations will check all persons held in custody in police cells when inspecting stations and posts under their command to ensure that there is legal authority to cover their detention and that they are being correctly treated. They will record the results of these inspections in the Officers Visiting Book. This includes Sub-Divisional Commanders. In this connection you are to see also that Force Standing Orders, Section XX, paragraph 7—Prisoners—treatment and control of—are strictly followed.

7. Provincial/Area Commanders will ensure that a copy of this instruction is given to every officer of the rank of Assistant Inspector and above who is not included in the distribution and that its contents are read out in Swahili to the Rank and File at Weekly parades every week for four weeks following receipt of the instruction. A Swahili version is attached for this purpose.

8. The instruction will also be reproduced as an Appendix to the next issue of Force Orders, both in English and in Swahili.

(Signature)
R.C. Catling
Commissioner

Enclos:
Copies to All Officers in Charge of Stations and Posts
RCC/PJM

Appendix V

SECRET

PART II

Operational Intelligence Summary

Period 12/5/55 to 26/5/55

A. General

82/55 It has been possible to detect some movement by terrorist gangs westwards through the Naivasha District:

(a) A gang led by MBURO MUKONO, strength 40, with the possible addition of a Masai gang 28 strong, has moved along the following route:

River Wabora	HZR 1003
Johansen's Farm	HZP 9406
Water Hole	HZP 8001
Akira Ranch	HZP 7489
Hell's Gate	HZP 6801
Mt. Orgaria	HZP 6302

(Here the gang appears to have split up. One party moving Southwest across the Masai Border and the other group heading North.)

(b) A gang, possibly Kibe Kimani, has moved through:

Van Rensburg	HZP 9021
Manera Railway Lhandie	HZP 7923
Hopcraft	HZP 6921
Denning	HZP 6620
Eburru	HZP 6226

(c) The gang lead by NGOME KARIUKI, which normally moves in the country between Eburru and Kipipiri, was contacted at HZP 401281 where Ngome was killed.

83/55 Informer information and also reports from farms have shown that there have been several visits by small parties of terrorists from the forest to farms in the Kunyu (HZP 9213), North Kinangop (HZP 9036) and 01 Magogo (HZP 3138) areas.

84/55 Apart from stock thefts, dealt with separately, terrorist activity has taken place in the following areas:

Karati and Armstrong's Gorges.

(a) Potatoes were stolen from shambas on Knight's (HZP 9351 8) and on Weaver's (HZP 931152). Some of this may be labour stealing from each other but it usually means labour stealing for Mau Mau—caches of potatoes marked by signs have been previously found in the vicinity of these farms.

Bamboo Forest

(b) Potatoes were stolen from shambas on Grimwood's farm (HZR 0008). It is all too clear that this farm provides a constant food supply for terrorists in the Bamboo Forest.

(c) A gang of food carriers was reported in the forest at HZR 0613. Another gang, estimated at about 100 strong, was reported at HZR 0100.

North Kinangop

(d) A gang of unknown strength attempted to raid the Dairy on Gledhill's farm EZR 0238. The terrorists were driven off by the Farm Guards.

(e) A patrol of the Royal Irish Fusiliers surprised a small gang in a hideout at HZR 081297. The patrol killed one terrorist and recovered some useful documents.

Lake Naivasha

(f) A gang, some 30-plus strong, raided the Manera Lhandie, stealing money, clothing and food. This Railway Lhandie, like the others in the District, though wired in, present easy targets to the terrorists because:

1. Of their isolated positions.
2. The wiring is not good enough.
3. The Lhandies are not guarded.
4. They are well supplied with food, and money.

(g) A farm guard who was wounded at Hopcraft's farm (HZP 6922) and had his shotgun taken from him by a party of terrorists was walking along on his own—contrary to standing orders for armed farm guards, who are supposed to travel in threes.

85/55 Report from European Farms

There have been eight reports from European farms giving useful information on terrorist movements. Usually in the form of strangers having been seen on the farm or tracks discovered which have not been made by the local labour. One such report by herd-boys on Nazers farm (HZP 7610) led to the discovery of an important gang that had left the Bamboo Forest and was making its way to Southern Province through the Naivasha District. The gang was contacted successfully, three terrorists were killed and two captured. One of the captures was also made possible by information received from a Meru on Carnelly's farm (HZP 6511).

86/55 Mau Mau Aims

Gangs now realise what strengths they have to contend with at bomas and come prepared to deal with the two or three guards. They usually make a noise to allow the Farm Guards to fire then before the guards can reload, a slow process with their type of gun, they rush them. The noise made is sometimes deliberate to draw fire, whilst the raiding party are busy at another point of the boma.

Self-styled Brigadier MWANGI WANGAI gave the following information which throws some light on terrorist intentions:

(a) He claimed STANLEY MATHENGE was now their overall leader.

(b) STANLEY MATHENGE had issued them with these orders:

1. To avoid contact with Security Forces.
2. Not to fight with anyone except when there was a chance of getting arms and ammunition.
3. To steal the food they required.
4. Not to hurt women and children anymore.

(c) DEDAN KIMATHI was opposed to these instructions and wanted them to fight.

(d) They had left the Bamboo Forest because of bombing and were going to rest in the Mau.

(e) He had been forced into Mau Mau and did not like it at first but later liked the life and preferred to live in the forest, than to work in the Reserve or Settled area.

87/55 C Terrorist Organisation and Identifications

A terrorist, WAWERU CHEGE, killed by a patrol of the Royal Irish Fusiliers at HZR 081297 on 20th May 1955 had documents on him, which showed he was a Brigadier and in charge of a gang called 'E' Company. There were nineteen names listed with his and a quick check showed them to be mostly people from the Fort Hall District. A letter carried by WAWERU had been written by a MUTUTA MACHARIA. An interesting point is that the terrorist 3rd Army under KAMAU KARICHU is split up into sections—not companies. It is therefore reasonable to say that the 3rd Army's sphere of influence must end around about Fey's Peak and possibly another terrorist formation split into companies lies to the north of the 3rd Army. (A detailed list of names has been forwarded to interested addressees.)

88/55 A terrorist killed at HZP 905115 by a patrol of the Royal Irish Fusiliers on 20th May 1955 had documents on him which showed he belonged to a section of ten under a GICHIMU MWAMBIRU. This was probably a section of the 3rd Army foraging for food in the settled area.

89/55 Information received from three terrorists captured during the fortnight, all from the same gang, can be summarised as follows:

MWANGI WANGAI Captured at HZP 652409 on 26th May 1955
GATHUMI KIMANI Captured at HZH 7489 on 24th May 1955 and
  subsequently died.
GATHONI KARIUKI Captured at HZP 687016 on 25th May 1955.

The gang was in the headwaters of the River Wabora (HZR 0903) at the end of April this year. Their leader WARUINGI was with them and altogether some 350 terrorists were there.

Their camp was bombed and many terrorists were killed. Some 40 terrorists were never seen again after the bombing. The section led by MBURU MUKONO, some 42 strong with a Masai called KIPKOSKE as guide, decided to leave the Bamboo Forest for the Mau.

They went via Johansen's (HZP 9406) where they stole one cow and then along the route mentioned in para. 82/55 (a).

90/55 Before leaving the Bamboo the above gang met a gang of about 25 terrorists led by NYAGA who commands a section of MWAURA's gang. This gang had three cows with them which they claimed to have recently stolen from Van Fey's (HZP 9918).

91/55 An analysis of the stock thefts during the last fortnight shows the following points of interest:

(a) Cattle lifted	125
(b) Cattle recovered	118
(c) Lost to terrorists	7

(d) The worst loss was from Van Fey's where three cattle were lost to the terrorists in the Bamboo Forest. Of the remaining four cattle lost in the District, two were possibly lost to Masai from Maiella Farm and the other two gangs moving in the settled area.

(e) Perhaps the most cold fact to note is that the terrorists in the fortnight have made nine attempts to get cattle and not one terrorist was killed as a result.

(Signature)
for Chairman
District Intelligence Committee
Naivasha

Appendix VI

No. 9. T.C.T.

SECRET

'Saving'

To: Officers in Charge, Police Stations, North & South Kinangop, Gilgil, Naivasha and Kijabe

(with sufficient copies for distribution to all Police Posts in your area)

Ref: C.170/K/72/55

I append below copy of a letter from the Commissioner of Police, Ref. Sec. 519/98 dated 27.10.55 for your information and compliance.

Please obtain receipts from your Post Commanders and return to this Divisional H.Q. as soon as possible.

(Signature)
Supol
Naivasha

Pseudo-gang Operations and Patrols

The following instructions are issued to ensure that the fullest possible precautions are adopted for the safety of personnel engaged in pseudo-gang operations and as a guide to those who engage in such operations:

1. Clearance

(a) In the case of pseudo-gang operations planned at Divisional level, the procedure for clearance will be as follows:

(i) Warning of clearance will first be passed from the Divisional Ops. Room to the Security Force units in any way involved in the area of the intended operation.

(ii) The patrol leader (or leaders) conducting the operation will then personally check that the Security Force Commanders concerned have received the warning order accurately and satisfy himself that the required clearance is being effected.

(iii) The patrol leader will then confirm to the Divisional Police Commander, or his deputy, that he (the patrol leader) is satisfied that the area will be cleared and that he can carry out the operation as intended.

(iv) No operational area will be declared open until the Divisional Police Commander or his deputy has satisfied himself that it is safe to do so.

(b) In the case of short pseudo-gang reconnaissance patrols by Special Branch officers in a Station or Post area, the clearance procedure will be that the patrol leader, himself, will be responsible for contacting the Police Station or Post Commander concerned to advise him of the intended reconnaissance and ensure that the area is clear and that where necessary, Security Force Commanders therein are warned. Under no circumstances will a patrol leader embark upon his reconnaissance unless he is satisfied that the fullest precautions for clearance have been taken.

(c) Wherever possible boundaries will be defined on the ground as opposed to the map.

(d) Physical features will be used whenever possible.

(e) The importance of ground reconnaissance prior to planned operations being implemented cannot be over-stressed. The reconnaissance must be carried out by, or in conjunction with, officers who know the area well.

(f) Where necessary, patrol leaders should be briefed, as to boundaries, on the ground.

(g) Appreciating that riverbeds or valleys often hold terrorist elements, operational areas should be defined, where possible, to include such features well within the boundary.

(h) In planned operations (as opposed to short reconnaissance patrols) it is important that boundaries are charted accurately (by map reference) for record purposes.

2. Operational Orders

In planned operations, it is most important that clear, comprehensive and accurate orders are issued by the Divisional Police Commander or his Deputy and that such orders are understood by all Security Force commanders involved directly and indirectly or in any way connected with or affected by such operations.

3. General

Appreciating that leaders of pseudo-gang patrols and their men are assuming considerable personal risk in their operations, it is of vital importance that leaders are entirely satisfied with all the aspects detailed in paras. 1 to 3 above before they are required to embark upon operations.

4. Safety Precautions

The following points will be brought to the attention of pseudo-gang leaders—particularly those who are new to an area in which they are operating:

(a) No pseudo-gang operation should be carried out during the hours of daylight in settled areas or the Reserves if the object could equally well be achieved by an operation carried out at night.

(b) Sentries or scouts must be posted at all times, particularly when resting.

(c) Camp sites must be so chosen as to obviate detection and surprise.

(d) If a pseudo-gang patrol is seen the patrol should retire without delay.

(e) In the event of a pseudo-gang patrol being encountered and being unable to retire, as in sub-para (d) above the patrol leader will endeavour to establish his identity by word of mouth or removal of his disguise.

R.C. Catling
Commissioner of Police

Appendix VII

SECRET

PART II

Operational Intelligence Summary

period 26/10/55 to 11/11/55
A. General

306/55 The period in question has been a quiet one and definitely a good one for Security Forces. Statistics of losses are as follows:

> Cattle 4
>
> Sheep 3

A few potatoes were also stolen.

Security Force successes have been as follows:

> Terrorists:
>
> | | |
> |---|---|
> | killed | 16 |
> | wounded | 2 |
> | captured | 3 |
> | surrendered | 3 |
> | Ammunition recovered | 48 rounds of assorted |
> | Weapons recovered | 2 x .303 |
> | | 1 shotgun |
> | | 1 pistol |
> | | 2H/M guns |

Details of Incidents and Contacts

307/55 On 25th October at HZP 763555 a gang of 3 was spotted by K.P.R. Airwing. A patrol contacted this gang, killing one, wounding one (who later died) and capturing one.

308/55 On 26th October at HZP 923565 a lone gangster was killed in his hide. Security Forces were lead to this contact by a surrenderee.

309/55 On 29th October at HZP 8613, Marula Estate, two farm guards were shot at by gangster, losing one shotgun. Later, on 3rd November in the same area a gang fired into a farm guard hut with shot guns. These actions are attributed to KIBE KIMANI.

310/55 During the military operation *Excalibur* on 2nd November, one gangster was killed and another captured. Information from the capturee led to a further military operation, indirectly resulting in contacting this gang again.

311/55 On 2nd November a gangster from MACHARI KIMEMIA's gang surrendered at HZP 3837. He led Security Forces back to his hide, HZR 0931, where KARIOKI NDUATI was killed and 4 precision weapons recovered together with a quantity of documents. Among those in the hide were:

MACHARI KIMEMIA
KABANG GATHATWA
MWANGI GICHIMU
KAMAU KERICU
NDONGA MURERE
GICHIMU MWAMBURA
GAKURE KARURE

The 3 sheep which were stolen from Nightingale's farm on 4th November were taken by this gang. Interesting facts are to be revealed by the documents which were captured during this action.

312/55 On 7th November at HZP 7745, on information, a gang of three was contacted and eliminated. Two gangsters being killed and the third being captured. The capturee lead Security Forces to the capture of a further two members of his gang on 10th November at HZP 9150.

B. Mau Mau Aims

313/55 To live off ripening crops; to attend ceremonies and follow preachings from local gang witch-doctors, and to avoid contact with Security Forces at all costs. KIBE KIMANI is the exception to this. His recent aggressive acts and successes in capturing 2 shotguns will have renewed his self-confidence and may encourage him to perpetrate further acts of aggression.

C. Organisation

314/55 The organisation of the 3rd Mburu Ngebo Army seems to be less cut and dried than of late. Sections may be combining with one another as a result of casualties and disorganisation caused through constant harassing by Security Forces. Opinion now varies greatly over individual section numbers.

D. Unit Identifications, Strengths, Locations

315/55 Ex CHEGE MAKUNDU This gang which was under the leadership of GICHENJE KIMEMIA has been contacted three times during the period. Its stamping ground would appear to be in the Ol Magogo, West Kipipiri area. During the past fortnight eight of its members have been accounted for, including the new Section Commander and 2 i/c. Strength 15?

316/55 NDONGORA MACHARIA Strength 18. Area HZP 9256. This is the commander of the 7 Section, 3rd Mburu Ngebo Army. His hide was found and one member of his gang killed as a result of information from a surrenderee.

317/55 KAGAI CHEGE Strength 35. Area HZP 0721. (MWITE RUGUNYA) This conjoint gang was contacted and identified twice during the period with a loss of 11 of its members. It is thought that it may have now fled to the Pencil Slats area of the Aberdare forest. KAGAI CHEGE has now been killed and 10 Section, 3rd M.N.A. has now been taken over by

MWANGI MACHARIA. MWITE RUNUNYA, a section commander of KIBE KIMANI has joined with 10 Section, 3rd M.N.A. temporarily to receive advice and sacraments from a visiting witch-doctor. An interesting point is that he and his gang may have split from KIBE KIMANI owing to the latter's disassociation from witch-doctors, their advice and teachings. It is learned that Mwite is looking for a new hide in the Kijabe forest area.

318/55 MACHARIA KIMEMIA Strength 20. Area 0931. Together with 7 important Fort Hall gang leaders, he was contacted as a result of information from a surrenderee. There are two moves resulting from this contact which may be possible. One that he and the gang will move to Kinari (Bamboo Forest) area. Two that the gang will move to Kipipiri. The later has been hinted in captured documents. It is interesting to note that KAMAU KARICU (lost for 3 months) from the Bamboo Forest was among this gang.

319/55 MWANGI KABEBEI Strength 15. Area HZR 0256. This is the supposed leader of No. 2 and 14 Sections, 3rd M.N.A. A wretched and emaciated member of his gang was captured on 8th November at HZR 053552.

(Signature)
Chairman
District Intelligence Committee
Naivasha

Appendix VIII

An excerpt from of F.D. Corfield's official report for the Kenya government: *The Origins and Growth of Mau Mau*

26. It cannot be denied that the congestion of the land in many parts of Kenya has been one of the most serious problems facing both the Government and the people of Kenya, but it is not within the scope of this historical survey to discuss in any detail the steps taken by the Government to deal with this problem. All that might be said, so far as the Kikuyu are concerned, is that the Government did not perhaps give sufficiently early consideration to future needs, expressed by the Carter Commission in the following extract from the Summary of its Recommendations (paragraph 2077):

The greatest disservice we could do to the country would be to compromise future development by locking up rigidly in tribal departments land not yet required by the tribes, because we apprehend that at some uncertain date in the future it might be required ... Tribes must be given only land for their present and future requirements and their claims of right must be satisfied; besides this there must be facilities for expansion either by the acquisition of more land tribally, or by individuals or families leaving the tribal territory and leasing land elsewhere; or by the inter-penetration, inter-tribal leases, or otherwise.

But the financial difficulties which faced the Government in giving effect to this recommendation were very great. The beneficial utilization of the extensive uninhabited and undeveloped areas in Kenya needed capital and the provision of capital through such agencies as the Colonial Development and Welfare Fund was still in its infancy.

My more limited objective has been, by recounting once again the true origins and background of European settlement, to show quite clearly, firstly that this settlement was undertaken not by the indiscriminate seizure of land by unscrupulous Europeans from the defenceless and primitive African, but as the result of the predetermined policy of H.M. Government which, in the circumstances then ruling, was eminently necessary to the needs of Kenya; secondly, that the area of land which was alienated for European settlement and which might not have been so alienated had more been known of local land usage amongst the Africans, did not exceed 110 square miles, an area of 10 by 11 miles, in the vastness of Africa; and, thirdly, that the Government, by accepting the recommendations of the Carter Commission, made full restitution for this alienation.

As I have said in paragraph 10 above, I do not expect that this plain statement of truth will have much influence on African thought, as the African's attachment to land is so emotional that it is almost impossible for him to take a detached view whenever land is mentioned. But, in the words of Mr. A. Lennox-Boyd in the House of Commons in February, 1952, when replying to an adjournment debate on the White Highlands:

Some of these facts ought to be known, and I hope hon. Members of the House, who have lent themselves to wild and inaccurate statements, will do their best to bring the true facts not only to the people of their friends in Africa but also to the people of the United Kingdom as well.

Appendix IX

Declaration of a State of Emergency

On Tuesday October 21st 1952 Kenya's governor and C-in-C, Sir Evelyn Baring, broadcast the following announcement:

1. A State of Emergency was declared throughout the Colony and Protectorate of Kenya by proclamation signed by me yesterday.

2. This grave step was taken most unwillingly and with great reluctance by the Government of Kenya. But there was no alternative in face of the mounting lawlessness, violence and disorder in a part of the Colony. This state of affairs has developed as a result of the activities of the *Mau Mau* movement. There is every sign that these activities have followed a regular course in accordance with a considered plan. There is a pattern in the acts of violence; and there can be no such pattern unless someone has made a plan. In order to restore law and order and to allow peaceable and loyal people of all races to go about their business in safety the Government have made emergency regulations to enable them to take into custody certain persons who, in their opinion, constitute a danger to public order.

3. Many have suffered from the attempts of the members of the *Mau Mau* society to gain their aims by widespread and carefully planned violence and intimidation; and most of the sufferers are peaceful and law-abiding Africans. Many African chiefs, headmen, missionaries, Government servants and teachers have shown the greatest courage and devotion to duty by continuing their work for their people in the face of constant threats and frequent attacks. Unfortunately, at first gradually and now swiftly, the *Mau Mau* crimes have increased in number, in daring and in savagery. Recently persecution of Kikuyu Christians has increased in severity, churches have been desecrated, missions have been attacked, and teachers and children in mission schools have been assaulted and threatened. At one time most of these crimes were committed by stealth, now one of the best-loved

and most revered African chiefs in Kenya has been assassinated on the high road in broad daylight by a band of armed men. In short, within a restricted but important area this movement which shows every sign of careful planning by clever and cruel men, has either by direct or indirect means produced a serious state of disorder.

4. Such is the position today in a part of Kenya; and Kenya is a country with many and peculiarly complex problems. It is understandable that many people in this country nurse grievances, but it is wrong that they should attempt to remedy those grievances by force and by secret plotting against society and the State. Problems of the nature and complexity of those of Kenya cannot be resolved suddenly and by violence.

5. The Government have, therefore, with the full knowledge and concurrence of the Secretary of State for the Colonies, taken drastic action in order to stop the spread of violence. This has been taken not against men who hold any particular political views, but against those who have had recourse to violent measures.

6. This is in the interests of all. It is in the interests of Africans in those wide areas of the Colony which have remained peaceful and of loyal Kikuyu who have been the main sufferers. It is in the interests of Asians who have been the object of attacks by criminal gangs, especially in Nairobi, but who have shown commendable steadiness under the strain. It is in the interests of Europeans whose persons and property have more recently been subject to outrage and who have very properly shown great restraint.

7. Kenya has before it a bright future with a good prospect of a rising standard of living for people of all races, provided that there is peace and order. In peaceful conditions plans were being made for economic development and particularly for help to the poorer inhabitants of this country. There were, for example, good hopes of accelerating the pace of the construction of houses for Africans, of expanding African education and of improving the position of Africans in the

Civil Service. All these things will be impossible of realization if conditions of disorder continue. Disorder leads to lack of confidence and where there is no confidence there is economic stagnation. In a state of economic stagnation the standard of life falls and social services, such as education and health, suffer.

8. But once peace and quiet have been restored, Kenya should enjoy an expanding economy; and before the present disorders there were most encouraging signs of this. The Government have every intention of continuing work on their plans, and indeed of speeding them up.

9. I now appeal to citizens of all races to keep calm, not to believe all that they hear and, above all, to be careful not to create alarm by passing on rumours. There is no doubt that Kenya is facing trouble. But the difficulties of the moment can be overcome. I hope that we shall look back on the events of these last months of 1952 as a sad but a passing phase.

Appendix X

Emergency statistics up to the end of 1956

	Killed	Captured wounded	Captured in action	Arrested	Surrendered
Terrorist Casualties	11,503	1,035	1,550	26,625	2,714
				Killed	Wounded
SECURITY FORCES CASUALTIES European Asian				63 3	101 12
African				101	1,469
LOYAL CIVILIANS European Asian African				32 26 1,819	26 36 916

Cost of the emergency up to 30th June, 1959:

a) Grants from Her Majesty's Government: £24,250,000

b) Interest-free loans from Her Majesty's Government: £5,250,000

c) Borne by the Kenya Government: £26,085,424

Appendix XI

British military units that served in Kenya during the Mau Mau emergency

Lancashire Fusiliers
Gloucester Regiment
Rifle Brigade
King's Own Light Infantry
Black Watch Regiment
Royal Engineers
Devons and Buffs
Royal Northumberland Fusiliers
Royal Iniskilling Fusiliers
Oxford and Buckinghamshire Light Infantry
Royal Air Force
Kenya Regiment
King's African Rifles